WITHOUT
HONOUR

ROB TRIPP

WITHOUT
HONOUR

THE TRUE STORY OF THE SHAFIA FAMILY
AND THE KINGSTON CANAL MURDERS

HARPERCOLLINS*PUBLISHERSLTD*

Published by HarperCollins Publishers Ltd

First edition

HarperCollins books may be purchased for educational, business,
or sales promotional use through our Special Markets Department.

HarperCollins Publishers Ltd
2 Bloor Street East, 20th Floor
Toronto, Ontario, Canada
M4W 1A8

www.harpercollins.ca

Library and Archives Canada Cataloguing in Publication
information is available upon request

ISBN 978-1-44341-061-8

Printed and bound in the United States
RRD 9 8 7 6 5 4 3 2 1

For my children, and for Sarah, who inspires and loves me, brilliantly.

Contents

Author's Note

The material in this book is derived from author interviews, observations, official records, court proceedings and transcripts. Some conversations have been recreated based on these sources. There are four surviving Shafia children. Hamed is in prison, the other three surviving children are referred to here by pseudonyms, Mina, Zafar and Fereshta, to comply with permanent publication bans. Names and some identifying details involving some other characters have been changed. The spelling Shafia has been adopted to be consistent with court and police records, although a variety of sources indicate that this is an erroneous Canadianization of the name, which would more accurately be transliterated from Dari as Shafi.

Every effort has been made to be faithful to transcripts used in the book. Some punctuation in quoted excerpts has been simplified. Intercepted communications of the Shafias, recorded by police, are reproduced throughout the book based on transcripts of the Dari conversations that were translated to English and were made exhibits at trial. All parties agreed to the accuracy of the transcripts. Portions of the transcripts that indicate some conversation was unintelligible are denoted here with [u]. The transcripts include inserted words and footnotes that were not part of the audio recordings. These additions are not reproduced in the book, but the context they were intended to provide has been woven into the text wherever possible.

Washerwoman

THE WOMAN SPRINKLED THE FINE GREEN POWDER into the basin. As she stirred, the *sidr* water turned the colour of bleached grass.

Norma Sargi had created this mixture from crushed lotus leaves hundreds of times before, for daughters, mothers, sisters, but never for *so many* at one time.

Twenty years of washing the dead.

Never three sisters.

Never four bodies.

The water swirled.

Sargi usually used it to flush away residue—glue, tape, dried blood—stigmata that marked the dead with signs that the living had fought to save them. She found no signs on these four, though their torsos were unmistakably scored in that way that revealed they had been examined after death. She could not erase those marks.

The short, sturdy Lebanese woman had arrived at the private funeral parlour expecting to conduct the ritual washing and wrapping of one body. Instead, she found the slender bodies of three teenaged girls and a middle-aged woman, perhaps their mother, or aunt. She understood now why the sheikh had not sent her to the Islamic funeral parlour. It had facilities for the washing of only one body at a time. The work would have been too time-consuming there. It was important to complete the task as soon as possible, in keeping with the teachings of the Prophet. Some Muslims were buried on the same day they died. These four had already been dead five days.

Sargi and her assistant began to cry before touching them.

The sadness was good, she knew, expected even. It was an important part of the process, a reminder for all Muslims of the inevitability of death and the importance of doing charitable work before that time came. One day, Sargi would be awaiting judgment, hoping for the respect and caring she offered others in death. This day, the sadness pressed down with a weight she had not felt before.

The naked girls were on their backs, covered only by plastic sheets. They were lying on the washing tables, waist-high white porcelain platforms that each stood on a single thick stalk. There were only three tables, so the body of the older woman remained in an adjoining room.

Sargi, hidden beneath a dark cloak and headscarf, peeled away the sheet on the first body, Zainab's body, then gently draped a white cotton towel, skirt-like, across it. Looking at the dead girl's face, the mother of seven confirmed what she had initially thought: She did not know the girls. She had never seen them at the mosque. She had not met their family.

Sargi wondered how these strong bodies had been broken, though she knew it was not her concern. Her duty was to prepare them for the journey ahead, so they could return to the earth. Without her help, their souls could not be free.

There was no one to answer Sargi's questions. Though permitted, no relatives had come to help with *Al-Ghusl,* the washing, and *Al-Kafan,* the wrapping. These were unpaid virtuous acts, to be performed only by trustworthy and honest Muslims who would profit from their kindness in a manner that could not be measured.

Though it was unusual, Sargi was not concerned that no one had come to share the duty. She knew there were many good people too frail of heart for this. This was her obligation. As long as she could, she would help the dead.

Sargi began to recite the Qur'an, the Arabic verses flowing together in singsong cadence:

Bism-illah-ir-Rahman-ir-Rahim.
Al-Hamdu lillahi Rabbil-alamin.

Her voice, low and soft, had a dark timbre.

Sargi serenaded Zainab with the holy words as her thick fingers massaged the green water through the girl's long mane of chestnut hair. There was too much to contain. Damp strands slipped away from the porcelain and plunged toward the floor. Sargi captured the tendrils and placed them back on the table.

Her fingers discovered the semicircle of staples that stretched from the left ear around the top of Zainab's head and down to her right ear. The washerwoman cleaned gingerly around the incision where the girl's scalp had been bound back together.

Ar-rahmani ar-rahim.
Maliki yawmi d-din.

She began to wash the right side of Zainab's body, from the top of her shoulder down to her foot. Sargi scooped the cleaning fluid from the basin with a plastic pitcher and poured a small amount over the pale flesh. She stroked gently with her gloved hand, pushing the water. Zainab's skin was cool, soft. Droplets flowed toward the centre of her body, following a stapled incision, the left branch of the Y.

Zainab watched, felt the washerwoman's touch, Sargi believed. Her spiritual certainty guided her delicacy. She caressed the skin. She did not scrub or scour. The dead would know if her touch were coarse, unkind. Zainab's soul was eager for its moment of supplication. A pure and honest act, this cleansing and wrapping would cast Zainab in the same simple form as every other Muslim who departed to face judgment.

Sargi's helper stepped in and rolled Zainab onto her left side. The woman held the body while Sargi washed the right rear, from shoulder to foot. The process was repeated on Zainab's left.

The remaining *sidr* water was dumped from the bowl and replaced with fresh water and camphor. Sargi rinsed Zainab with this solution and then bathed her body a third time with clear water. Towels were used to dry the damp skin. The washing complete, Sargi folded Zainab's arms across her chest.

Sargi's helper brought three pieces of *kafan*, plain white cotton that would be used to shroud the eldest sister, to dress her in death as all Muslims are dressed, symbolically pure and equal.

They pushed the first piece of *kafan* beneath her. The cloth was large enough to encircle Zainab from chest to knees. Sargi bundled Zainab's hair behind her head and, using the second piece of fabric, fashioned a head covering that left only Zainab's face exposed.

The final piece of cotton, rectangular and several feet longer than Zainab, was pulled beneath her. The sides were folded up so that the fabric cocooned the girl. At each end, Sargi tied the wrapping closed with a belt-width strip of fabric so that the body was completely hidden.

Zainab was done.

Sargi and her helper moved on to the second girl.

Thirteen-year-old Geeti had the markings of adulthood—painted nails, pierced ears and a pierced navel—but the women saw a child.

They wept again.

When Geeti was done, they moved on to Sahar, and then lastly Rona.

When Sargi tied the final cord on Rona's *kafan*, three hours had elapsed from the moment she had first begun to bathe Zainab with cleansing fluid. She had caressed the curves and angles of each damp body with gentle fingers and had found no clue why four were taken together.

Knowing that only Allah can determine the time and place of a Muslim's death did not dull the sadness or her desire to understand the cause of such a tragedy.

As Sargi left the funeral parlour, she asked the clerk working in the office how the four had died.

"I think it was a car accident," she answered.

It seemed a reasonable explanation.

PART ONE

Family Roots

"If you love someone, it's a crime."
—Zubaida Siddique

1

"*If He Is a Good Man*"

EIGHTEEN-YEAR-OLD RONA AMIR and Mohammad Shafia were a picture-perfect bridal couple, the beautiful eldest daughter of a retired army colonel and the handsome Kabul businessman. Shafia, accomplished at age twenty-five, smiled for snapshots with his porcelain bride on his arm. It was 1978, the year that Rona would later lament that her lot in life "began a downward spiral." That day, in the crush of well-wishers and glare of flashbulbs that froze her mask of happiness, she did not see the turmoil ahead.

Many people attended their elaborate wedding at the Intercontinental, the finest hotel in Kabul. The surroundings were posh, adorned with chandeliers and carpets in rich red tones. The teenaged bride wore a gauzy baby-blue dress. Two blue roses, fashioned from the fabric, protruded from the satiny waves of dark hair near her left ear.

It was a refined beginning.

Shafia's mother, Shirin, had arranged the marriage two years earlier. She had found him this good girl when she attended the wedding of a distant relative, Noor. At the reception, Shirin noticed the bridegroom's younger sister Rona. The slender sixteen-year-old had beautiful skin and a round face with delicate features. She was quiet and reserved, perhaps even timid. Shirin was pleased. This girl was attractive, and she came from a reputable, middle-class family. Rona would surely make a good wife for Shafia and mother for his children.

Shirin was careful to comply with the strict tradition of *khwastgari*, the ritual that dictated rules of betrothal. First she asked Rona's family for the girl's hand in marriage for her son, and then she visited Rona's home several times to see the girl with her family. The visits did not diminish her first impression that Rona was a good mate for her son. Rona and her family were also invited to Shirin's home, as custom required. The visits afforded Shafia a chance to get a good look at the girl that his mother had selected for him. He approved.

Rona's elder brother asked her if she would accept the proposal to marry Shafia. Rona didn't fully comprehend what it would mean to become a wife, but she recognized that it was her fate to be given away to a man she did not know or love.

"Give me away in marriage if he is a good man," she replied. "Don't if he is not."

And so Rona's family investigated Shafia. They learned that his father, Akbar, had died in a car crash when Shafia was only two. Shafia had completed Grade 6, but in the absence of a patriarch in his family, and out of economic necessity, he was thrust at a young age into a position of leadership and responsibility. He began apprenticing with extended family, learning to repair televisions and radios. By the time Shafia was a teenager, he had opened a small electronics shop with a loan from his grandfather. Shafia proved adept at electronic repair and was soon able to open a larger shop in downtown Kabul. He expanded from selling primarily radios to importing and reselling other electronics.

Learning this, Rona's family decided Shafia was a simple, hard-working young man who would succeed in business—an acceptable suitor. With the blessing of her family secured, the bright young high school student who had just completed Grade 11 was betrothed to a stranger seven years her senior. In a country where girls as young as two were offered up by their families as wives for men in their sixties and seventies, it was a reasonable arrangement viewed as a highly compatible match.

And so, in 1978, Rona and Shafia were wed, beginning their new life together in the same year that Afghanistan began its descent into three bloody decades of war and chaos that would reduce Kabul to rubble and displace millions of Afghans. President Daoud Khan was assassinated in a coup in which thousands died. War planes fired on the presidential palace in Kabul as military units loyal to Daoud battled troops sympathetic to the Soviet Union, which had long provided financial and political support to Afghanistan.

Rona and Shafia were still relative newlyweds when Soviet troops invaded Afghanistan in December 1979. Soviet commandos stormed the palace and killed the president, setting the stage for the installation of a puppet leader and a deadly, decade-long occupation that would see one million Afghans die.

In the Shafia home, an unexpected problem was festering: Rona could not get pregnant. At first, Shafia was not troubled by her failure to give him a child. He was busy with his expanding business empire. He launched a company, Babul Ltd., to import and distribute products from Japan. Rona visited several doctors, received injections and assurances, but still failed to conceive. Shafia took her to India for treatment from experts, but the expensive intervention did not help.

After several childless years, Shafia began to hear derisive jokes from his acquaintances and business associates. People were ridiculing him for his failure to impregnate his wife. Maybe something was wrong with *him*, they were saying. There were crude taunts about farm animals.

Shafia trained his anger upon his barren wife. He began to snipe at Rona and became more controlling, telling her to stop leaving the home to visit her mother. "He would find fault with my cooking and serving meals and he would find excuses to harass me," Rona would write in her diary, years later. Until that point, she had considered his treatment of her to be kind. But Shafia could not contain his growing bitterness over his wife's failure to give him children.

Rona's younger sister Houma arrived for an overnight visit. She was sitting with Rona when Shafia came into the room and snapped at his wife.

"You are a land without crops," he complained. "You cannot give me kids."

Houma spoke up: "Shafia, you shouldn't say these kinds of things to my sister. This is from God."

Rona would not let the slight pass. "Please don't say these things in front of my sister," she implored, challenging her husband.

Shafia stepped forward and began slapping Rona on the face. Horrified, Houma retreated to her room. She did not confront Shafia and she never spent the night at her sister's home again. Houma feared for Rona but custom dictated that she should not meddle in the affairs of another family.

Rona's frustration with her husband's resentment and anger led her to a distasteful but, she believed, necessary decision. Feeling there was nothing else she could do, she told Shafia to marry again.

"I will take a second wife but you also I will have treated," Shafia said, promising to continue to seek a medical solution to Rona's infertility.

As Shafia recalled it, he did not have to look far for a second mate. The wife of his longtime friend Aziz visited the couple's home in Wazir Akbar Khan, an affluent Kabul neighbourhood. She noted that the big house Shafia had built was quiet, devoid of the sounds of scampering little feet on the tile floors. The woman suggested her seventeen-year-old sister Tooba would make a good bride and mother. The educated girl, one of seventeen children of a well-to-do pharmacist, met with the suitor in a restaurant, according to Tooba's recollection years later.

"I have a good life but I have no kids," Shafia told her. "If you're not in agreement, no one can force you and I don't want this marriage to be forced."

Other family members have a different recollection of Shafia's introduction to Tooba. Tooba's brother Fazil Jawid, who fled Afghanistan in 1992 and who now lives in Sweden, and Tooba's uncle, Latif Hyderi, who moved to Canada in 2000, say that Shafia was imprisoned in an Afghan jail for several years in the early 1980s. It was a time of political upheaval and violence as feuding groups jockeyed for power while mujahedeen rebels waged a guerrilla campaign against the Soviet occupiers.

Hyderi said, in an interview years after the events, that Shafia was caught up in a dangerous scheme of bribe-giving and -taking, in which people affiliated with warring political factions were jailed without cause and then released if money was paid to the right person. While behind bars, Shafia met Aziz, who listened sympathetically to his story of failing to sire children. The pair remained friends after their release, and the man told Shafia he had an unmarried sister-in-law who might make a suitable spouse.

Whichever version of the story is true, Shafia and Tooba Yahya were married in 1988. Shafia presented his new bride to his family and friends in a familiar setting, one befitting his status as a successful businessman: the grand banquet hall at the Intercontinental Hotel.

The family album grew to contain snapshots of two picture-perfect brides. In the second set, Tooba was striking in an elaborate white gown, cinched snugly at the waist. Her layered skirt skimmed the floor. She was doll-like, with bright red lips, rosy, blush-dappled cheeks and green-shadowed eyes. As a sign of her husband's wealth, she wore an elaborate gold necklace and dangling gold earrings. Her thick hair was rolled on top of her head. A veil hung around her shoulders.

The newlyweds walked arm in arm, Shafia dressed in a crisp dark blue suit, light blue shirt and simple diagonally striped tie. To an outsider, it would have appeared to be a traditional western celebration, save for one significant aberration. As the couple walked, Shafia clutched another woman tightly to his side, his left arm linked with hers. Rona wore a shimmering, pale green dress that fell below her knees. She too wore a conspicuously large gold necklace and earrings.

Twelve months after the union, on September 9, 1989, Tooba gave Shafia what he wanted. He took her to India, where he believed medical care was superior, so that she could deliver the couple's first child, a girl they named Sadaf. Everyone came to know her by her second name, Zainab.

The birth secured Tooba's place as the dominant wife. Shafia denied Rona an opportunity to bear children. While the three were in India, Rona visited a doctor who told her that surgery could overcome her infertility. Shafia would not permit it. The group had only fifteen days left on their visas before they must return to Afghanistan. Shafia told Rona that he feared she would not get good care if there were any post-surgery complications, because there were no good doctors in Kabul.

They returned to Kabul and, fifteen months after Zainab's birth, Tooba gave Shafia a son. Hamed was born December 31, 1990. It seemed a turning point. Rona believed that Tooba was growing resentful that Shafia continued to treat the two women equally.

When Hamed was seven months old, catastrophe struck. Rona was sitting on a glass skylight on the roof of the family home, cradling Hamed in her arms, when the glass gave way and they plunged to the floor below. Hamed's head and Rona's head, arm and leg were badly injured. They were treated by Shafia's half-brother, Dr. Anwar Yaqubi. The pair recovered fully, but Shafia blamed Rona.

"You dropped my son," he complained repeatedly.

"I didn't do it on purpose, I was hurt too," she offered, but his reply was always the same.

"I don't care about you, you hurt my son."

Three months after the mishap, on October 22, 1991, Tooba gave birth a third time and, to Rona's surprise, handed Sahar to Rona to raise as her own. Rona was thrilled, but she did not realize that gaining a daughter would mean losing her husband. A few months after Sahar's birth, Tooba announced that Shafia would begin spending three out of every four nights with her. Rona did not resist because Tooba had given her a child. She loved Sahar dearly and cherished the other children. She had spent countless hours helping to raise them and tend their home.

By the summer of 1992, when Sahar was eight months old, the civil war in Kabul had intensified, and Shafia and Anwar Yaqubi hastily packed their families into vehicles and fled together across the border to Pakistan. Three more children were born there, Mina, Zafar and Geeti, before Shafia relocated his family again in 1996, to Dubai, a prosperous Islamic state on the Arabian peninsula. They would remain there for a decade. Tooba gave birth once more, in 2000, to Fereshta.

By this time, Rona felt miserable and alienated. "We were very happy for some time after we arrived in Dubai because there was a change in our lives, but this happiness was short-lived because Tooba, little by little, implemented all the schemes and drove me into misery without allowing any censure or blame to attach to herself," Rona would write in her diary.

Tooba learned to drive, took control of the household finances and severed any thread that connected Shafia and Rona as husband and wife. Shafia stopped sleeping in the same bed with Rona.

"Miserable me, who wouldn't question Shafia in regard to anything, swallowed everything without a word, because I had no option," Rona would write. She felt trapped and tortured by the emotional push and pull. She could not imagine leaving the children she loved, yet she dreamed of a better life. Instead, her misery grew. Shafia would soon blame her for another misfortune.

In 2001, Shafia moved the ten-member family to Australia, after his application to enter New Zealand was denied because Rona had failed a required medical examination. In January 2002, the Australian government denied Shafia's request for a business visa that would allow him to remain in the country for five years. He had been caught sending his children to publicly funded schools in violation of their short-stay holiday visas. Rona's status as Shafia's first wife had not been declared. Shafia was told that he and his family no longer had any lawful reason to remain in the country.

The family retreated to Dubai and took up temporary residence in a hotel for three months. Shafia blamed Rona for the costly episode: "This is all because of you. We had been accepted in New Zealand but all this loss we have incurred because of you," he said, according to Rona's diary.

One day, he angrily suggested she leave. "Go back to Kabul. I can't keep you as my tail wherever I go."

"The Taliban are in power, how can I go back there?" Rona complained. "Many a lion-whiskered macho brute has had to flee Kabul and you want to send me there?"

Shafia responded to her defiance by hitting her. Some of the children came into the room and pleaded with their father to stop.

"I am beating her up because she swore at your mom and insulted her," Shafia said.

Rona wrote in her diary that the lie was meant to conceal his abuse: "In short, he had made life a torture for me."

SHAFIA EVENTUALLY FOUND A SUITABLE HOME for his big family, an apartment in Deira, an older area of Dubai. He rented a three-bedroom unit in the Al Yasmeen building, a modern, five-level complex of several hundred units near the burgeoning Dubai International Airport. The location would be convenient for Shafia's regular business trips out of the country, and the complex had amenities: a swimming pool, a fitness centre and a sheltered central courtyard with a playground.

Dubai seemed a good fit for Shafia, a man who was wedded to old-world traditions but who yearned for lucrative, modern business opportunities. The largest city in the emirate of the same name, Dubai was an anachronistic mix of fifteen-hundred-year-old Islamic strictures and modern hedonism. It was one of the wealthiest and fastest-growing regions on the Arabian Peninsula, a centre of commerce in the Persian Gulf. Oil cash had fuelled a four-decade orgy of construction in Dubai, which had become one of the world's biggest oil producers since the black gold was discovered there in the 1960s. Outlandish structures of glass and steel shaped like boat sails and space rockets sprouted in a conservative Islamic desert community dotted with mosques.

The royal rulers, sheikhs, had cancelled taxes and duties and thrown open their doors to wealthy Britons, Indians, Saudis, even Americans, to work and live in the expanding metropolis. Gleaming shopping malls were erected that sold body-baring fashions from around the globe, and pulsing nightclubs served alcohol to partying westerners. But visitors to Dubai were cautioned to dress and behave conservatively in public.

Al Yasmeen was functional if not ideal for the large Shafia family. Dubai barred immigrants from purchasing property, so Shafia could not buy a home more suited to the family's size. But there were friendly faces in the Al Yasmeen building. Old acquaintances of Shafia from Kabul, the Shahabis, also lived in the building with their two children, a son and a daughter.

Sanam Shahabi accompanied her mother on regular visits to the Shafia apartment. Four years older than Zainab, Sanam was polite and respectful but did not consider herself a friend or playmate of the Shafia children, despite their common background. The Shafias were a more traditional and strict family than her own. Sanam did not attend an Islamic school and, like her brothers, could choose her friends. Her father did not insist she wear a headscarf. Although the Shafia children enjoyed some of Dubai's modern luxuries, they had to adhere to some old-world ways.

Sanam enjoyed the hospitality at the Shafia home, particularly the *bolani* that Tooba often served when they visited. She munched on the fried flatbread filled with potatoes while her mother and Tooba talked. Sanam marvelled at how the family, ten people stuffed into one apartment, seemed blissfully happy. All of the children spoke lovingly of their parents, including Rona and Tooba, who both got cards on Mother's Day. Sanam couldn't imagine being equally kind to a stepmother who lived with you, but hadn't given birth to you. She had heard Rona and Tooba's story from her family.

As in Afghanistan, having more than one wife was acceptable in Dubai, as long as the man could provide for all his wives and didn't have more than four. In Dubai, local zoning rules barred the construction of more than one home on a single lot except in the case of men with two wives.

Sanam saw Rona and Tooba almost every day in the exercise room at the apartment complex, working out together. She also saw them together with the kids in the courtyard play area. She detected no signs of rivalry or discord between the co-wives.

On Fridays the brood often piled into their car for the drive to Safa Park, a sixty-hectare oasis of water fountains, rolling green space and sports facilities about ten minutes south in new Dubai. Shafia would slaughter a lamb for the barbecue. He seemed, despite his old-fashioned values, a caring father, the head of a happy household. There did not appear to Sanam to be a facade of family happiness, so she was shocked by the events that unfolded years later.

2

Popular Girls

"GEETI, QUIET PLEASE!" the teacher snapped.

Hamida covered her mouth with her hand to conceal a smile. She knew where this could be heading.

Geeti dismissed the reprimand with a glance. She kept on talking to her classmate, about nothing in particular. *Uh-oh,* Hamida thought.

"Geeti!" the teacher barked, louder, more urgently.

The chatty ten-year-old was still jabbering to her pal, smiling, ignoring the commands. Her defiance had an inevitable outcome and Geeti knew it.

"Geeti, go and stand out for the rest of the class," the teacher ordered. The climax had come swiftly.

Hamida held her breath.

Geeti stared at her punisher and began to laugh defiantly.

Hamida giggled. This was the way it had gone before, many times. Some of the other twenty-five girls in the Grade 4 classroom began to laugh. It became a cacophony of squeaky, prepubescent cheering.

Geeti was always "messing with teachers," as Hamida thought of it. Many of Geeti's schoolmates regarded her as cool because of it. Hamida wished she could spend more time with Geeti, but their parents were strict and didn't allow them to socialize outside of school. She didn't find it strange. It was just the way life was with traditional, conservative parents. Neither girl had visited the other's home. They did not hang out at the park together. School was their playground.

Hamida considered Geeti her best friend. She really liked her, although sometimes Geeti seemed too confident, too cocky. She came off as rude with some of the shy girls who weren't willing to join in or cheer the mischief. And sometimes, Geeti seemed to push too far against adult authority.

Still, Geeti had been kind when Hamida arrived in Dubai a year earlier from Afghanistan. It had been a scary time for a nine-year-old, arriving in a strange new city and beginning studies at a big Islamic school where everyone wore uniforms and studied Arabic and the Qur'an but spoke English in science and math classes.

"You're not odd," Geeti reassured Hamida many times. "Don't worry about it. You'll learn English fast and nobody here looks down on Afghans."

The kindness cemented their friendship.

"We'll be friends till we're old," Geeti told Hamida. "I hope we can be together forever."

Friends seemed important to Geeti, who smirked at her classmate as she got up from her seat and headed for the door. Her performance was complete and the laughter was subsiding. With the leader banished, the brief rebellion ended. Hamida watched admiringly as Geeti left the classroom.

She's pretty, popular and confident, Hamida thought. *I'd like to be just like her.*

ZAINAB'S FRIENDS BEGAN TO SNICKER as soon as they saw her.

They weren't sure she would be bold enough to follow through on the dare, especially after the teacher's pointed warning the day before, but they weren't really surprised. Her mischievousness endeared her to her crew, who could always count on her to make them laugh.

She's the kind of girl you always want to be around, Zubaida thought.

The teacher had said any student not wearing the proper uniform— standard grey dress over a white T-shirt and white trousers with a plain white headscarf—would not be permitted to write the exam. But there

Zainab was, strutting down the corridor with her familiar Mona Lisa smile, wearing a black headscarf and, beneath her uniform dress, a black T-shirt and jeans.

"Zainy, you're crazy, you're not going to be allowed to do the exam," Fatma pronounced breathlessly. Zubaida giggled next to Fatma.

Zainab dismissed her friends, though she was emboldened by their anxiety. She was simply following through on Fatma and Zubi's challenge.

"C'mon, it's your turn," they had goaded. "Do it. Tomorrow. Just wear a different colour pant or shirt." They played a never-ending game of dare and now Zainab had one-upped them. The exam supervisor approached Zainab immediately, demanding to know why she was not wearing a proper uniform.

Fatma and Zubi eavesdropped from a few metres away.

"I'm sorry," Zainab offered, feigning remorse. "I forgot to get my mom to wash my T-shirt and my scarf and that . . . and I was so busy preparing for my examination."

The teacher grudgingly agreed to let Zainab write the exam, but cautioned her not to show up again in black. It wasn't much of a scolding for what seemed, at least to the girls, a transparent lie. Once the trio was out of range of the teacher, they laughed.

"See, I bet you I could get away with it," Zainab announced triumphantly.

It was another small victory for the Top Girls, as they called themselves. They believed that their reputation was a shield against rules and retribution. After all, they all got top grades, and they were pretty, fashionable and funny. Most teachers liked them, despite their mischief. It was harmless girly stuff, Fatma believed. They feared their parents, so their misbehaviour didn't stray into dangerous territory—boys, smoking or alcohol. None of them had boyfriends. It was forbidden.

Zubaida considered them sisters, particularly Zainab. She liked it when teachers remarked that she and Zainab looked alike and even talked alike. The trio of fifteen-year-olds, Zainab, Zubaida Siddique and Fatma Kassim, were the core of the TGs, though several other girls drifted in and out of the group.

"We were like sisters, so she used to share everything with me," Zubaida recalled years later. She knew that at home Zainab could not share her secret crushes on boys, her dreams of romance and her pride for the pranks that went unpunished.

Zubaida felt sorry for Zainab, who had lived a strangely nomadic life—three years in Kabul, four years in Pakistan, five years in Dubai, nine months in Australia, then back to Dubai. She was an Afghan who did not know Afghanistan. She didn't know anywhere as home, really.

Now, Zainab had found something to hold onto, something to give her purchase in life, this whimsical band of wannabe bad girls who encouraged her minor misdeeds and who appreciated her defiance of adult authority. Fatma and Zubaida marvelled at how Zainab would offer to take the blame if the Top Girls were accused of causing trouble in class, talking too much, being disruptive, skipping. Like a protective den mother, she was always willing to sacrifice herself for the group, a trait that might have had something to do with being the eldest of five sisters.

"It was kind of a family for us," Fatma said, years later. "We were the popular girls in fun and naughtiness."

KHADIJA THOUGHT SAHAR LOOKED A BIT STRANGE, dressed in skinny jeans, a short-sleeved top and a headscarf that wasn't wrapped around her hair. It drooped around Sahar's neck and shoulders, like an accessory.

It was parent–teacher night, so the girls were permitted to shun their shapeless school uniforms.

"Short sleeves and a scarf isn't really a fashion statement," Khadija teased. "You look like a fob!"

Sahar laughed off the mocking immigrant slur from her Somali friend. She wasn't "fresh off the boat." Her family had been in Dubai for years.

"I don't care," Sahar said dismissively.

There was nothing angry about the response. Needling was a regular occurrence between the girls, although they weren't classmates. Khadija was two years younger than Sahar but thought her older schoolmate was the kindest person in the school to her. Sahar was friendly and outgoing, but calm and thoughtful. To Khadija, Sahar always looked like she was thinking things through carefully. She got good grades and rarely misbehaved, unlike her sisters.

Whenever Khadija scoured the hallways for her cousin, who was in Sahar's class, Sahar would eagerly join the search. Sahar was so different from her younger sister Geeti, whom Khadija also considered a friend. She couldn't quite figure out the girl who was known around the school as the naughtiest Shafia. Geeti was exuberant and outspoken, a class clown who got poor grades and made frequent trips to the principal's office. Geeti's sisters Mina and Zainab also had a reputation for getting into trouble, but they managed decent grades and their pranks were different, less threatening. Geeti could be nasty. Like that time she slapped her English teacher, and the time in the hallway at lunch.

Khadija had been startled by what she had seen, but not really surprised. Geeti *hated* that teacher. The corridor was crowded with girls and teachers, including the middle-aged woman who had been riding Geeti about her behaviour, chastising her incessantly for weeks: *Where are your manners? You're such a shame.*

Khadija had watched Geeti weave stealthily through the bodies until she was almost behind the teacher, who was walking to another classroom. Geeti suddenly stepped close, cocked her leg back and kicked the woman quickly but firmly. The teacher yelped and wheeled round to confront her attacker, but Geeti had darted to the other side of the hall. She was leaning against the wall, smirking, by the time the teacher pivoted. The woman confronted Geeti, but the girl bristled with denial.

Lacking proof, an eyewitness or a confession, the teacher gave up and stormed away.

Geeti thought she had gotten away with it, but schoolmates didn't universally admire her defiance. Several students snitched and told teachers what they had seen. Geeti was suspended.

Khadija never considered whether the slapping and kicking incidents might have been a sign of something else going on in the young girl's life, maybe something troubling at home. To the unsophisticated thirteen-year-old, Geeti just seemed to be looking for attention.

She liked being talked about, Khadija figured.

GEETI ACQUIRED A REPUTATION at Al Sadiq Islamic English School as a troublemaker, but many students regarded her and her sisters as kind, loyal and likable. Good looks secured their popular status.

All of the Shafia girls had it. Zainab, Sahar, Mina and Geeti were pretty Afghans who stood out among the dozens of ethnic and racial groups represented at the fifteen-hundred-student school, one of more than 130 private schools in Dubai that teemed with children whose families had flocked to Dubai from South Asia and the Middle East.

The Shafias, with thick, dark hair, big almond eyes, soft oval faces and full lips, were striking. All of them, even little Fereshta, who attended the primary section, had the symmetry and suppleness of classic beauty. Classmates couldn't agree on who was the most attractive of the sisters. Some believed Mina, with her slender frame, was the prettier girl. Some schoolmates adored Sahar, with her captivating brown doe eyes.

Many boys coveted the Shafia girls, but they were perpetually frustrated window shoppers. At Al Sadiq, girls and boys studied in segregated wings from Grade 4 on. The sexes mixed only on rare occasions, like sports day. Admirers also knew they'd have to contend with the Shafia brothers, Hamed and Zafar, who were protective.

The school's Islamic code, and the parents of most students, forbade almost any contact between girls and boys, particularly teenagers. This didn't mean that the boys, seemingly refined in their blue-grey uniforms of dark trousers, pale blue shirts and ties, didn't struggle with hormonal urges. Zafar, who chastised his sisters for removing their hijabs, was twelve when he was caught at school with a CD of photos of naked women. He was ordered not to return to the school the following year, 2007. A teacher who was involved, Khurshid Khan, believed that Mohammad Shafia was humiliated by the incident.

Girls at Al Sadiq also grappled with biological anxieties. They spent long hours giggling over crushes on cute boys with whom they could not flirt. Older girls would lightly apply forbidden eye shadow and lipstick. They were almost always caught and required to scrub their faces.

For some older girls, the mandatory white head coverings were a daily experiment. Some would push their scarves back so that strands of hair escaped the concealing fabric to hang stylishly along their cheeks. Often, the scarf would hang open, allowing a view of colourful, dangling earrings. If she wanted to be more provocative, a girl could reshape her baggy uniform dress. A few careful hand stitches here and there would tuck the garment so that it was more form-fitting.

Many of these outwardly conservative girls owned skin-hugging True Religion jeans and Bench shirts bought in Dubai's vast malls, which bulged with pricey North American and European fashions. Some girls wore designer denim beneath their school dresses. Though the slacks were mostly unseen by teachers, the small act of rebellion was known to the perpetrators and acknowledged by schoolmates. The girls who wore jeans, painted their nails and tinkered with their headscarves considered themselves fashionable objectors. They drew satisfaction from small victories in a struggle against customs and rules imposed on them. They acquiesced, but only in the interest of keeping the adults happy.

Many of the transplanted girls at Al Sadiq knew old-world ways through the commandments of family and in the examples they saw in the adoptive Islamic society where they lived. Few girls were truly defiant. They acknowledged the rules their traditional families imposed and respected their boundaries, even though they often pressed up against them. Girls were aware of the wrath their behaviour could induce and most of them were concerned about it. Their concern was a mix of fear and respect.

The Shafia girls were no different. Though they too feared and respected their parents, they had not been raised in Afghanistan. The girls did not fully appreciate the traditional lives their parents had led, in which their two mothers, Rona and Tooba, were acquired by their father in arranged marriages brokered by their families.

THE TOP GIRLS SHARED EVERYTHING—clothing, makeup, jewellery. They pulled stunts together, "bunking" class and scampering off to the bathroom to giggle away an entire forty-minute period before sneaking back into the classroom. The girls were drawn to each other despite their dissimilar backgrounds. Zubaida, born in Pakistan to a liberal family, had been in Dubai for ten years. Fatma was born in neighbouring Sharjah to progressive parents from Tanzania. Zainab, born in Afghanistan in 1989, lived with rigid rules but still enjoyed some of the same freedoms as her pals. She was allowed to buy jewellery and fashionable clothing as long as she followed long-practised customs of modesty and propriety.

Zainab's parents were strict, her friends thought, though they didn't consider the Shafia rules harsh, at least not compared to what Abida faced. Their Pakistani schoolmate had tried to worm her way into their clique but the trio had rejected her. Even if the Top Girls felt some sympathy for Abida, they didn't trust her. She was the kind of girl who tried to turn friends against each other by spreading stories and gossip. The Top Girls were too tight, too protective of each other, to admit such an interloper. Abida seemed desperate to belong, perhaps because she knew her time was expiring. Her family would not permit her to complete further education after high school. She'd likely be required to spend most of her time at home until a suitable husband could be found. She had to wear a cloak and full face covering when she ventured outside her home. If she were caught talking to boys it would be *dangerous* for her, Zubaida knew. She was uncertain how far punishment might go, but she understood that Abida's family members, her father and brothers, might harm her.

Zubaida knew she'd never have to worry about such things in her family, and she didn't think Zainab had to worry about them either. Her friend had never even hinted at family violence and Zubaida saw no evidence to contradict this, though she had rarely been to the Shafia home. Like Abida's house, it was not a welcoming place for outsiders. Zubaida had met Zainab's mother many times and considered her pleasant, sweet even. Tooba often picked up her kids at the school.

Zainab's father seemed polite when Zubaida met him a few times at school. Mohammad Shafia always smiled and offered a *salam*. But Zubaida understood that Zainab's father wanted his eldest daughter to follow the family's tradition of arranged marriages. A partner would be chosen, but not based on love. Zubaida knew what this meant for many girls, including Zainab: *If you love someone, it's a crime.*

AS ZAINAB'S GRADE 10 SCHOOL YEAR WAS WINDING DOWN, she delivered shocking news to her friends: Her family was moving to Canada in June.

"I'm so happy here," Zainab told her girlfriends. "I love you guys. I don't want to go. I don't want to be with my family. I don't want to see my cousins in Canada."

She relayed to them what her parents had told her: "My mom and dad want a better future for us."

Shafia would later offer a vague claim that the departure from Dubai had something to do with Zainab turning eighteen and not having citizenship, which was nearly impossible for visitors to acquire in the United Arab Emirates. But none of Zainab's non-citizen schoolmates suddenly moved away, and Shafia never publicly discussed the embarrassing expulsion of his younger son from Al Sadiq.

Zainab saw her dreams evaporating.

"I thought I'd get married here," she said. "I want to stay near you guys."

She was angry and frustrated, so she gave up on school and stopped studying or completing homework. "What's the use," she told Fatma and Zubaida. "I mean, I'm going to do it here and when I go over to Canada, I have to do it again."

Her friends couldn't understand why the family was moving again, five years after returning to Dubai from Australia. They knew that Zainab's father still did business in Dubai and regularly made trips to Afghanistan and other nearby countries. They saw no logical reason for the upheaval, but they knew Zainab would have to go.

On June 13, the girls were dropped off by their parents at the Al Yasmeen building for a rare visit to Zainab's home, on her last night in Dubai. The family's flight was scheduled to leave at nine the next morning.

The trio spent hours roaming the apartment complex, searching for a suitable backdrop for their farewells. They reminisced about the exploits of the Top Girls. They tried to count the number of times they had skipped introductory Arabic class. They struggled to remember how many times they'd been ordered to scrub away nail polish or tuck runaway strands of hair back into their headscarves. They laughed at the memories and imagined that one day they'd all be together again.

At midnight, the girls hugged goodbyes in the doorway. Zainab's eyes glistened but she did not cry.

"As soon as I can, I'll come back," she told them.

PART TWO

Canada

"be aware of my bro"
—Zainab Shafia

3

Home

LATIF HYDERI FELT A SENSE OF OBLIGATION to meet the Shafia family at the airport in June 2007. Only a handful of Afghans lived in Montreal, and he knew that a fellow countryman would be a welcoming sight for newcomers. Indeed, Hyderi was happy because it would be a reunion of sorts for him. He had lost contact with much of his family. Like many Afghans who had fled violence and extremism, he and his family had scattered throughout Europe, the Middle East and North America. Hyderi, who had spent four years in prison during the Soviet occupation, had brought only memories and a few scraps of mujahedeen memorabilia to Montreal in 2000. He treasured the snapshots that showed him and camouflage-clad compatriots toting Kalashnikov rifles, but he embraced the ideals of his new home. He believed Canada was a good place for his two sons and two daughters to grow up, a country where they would have opportunities and choices that would never have been available to them in his birthplace.

Mohammad Shafia gave these opportunities as his reason to uproot his family again. Canada was a safe country, where they could easily secure citizenship and trusted passports and where there were good schools for his children. He would say, years later, that "wherever I went, to any place, I just went for my family."

The Shafia family home in Canada was a rented, four-bedroom flat in a brick building on a pretty suburban street in the borough of Saint-Léonard, in the east end of the Island of Montreal. Towering maple trees shaded the building's front. A thick cedar hedge traced the property's northwest corner. Bright orange azaleas bloomed in the shrubbery.

Saint-Léonard was a popular destination for newcomers to Quebec's biggest city. The area had grown dramatically through the mid-twentieth century as Italian immigrants flocked there. Now, four of every ten of the borough's seventy-one thousand citizens were immigrants, including more than five thousand of Arab background.

The Shafias joined a very small and tight-knit group. Only a few hundred of the area's transplants were from South Asian countries such as Afghanistan and Pakistan. And few among them were wealthy entrepreneurs who could afford to buy their way into the country as had Mohammad Shafia. He and his family qualified immediately, under the province's immigrant investor program, for permanent residency. As part of the program, Shafia had given $400,000 to the Quebec government. The province would keep the cash for five years, retaining any interest earned but returning the principal at the end of the period. Shafia made it clear he was an ambitious businessman. He had registered a business in his name in 2006, before the family even arrived in Canada. In the year after his arrival, he registered three more businesses in Quebec.

The complex at 8644 rue Bonnivet was typical of the working-class neighbourhood. It was a flat-roofed, three-storey building containing six apartments. The Shafias took the middle unit on the west end of the building. They filled the garage with disassembled furniture, boxes and clothing shipped from Dubai, most of which remained unpacked. Shafia did not plan to stay long on Bonnivet, even though more than half a dozen relatives lived nearby, including Tooba's elderly mother and Hyderi, her paternal uncle.

When Hyderi met the Shafias at the airport on June 14, one member of the family was missing: Rona did not make the trip to Canada. She left Dubai on the same day as the nine other family members and flew to France to visit her sister Diba, whom she had not seen for fifteen years. Rona had been packed off to Europe because Shafia needed time to figure out how to get her into Canada. He knew that polygamy was illegal and so he could not bring two wives to the country. In his immigration application, Shafia had named Tooba as his wife.

After their arrival, Hyderi extended an invitation that he hoped would help draw the families closer. He invited the Shafias to attend the summer wedding of his daughter. Tooba asked for help to get suitable clothes for her children to wear to the event, so Hyderi's nephew took her on a shopping trip. Hyderi was eager to host the niece he had not seen in a decade, and her family, and to share the joy of his daughter's big day. Places were reserved for the entire Shafia family, but when the day arrived they remained empty. None of the Shafias showed up.

Hyderi was told later that Mohammad Shafia had used scissors to angrily shred the clothes that were bought for his children while complaining that the outfits, some without sleeves, were inappropriate and too revealing. Hyderi was disappointed and felt insulted, but he did not dwell on it. Tooba was his niece and he would not hold this against her. He knew that Shafia was a strict and domineering man who would not easily adapt to a liberal society.

SHAFIA DENIED HIS CHILDREN the chance to wear sleeveless outfits and attend a wedding celebration, but he packed them off to public schools that were incubators for adolescent hormones, where teenagers preened and strutted, and pursued pleasures that promised admission to adulthood. He did not appreciate the powerful spell this new environment would cast over his naive brood.

Unlike that of Dubai, education in Quebec was not a one-stop proposition for the Shafia children. In the UAE, they had all attended one school from kindergarten through senior high school. Now they were split into three groups. Geeti, who was eleven, and Fereshta, seven, were enrolled at École Gabrielle Roy, an elementary school only a few blocks from their home. Sahar, almost sixteen, her sister Mina, fourteen, and brother Zafar, thirteen, were enrolled at Antoine-de-St-Exupéry, a big public high school about two kilometres south of their apartment. Zainab, who turned eighteen in September, attended St. Pius X, an adult education centre fifteen minutes by car from their apartment. Her brother Hamed, who would turn seventeen in December, also enrolled at St. Pius. He would drive Zainab, who did not have a licence, back and forth to school each day.

At Antoine-de-St-Exupéry high school, body-hugging jeans and hallway embraces supplanted concealing, shapeless uniforms, segregation and the absolute prohibition on inter-sex socialization that had dominated Sahar's school life in Dubai. She was awed by her new surroundings.

Sahar, Mina and Zafar were placed in a reception class for newcomers with a limited grasp of French. Immigrant students were required to study francophone culture and history and, most importantly, to learn to speak, read and write French. The students were forced, with a firm but polite push, to integrate into Quebec society in a way that no other Canadian jurisdiction demanded. Sahar was eager to learn French. She wanted to integrate, to be just like the other girls.

At St-Ex, as it was known, the number of reception classes grew each year. The school boasted more than seventy nationalities in the student body. The reception classes sheltered newcomers, to a limited extent, from the chaos of a suburban two-thousand-student school, at a time when there were many other pressures.

Most of the kids in reception classes at St-Ex were getting their first taste of Canadian schooling in an adoptive new home where they did not speak the right language. Many of the teenagers arrived wondering how they would fit in and whether they'd find someone they could talk to, someone to trust. Some spoke English. Some had a rudimentary understanding of French. Sahar knew some Urdu, acquired during the four years her family lived in Pakistan. She spoke a little Arabic, Dari, her first language, and fluent English.

The thirty kids placed in Sahar, Mina and Zafar's group immediately set about pigeonholing faces and personalities. There was Jake Suarez, the mysterious Colombian; Ray Hernandez, the shy Dominican; Lucy Lastragui, the gregarious Mexican; Herna Paul, the brash Haitian. Herna was intrigued by Sahar, the petite, quiet girl with big brown eyes. She seemed to glide through the room. Herna was reminded of a classical Japanese dancer, energy radiating from her core to her arms and out through expressive hands. She thought Sahar looked *elegant.*

Although the girls both spoke English, they didn't talk much in the first days of the school year. But the pair soon realized that they had something in common, besides their immigrant status—a crush on Jake, a dreamy boy with spiky black hair and a mellow, mysterious manner. Even his name was cool.

"He's hot," Sahar would say, in a small voice.

"Oh yeah, so *hawt,*" Herna gushed.

It went like this, a lot.

The girls would hurry out of their classroom into the corridor during breaks so that they could watch Jake, hanging in the hallway. He'd be standing around, talking with his Spanish-speaking bad-boy pals. The girls couldn't tell if he was truly uninterested in the girls who buzzed about him, or who ogled him from across the hall, or if he was playing a game of hard-to-get. And they couldn't figure out if he was a bad boy himself, or had just associated himself with the sketchy crowd for the sake of building a rep. Occasionally, Spanish-speaking girls who were not in the reception classes, but who had seen Jake at school—who had recognized his *hotness*—swooped in during breaks, hoping to interest him.

Sahar and Herna watched the intruders, who shared Jake's cultural background. He greeted them with a soft peck on each cheek.

Sahar and Herna cringed enviously.

"I hate them," they'd say. "I wish they'd get lost."

Although Sahar knew the double kisses were sexless, they were fascinating and unlike anything she had seen in a school corridor. They inflated the aura of mystery around Jake. He spoke English, so Sahar and Herna tried to talk with him, but the meaningless chatter never evolved into meaningful conversation.

"Hey," the girls would say, hopefully.

"Hey," Jake usually replied and then, typically, "I'm leaving now. Catch you later." And with that, it was over, leaving the awestruck duo whispering again that he was "Sooo hot." Jake's dull banter didn't put them off. They couldn't get enough out of him to decide whether he was annoying and they got just enough to conclude he was intriguing.

As Sahar grew more comfortable in her new surroundings, she began to mingle with her classmates, to chit-chat in the corridor with the other girls and to *hang*, doing nothing but being in a place where you could see and be seen.

A few weeks into the school year, one morning before class, Sahar was hanging with several other girls in the hallway when Jake approached. There were grins and giggles. Jake leaned in to a girl in the group, said hi and kissed her cheek. Before Sahar had a chance to recoil, Jake moved toward her. He leaned in, closer to her than any boy had come before. His lips caressed Sahar's cheek, softly, for just a second, before he moved on to another girl.

Sahar blushed and grinned. Jake thought her reaction seemed a mixture of delight and anxiety, like she was nervous or afraid. He kissed the cheeks of smiling girls dozens of times every day. They knew it was just his way of saying hello and most of them appreciated it, without complication. Jake couldn't figure out what Sahar was thinking.

The next day, when Jake arrived for school, he discovered that his purposeless little kiss had turned into something bad. The teacher told Jake that Sahar was outside the classroom and wanted to speak to him. Jake followed his teacher into the corridor, to a secluded spot where Sahar was waiting. She was crying.

"You're the first guy who ever got that close to me and kissed me like that," Sahar told him. "My little sister saw and she told my dad."

Jake was stunned.

"He got really mad and he slapped me."

Slapped me. Jake heard what she said but couldn't believe what she was telling him. He'd never, ever caused any trouble before with one of his harmless kisses, and here was this sweet girl, not his girlfriend, not someone he flirted with, telling him it was a big deal.

"So if my sister is around, you can't get that close to me," Sahar said.

Jake mumbled an apology and said he understood, though he didn't. The teacher asked Jake to stay at the end of the day so she could talk to him. After class, the teacher gave Jake advice, not instruction. She told Jake that Sahar might get into more trouble at home if her sister saw her doing things at school that her family didn't consider appropriate. The woman did not tell him that he should not hang around Sahar or that he should not kiss her again. She simply said that he should watch out for Sahar's sister.

BEFORE ANYONE COULD FIGURE EVERYONE OUT, the reception group was divided because it was clear that some students could pick up French faster than others. Ray and his new pal Benjamin, both Dominicans, were separated when Ray was moved into the advanced group with Sahar and Herna. Zafar and Mina, Sahar's younger siblings, ended up in the basic group with Jake. Jake didn't mind the split. It made it easier to keep his distance from Sahar.

Ray and Benjamin shared a common language and culture but they were an odd pair. Ray was slight, well-groomed and thoughtful. Benjamin was a 250-pound fifteen-year-old with long hair and shabby clothes who liked to *chill*. He called himself a loser. Herna, who spoke Creole and English and was born in New York to Haitian parents, was worldly-wise and independent, the product of a fractured family life with a drug-addicted father who was frequently in trouble with the law. Herna befriended Patrick, another American-born Haitian, among the fifteen students in the advanced class.

Most of the kids were going through *something* at home, and their school clique became their refuge. Many of them peppered their banter with F-bombs and multilingual cusses they eagerly gobbled up in the ethnic stew of St-Ex. Sahar giggled at the foul language and remarked that her classmates were *so bad*.

Herna would laugh at her in return.

"You're so sweet," she would say.

The advanced kids liked their teacher, Antonella Enea, because she treated them more like her children than her charges. She was gentle and welcoming, and she seemed to truly care about them. Many of the students began to trust her and to regard her as their den mother.

Where Sahar's peers perceived shyness, Enea sensed sadness. As soon as an opportunity arose, she took Sahar aside from the rest of the students and asked her if she was all right.

"No," Sahar replied.

"What's wrong?" the teacher asked. "Is there a problem at home?"

"Yes," Sahar said.

"Do you want to tell me about it?" Enea gently prodded.

"It's just—I can't, my family is strict," Sahar explained. "I can't have a normal life. I can't have the friends I want. I can't go out. I can't do stuff that other girls do."

The teacher said she might be able to help.

"No," Sahar replied quickly. "It's just the way things are. There's nothing you can do, but thanks."

ALTHOUGH SAHAR AND JAKE WERE NOW IN SEPARATE CLASSES, she couldn't stop thinking about him. She told Herna that she wanted to get Jake a gift for his birthday, coming up early in October.

"Like what?" Herna asked.

"I don't know," Sahar said. "Maybe a chain or something. But I don't know how I'm gonna do it, 'cause if my dad knows I want money to buy something for a guy, he'll never let me. And somebody's always with me."

Herna was surprised by Sahar's plan. She considered her friend shy and this was bold. But Sahar was smitten and intoxicated by the idea of liking a boy—at the very least, she would make sure that he knew how she felt.

SAHAR DID NOT EXPLAIN HOW SHE HAD DONE IT. She carefully lifted the piece of jewellery from the bag, just far enough that Herna could see it was a sparkly silver bracelet.

"I'm going to give it to him," Sahar whispered to Herna. "Maybe next break."

It had been several weeks since Sahar had started talking about her scheme to get Jake a gift. His birthday had passed, but Sahar was determined to make the offering. At the next break, Jake got a message from a girl that Sahar wanted to talk to him by the lockers. It was a relatively secluded spot. When he found her, Sahar grabbed Jake's hand firmly and dragged him behind the lockers.

"I have something for you," she said eagerly as she handed him a dark black and brown scarf and a silver bracelet of intertwined links. "I know it's late, but happy birthday."

Jake was surprised. He had a girlfriend, as Sahar knew, and he had tried to keep his distance from her since the incident in September. He had been afraid, both for her and for himself, though he did not admit it to anyone.

Now here she was, this quiet, kind girl, demonstrating her bravery. Jake rewarded it by kissing her on both cheeks and then drawing her close to him in a gentle hug that she did not resist.

When Sahar returned to the classroom and sat down near Herna and Patrick, she looked angry.

"I gave it to him but my little sister saw me," she harrumphed. "She's gonna tell my dad and I'm going to get in trouble. She's always telling."

"I hate her," Herna commiserated. "She needs to just shut up."

"What's her problem?" Patrick added.

Sahar said she hadn't realized that Mina was in the corridor, watching her.

"If your parents could see us, they'd realize what an angel you are," Herna said.

In the weeks after Sahar exchanged a bracelet for two small kisses and one hug, her whole family stopped talking to her, on orders from her parents, as punishment for her transgressions. Sahar felt completely alone.

Rona, who always took Sahar's side in these battles, hadn't yet come to Canada, and Sahar's parents had warned her not to discuss private family matters with others. But there was too much anguish to conceal: Sahar's friends could see her sadness. Some days she cried and they struggled to cheer her. She told them about the shunning.

Benjamin, who sometimes hung out with Sahar's younger brother, Zafar, asked him about it.

"Hey, dude, why are you not talking to your sister?" he asked. "She's your sister."

"I don't know, it's a rule," Zafar said, refusing to provide any more explanation.

Benjamin turned the answer over in his head. It's a *rule?* That didn't sound right. *You can't do that to a kid,* he thought.

FOR THE FIRST FEW CHAOTIC MONTHS OF THEIR NEW LIVES in Canada, the Shafia children lacked a significant stabilizing force that they had known since birth. Rona was still missing. For Sahar, Zainab and Geeti particularly, Rona had often played the role of intermediary, backing them in disputes with their parents over strict rules and limitations on their freedoms.

Shafia did not find a way to bring Rona into the country until November, five months after the rest of the family. To conceal her status as his first wife, Shafia signed a document declaring that Rona "works for my family since my marriage in 1990 and takes care of my seven children and of my house."

Rona was anxious to see the kids again. She had found the separation unbearably painful, and she was willing to accept the humiliation of being passed off as Shafia's housekeeper and nanny so that she could be reunited with them.

Latif Hyderi extended a warm greeting to Rona after her arrival. He told Rona that although he was Tooba's uncle, she was part of the Shafia family and he would treat her too as his niece. She was free to visit his home anytime. Although Rona welcomed the kindness, Hyderi learned that the Shafia family did not appreciate it. Tooba told Hyderi that he should not speak to Rona when she or her husband was not present.

"You have taken her husband," Hyderi said. "You have kids. She has nothing. She has no husband, no kids. What has she taken from you?"

"You don't know her," Tooba responded. "You don't know what kind of person she is. If I'm there, you're allowed to talk to her, but if I'm not there, please don't talk to her."

For the sake of family harmony, Hyderi accepted what Tooba said without pressing further.

MOHAMMAD SHAFIA HAD FOUND THE PLACE he really wanted to call home.

Domaines de la Rive-Sud was an enclave of estate properties in Brossard, a suburban neighbourhood twenty-five kilometres southeast of Saint-Léonard in an area known as the South Shore because it was across the St. Lawrence River from the Island of Montreal. Rive-Sud was an exclusive subdivision where streets named Rome, Leningrad and Liverpool wound around two artificial lakes. A half-acre lot alone cost more than half a million dollars. Perfectly manicured lawns surrounded brick and stone mansions with copper-domed turrets and swimming-pool-sized fountains.

Shafia bought a lot on Lisbonne Street and, in December, he found an architect, a fellow Afghan who was living in Montreal, to design his home. Nabi Neda and his wife, Nasrin, had emigrated with their two children from Kabul to Montreal in 1999. Dreaming of new opportunities, the architect and doctor had found exactly the opposite: their Afghan credentials were not recognized. Nasrin needed years of expensive university upgrading before she would be allowed to practise medicine in the province, so she gave up her dream of returning to that career. She learned French and secured a steady job in a government office. Neda wasn't willing to abandon architecture. He completed a second master's degree at a Montreal university and was on his way to completing the thousands of hours of internship required to get full certification to work in the province as an architect. He had taken time away from the internship because he felt a duty to help rebuild his home country, and had just returned to Canada from Kabul, where he had worked in the international reconstruction program that was repairing the war-shattered city. Neda brought back a congratulatory framed photo of himself standing next to President Hamid Karzai.

Money was tight when Neda got a phone call from a friend asking if he wanted to design a house for a rich man. Nasrin urged her husband to keep doing what he loved, working on his internship so that he could land a good job with an architecture firm.

"This is not for you, Nabi," she told him. To her, it didn't feel right.

Neda convinced her that the house would be a short-term project that would provide the cash they needed; moreover, this businessman was a fellow Afghan new to the country who did not speak English or French. Neda felt sorry for Shafia, who seemed a simple but ambitious and hard-working man. He did not know that his new boss was a tight-fisted schemer who would try to drag him into bigger ventures.

SAHAR KNEW THAT ENJOYING THE COMFORTS that her father could provide, like a luxurious new home, required obedience, but she desperately wanted to fit in. Many girls at St-Ex painted their faces and bared their legs. Sahar wanted to look pretty for the Christmas potluck party in Antonella Enea's class.

Herna was sitting in the classroom when Sahar came rushing in that morning, looking panicked.

"Herna, I'm so scared!" Sahar said urgently. "My dad just saw me with eye shadow on. I'm scared. I'm so scared."

"What did he say?" Herna asked.

"Nothing, but I'm scared," Sahar repeated.

Herna had noticed the makeup right away, although it had been lightly applied. She had not seen Sahar wear makeup before. Herna wasn't sure how to reassure her friend because she didn't understand the problem. The makeup was barely visible compared to the heavy eyeliner and shadow most of the girls wore at school every day. Herna told Sahar not to worry; everything would be fine. Maybe her father hadn't seen the makeup, she said, since it was so light. Even if he had, he certainly wouldn't do anything, Herna said.

Sahar explained that she'd been making her way to the classroom when she saw her father in the corridor. She had no idea why he was at the school. She was sure he had seen her, seen *it*.

4

Half Hijab

THERE WERE NO TOP GIRLS AT ST. PIUS. Zainab didn't have a posse in the cavernous, four-storey school, which was a maze of tiled passageways and garishly painted red and yellow stairwells. But she was not alone. Her younger brother Hamed, who drove her to school, was always around. He was in class with her in the morning and he hovered during lunch. When she left the classroom or the library, he was usually nearby, trailing her. He knew everything she did.

But he didn't prevent Zainab from noticing the boys who were *everywhere* around her. Some of them had lockers within arm's reach. They passed her in hallways and they sat just a desk away in the classroom. Like Sahar, she was amazed and tantalized, being so close to so many boys after years of attending school segregated by gender.

Ammar Wahid had immediately noticed the new girl at her locker, near his on the third floor. Long swirling strands of dark hair fell out of her hijab. It was pushed back on her head, not wrapped tight like head coverings he'd seen on many girls from strict Muslim families, including many in his country, Pakistan. It looked as if she didn't really want to wear the scarf but was making a half-hearted attempt, while trying to be stylish at the same time. She wasn't wearing any makeup, but he thought she didn't need any: her skin was flawless. Ammar could see a small mole on her right cheekbone. It looked like a perfectly placed beauty mark. He was surprised that such a pretty girl didn't appear to have a boyfriend.

"Hey, Wasi, did you see that new girl with the half hijab?" Ammar asked his best friend. "There's something about her. I'd like to meet her."

Ammar went to mosque every Friday, but he didn't consider himself religious or a particularly devoted Muslim. He smoked and partied like many guys in their twenties. His parents had brought him to Canada when he was nine and he thought he'd done a good job of integrating into Montreal's multiracial society. He'd learned French and English, and he still spoke Urdu. He had taken to spiking his black hair and sometimes he trimmed his beard into thin strips of black that traced his jawline.

Maybe the new girl came from a religious family? Maybe he shouldn't make a direct move? He thought he'd caught her staring invitingly at him once or twice, so he figured it was worth a shot. He approached one of the girls he'd seen her talking to in the hallway.

"Hey, I'm Ammar. You know that girl, light skin, she wears a hijab, half covering and half not?" Ammar asked. "I think you're friends."

"Yeah, that's Zainab," the girl replied.

"I want to get to know her, and I wondered if you could introduce me to her?"

"Sure, I'll ask her," the girl replied. "If she's interested, I'll let you know."

Ammar waited eagerly for word from the intermediary. A few days passed and he heard nothing, so he approached the girl again and asked if she'd spoken to Zainab.

"Oh yeah, she's not interested."

Ammar wondered if he should have approached her directly. But he didn't see her talking to other guys at school, so maybe she wasn't interested in dating or maybe she couldn't, for some reason. She wasn't in his class, so there was no opportunity for schoolwork-related banter. He wasn't sure if "not interested" was really a no. Maybe she was playing hard to get.

WHEN STUDENT COUNCIL ANNOUNCED THE ROSE-A-GRAM SCHEME for Valentine's Day, Ammar knew it was the perfect opportunity to make another nonthreatening approach to the girl in the half hijab. In the weeks since the initial rejection, he was certain that he'd seen her tossing him looks. He was puzzled but intrigued, and he thought she was gorgeous.

He paid one dollar for a rose and a chocolate to be delivered to Zainab in the classroom across the hall from his. He wrote a short note to attach to the gift, asking Zainab if she'd like to get to know him. He included an unusual suggestion about how she might signal her approval. It gave her an easy out if she wanted to blow him off without having to confront him. He suggested she wear white to school the following day if she was interested.

On Valentine's Day, hundreds of hopeful suitors in St. Pius waited anxiously for a sign that their gifts had sparked interest. Ammar didn't see Zainab's reaction. When the student council rep showed up in her classroom with a load of roses and Zainab's name was called to receive one, she was startled. As she sat down at her desk with the flower, she noticed her brother Hamed glaring at her. As soon as class ended, he demanded to know who had sent the gift.

"Just one of my girlfriends," Zainab lied. "She's being funny, you know."

The next morning, as Wasi steered his car into the parking lot at the rear of the school, he jabbed Ammar, who was in the passenger seat beside him.

"Look, look," he said excitedly. "Look up at the window."

He was motioning toward the big third-floor window that overlooked the lot from the end of the school's northwest corridor. Ammar looked up and smiled at the angelic image. He could see Zainab clearly, although the parking lot was a good hundred metres from the school building. She was standing at the window, dressed in white tights, a white skirt and a white top.

She was still there, near Ammar's locker, when he got to the third floor. As he approached, she looked at him, smiled and walked away. Ammar couldn't figure out this alluring creature. She was stunning in her all-white outfit, which seemed to be her way of shouting *YES* in response to his valentine, yet now she seemed to be playing coy. He scrawled a note asking Zainab to call him on his cell or to email, and had Wasi deliver it. He didn't see Zainab for the remainder of the morning.

Ammar and Wasi left the school at noon. Minutes after they pulled out of the parking lot in Wasi's car, Ammar's cellphone rang.

"Hi, it's Zainab," a timid female voice said. "I won't be able to call you during the weekend. I'm going to be home with my father and it's very hard for me to use the phone." She didn't explain what she meant.

"No problem," Ammar said. "What about email?"

Zainab said she thought she'd be able to send an email, and the brief, promising phone call ended.

WHILE ZAINAB AND SAHAR WRESTLED WITH RULES designed to bind them to their family, Rona had discovered that she was unwanted and powerless in Canada. Tooba and Shafia were keeping all of her documents, her passport and other identification, from her. Permitted entry into the country on a six-month visitor visa, she feared what would happen to her at the end of the term, since she had no means to prove that she was Shafia's wife. She did not want to return to Afghanistan.

Tooba made it clear she wished that Rona had not come to Canada.

"Your family got rid of you," Tooba mocked. She told Rona that she might remain in the country for a few years, but eventually she'd have to leave and perhaps be sent back to Afghanistan. Tooba exploited the humiliation that Rona felt at having to come to the country masquerading as the family's nanny and Shafia's cousin.

"You are not his wife, you are my servant," Tooba said. "Your life is in my hands."

With no family or friends in Canada, Rona felt isolated and afraid. She trusted only the children, particularly Zainab, Sahar and Geeti.

She soon began telephoning friends and relatives scattered throughout Europe, to seek advice and to complain about abuse, humiliation and alienation. She told her confidantes that Tooba told her she no longer had any right to intervene in the lives of the children or in the affairs of the home—her usefulness to the family was at an end.

"Tooba said, 'I don't want you to live with us anymore,'" Rona told her sister-in-law Rasia Hamiri, who lived in Sweden, in a phone call in January 2008.

Rona prayed regularly and considered herself a faithful Muslim, though she was a liberal woman who liked makeup and fashionable clothes. Tooba seized on this, telling Shafia that Rona was behaving immodestly and spending entire days away from the house, perhaps doing inappropriate things. Rona told Hamiri that Tooba's fabrications would ignite Shafia's volatile temper and he would swear and curse her.

Shafia berated Rona one day, in front of guests at their home, because she wore a short jacket, Hamiri heard. Shafia used foul and demeaning language that brought Rona to tears.

Rona told her sister Diba Masoomi, who lived in France, that Shafia's rage sometimes provoked violence and he would slap or kick her.

"When he hit me, I asked him for a divorce," Rona told her. "He said, 'I've already given you your divorce,' but I said, 'Please write this divorce in a proper paper.'"

When his fury was spent, Shafia turned to Tooba and told her, "I have to find another way for this."

Rona complained to her old high school friend Cima Nejat, who lived in Austria, that she felt hopeless.

"With all the thousands of problems and bad language directed at me, I still helped in raising the children from the bottom of my heart," Rona told Nejat. "Maybe one day people will acknowledge my efforts and the troubles I go through in this house." Nejat was told that Shafia was a "tyrant" who gave his teenaged daughters no freedom and treated them as if they lived in another century.

Rona related to her brother Wali Abdali, who lived in France, that one of the girls hoped that she and Rona could escape the family together. "When I get married, I'll take you with me to my house and I will save you from these cruel parents of mine," Sahar told Rona.

UNLIKE RONA, Zainab saw a way out. She sent an email to the boy who had sent her the rose-a-gram.

The message from miss.kabuli, with the subject line "hiiiiii," arrived in Ammar's inbox the day after their brief phone call.

> hey
> how r u
> thanx 4 the great v card.
> let me explain the rules of my friend ship
> fristly be aware of my bro
> than if sometimes wanna talk come in the library.
> and if my bro is around act like complete stranger
> i will call u when we r at skool from the public telephone
> but its wasi cell ??????????do u guys live in the same house
> coz if i call when i m at home i might not get u coz its wasi's
> cell
> ok than see ya monday
> i 11come near ur locker than we 11 talk if my bro is not
> around coz i don't want to give him the slightest idea that
> we r friends
> ok than
> bye
> from zainab

On Monday morning, Ammar found her in the corridor before class. He was careful to make sure Hamed was not around. Their conversation was just long enough to plan a lunchtime meeting in a secluded corridor on the first floor. Ammar asked Wasi to keep an eye on Hamed and to call Ammar's cell if it looked like he might head for the first floor and discover them.

Ammar thought Zainab seemed nervous when they found each other in the secret meeting place. She was wearing black jeans, knee-high boots, a simple beige top and no makeup. She wasn't making any effort to impress him. Now that he was close to her, she seemed more beautiful. He felt shy, unsure what to say first. They exchanged timid hellos and swapped profiles.

She: An eighteen-year-old Afghan, new to Canada, from a big, strict Muslim family, sometimes watches Bollywood movies, likes to dress in pretty clothes, into fashion.

He: A twenty-four-year-old Pakistani from Punjab living in Canada for fifteen years, from an average Muslim family, likes hanging out with friends, playing ice hockey.

They relaxed after a few minutes had passed without any sign that Hamed might find them.

"I don't go out much but I like to hang out with my friends," Zainab explained. "I don't have a lot of freedom."

Ammar did not press for an explanation, and he wasn't put off by the prospect of navigating her peculiar family situation. Before the lunch break ended, they agreed to meet again the following day.

When Zainab returned to class after her secret rendezvous, Hamed cornered her.

"Where were you the whole lunch?" he asked. "I was at the cafeteria the whole lunch and I didn't see you."

"I was in the library," Zainab said.

"I didn't see you."

"I was probably in the corner, or somewhere, doing my work. You didn't look close enough."

ZAINAB AND AMMAR MET CLANDESTINELY and talked every day that week, though sometimes there was time to exchange only a few words in the corridor. By the end of the week, they had perfected ruses that afforded them more time. They had morning classes at the same time on opposite sides of the same third-floor wing and they discovered that they could see across the hallway into each other's classrooms if they sat in just the right spot. Zainab would leave her classroom and head for the washrooms, passing slowly through the corridor to make sure that Ammar had seen her. Moments later, he'd leave his classroom, ostensibly for a drink or a washroom break, and trail her to a predetermined spot. Sometimes they'd hurry down to the poorly lit first-floor library, where they felt certain they wouldn't be discovered. Hamed was almost always a topic of conversation. Had he seen them? Had he followed them? Did he suspect she was seeing a boy?

"Even if he sees you, you don't have to be scared of him," Ammar told her. "I understand he's your brother, but you're not doing anything wrong."

"But you don't know my brother," Zainab said. "He'll tell my dad and then my dad's going to get mad at me."

"I understand that but—"

"If we get caught, then there's no way I'm going to get to see you, 'cause they're not even going to let me come to school," she interrupted.

Ammar didn't care that seeing her was difficult. He had surrendered to a growing feeling that he knew Zainab shared. There was something special between them. Ammar told Zainab he had liked her from the first day he saw her.

"Every time I would see you come to your locker and I'd be standing at my locker, I'd take forever to open my locker just to watch you," he said.

Zainab said she'd had a crush on him since the first time she saw him. Ammar was flattered but perplexed when he recalled how she had rebuffed his first, indirect approach.

"How come you said to your friend that you're not interested in me?" he asked.

"Like, I never said that to her!" Zainab answered indignantly. She insisted she didn't know what he was talking about.

Zainab grew wide-eyed as Ammar explained how her classmate had said she wasn't interested in meeting him. Zainab said she had asked the same girl to find out if Ammar was interested in her. The answer had been no.

Ammar wondered if they were fated to be together, given that they already had overcome a conspiracy to keep them apart.

IN MARCH, SAHAR SUDDENLY DISAPPEARED FROM SCHOOL. Tooba took Sahar
and Fereshta to Dubai, where they met Shafia, who was already overseas on
business. Sahar's classmates did not connect her absence with the events
they had seen or heard about in the first few months of the school year.
The incidents seemed trifling to most of the kids—wearing makeup, being
kissed in the corridor by a boy.

Some students barely noticed that she was absent from class for the
entire month of March. Herna Paul remembers asking around, wondering
if anyone knew where Sahar was, but no one had an answer and no one
was concerned.

Sahar's teacher, Antonella Enea, marked her absent without explanation. Enea did not know that Sahar's mother had whisked her ten
thousand kilometres away from Montreal. She had been marked absent
forty-eight times by the end of her first school year. Although Sahar was
a polite and attentive student who did well academically, her attendance
record suggested that something troubling was going on in the young
girl's life.

ONCE TOOBA AND SHAFIA WERE IN DUBAI, Zainab saw an opportunity. Rona
was home, but she knew Zainab's secret and she'd never tell. Rona was
always saying that the girls should have more freedom. Zainab's only concern was Hamed, but she figured she had a foolproof plan to elude him.
Her relationship with Ammar had blossomed in the three and a half weeks
they had been together. They had traded *I love you*s. They were sneaking
meetings at school every day.

Zainab told Ammar that her parents were out of the country so, for the
first time, he could come to her home in Saint-Léonard. They set the date
for Tuesday, March 11, because Zainab's class was scheduled to go on a bus
trip. Hamed would be on the trip, taking him far away from Saint-Léonard.

Zainab told Hamed that morning that she was ill and could not go to school. She'd have to stay home.

Zainab was waiting for Ammar at the door when he got to her home on Bonnivet. The couple, accustomed to snatching moments together, were full of anticipation. But as soon as Ammar stepped through the door and into the hallway of the apartment, Zainab began shooing him toward the central living room. She had a look of panic on her face and pointed toward a stairwell off the left side of the room.

"Go to the garage, down there, hide!" she said urgently. "My brother is coming."

Ammar, who'd had his back turned to the street as he entered the apartment, had not seen Hamed coming up the sidewalk. He had appeared out of nowhere, within seconds of Ammar getting to the front door.

Ammar scampered down the stairs into the ground-level garage. The perimeter was jammed with furniture and small packages but nothing that provided a good hiding place. Ammar crouched behind a box, concealing himself as best he could. He could hear people on the stairs and Zainab's voice.

"No, no, no, there's nothing down there," she was saying.

"No, I want to check," Hamed said.

Seconds later, Hamed was standing over Ammar. He extended his arm and took Ammar's hand and helped him up.

"Go, just leave," Hamed said. His voice was flat, emotionless. He pointed toward the big garage door as he pushed a button and the door began to roll up. Ammar left without saying anything to Hamed or Zainab.

Five minutes after Ammar left, Hamed's demeanour changed. He began screaming at Zainab for defying family rules that barred the girls from having boyfriends. Hamed told her she was confined to her room and would not be permitted to go back to school. Their parents would decide her fate when they returned from Dubai later in the month, he said.

The next day, Zainab called Ammar and told him what had happened after he left. She said that Hamed got very angry. He threatened to chase Ammar and confront him, but Zainab had convinced Hamed to stay put.

She began to cry as she explained that she wasn't permitted to leave the house, even for school.

"But I wanna see you one more time," she said. She pleaded with Ammar to come back to the house and he agreed. Three days later, Ammar skipped school and went to Saint-Léonard. Wasi had orders to watch Hamed and call Ammar's cell if there was any indication that Hamed was leaving St. Pius and driving back to the Shafia home.

Zainab bounded down the big concrete steps at the front of the apartment as soon as Ammar got near the building. He could see that she was crying as she leaped into his arms and squeezed him, telling him that she loved him. Their anxiety about Hamed, about being *seen,* getting *caught,* was washed away in a wave of emotion.

"This is going to be the last time we're going to be able to see each other," Zainab sputtered. "Most likely this is going to be the end of it." She sobbed as she spoke. "When my dad comes back, there's no way they're going to let me go anywhere."

She pushed her sleeve up to reveal her forearm and showed Ammar the soft underside. "But I'm never gonna forget you," she was saying. "I will always love you."

He was horrified. She had carved the letter *A* into her tender flesh.

"That was pretty stupid," Ammar said, trying not to be harsh. "Don't do things like this."

He was comforting her, sharing her anguish, but furious that this tormented girl had been driven to take a knife to her arm. *She doesn't deserve this,* he was thinking, but her words were still echoing. "The *end* of it," she had said. But they were just getting started, just finding each other, discovering where they might go, and now it was over. He was crying now.

He could see her pain and fear, and he accepted that he could not put her at risk. He decided he would not try to convince her to defy her parents to be with him. He wanted her to be safe. He told her that he loved her, kissed her and left.

5

Unbearable

BY THE TIME SHAFIA, TOOBA, SAHAR AND FERESHTA RETURNED to Canada from Dubai in late March, Shafia had heard about Zainab's disobedience and realized that he had big problems with not one but two teenaged daughters. He had always been able to control them, and though he could see no reason things would have changed, he did not understand the forces at work.

The girls, stifled for so long, had smelled boys, touched them, felt the intoxicating rush of their attention. And they had seen the power girls could wield, with a look or a walk or word. Zainab and Sahar saw that their schoolmates had the freedom to explore this terrain in a way they had only imagined, until now. They would not give up this ground easily.

Zainab tried to extricate herself with a ruse, recruiting a schoolmate at St. Pius, Muhja, to share the blame. Zainab told her parents that her friend had introduced her to Ammar. Shafia, Tooba, Hamed and Zainab met with Muhja in a restaurant parking lot near St. Pius.

"It's my friend," Muhja lied to them. "Like, Ammar is my friend. It's not Zainab's fault."

Shafia glowered at the teenager.

"You are not a good girl," he said, in a loud voice. "Why you did this?"

Muhja was startled by his aggressive and angry tone. She recoiled in fear.

"You did bad to our daughter," Shafia yelled, before turning toward Zainab. "You're not going to talk to this girl again."

Tooba joined the condemnation, calling Muhja a "bad girl." Muhja was frightened of the angry mother too.

Though Shafia seemed to believe Muhja, the ploy did not work. He told Zainab she would not be permitted to return to school. He ordered her to stay in her room. When she emerged for food or to go to the washroom, she was subjected to angry glares from Shafia and Hamed.

AFTER HER "VACATION" IN DUBAI, Sahar was kept at home another two weeks. She returned to St-Ex only after school administrators informed the family that attendance was compulsory for children under sixteen. Tooba and Shafia pleaded ignorance and insisted they didn't realize they should have notified school authorities in advance that Sahar would be absent for such a long period. But Sahar told her teacher that her parents had yanked her out of school for the seventeen-day trip to Dubai, apparently as punishment for her misbehaviour. Shafia barred Sahar from going on the Internet or making phone calls, but he had underestimated her. She wasn't cowed by the punishments and would not obey the edict that family matters must not be shared outside the home. She had reached a breaking point.

On May 7, Sahar told the teacher she trusted, Antonella Enea, what was happening.

"Life is unbearable, I want to die," Sahar confided to Enea, through tears. She explained that a week and half earlier, she had swallowed a handful of pills she found at home. Sahar said her mother had refused to come to her aid but Aunt Rona had helped her. When Rona found the groggy girl, she asked Tooba what was going on.

"She can go to hell," Tooba said. "Let her kill herself."

Over the past eight months, Enea had heard, one small bit at a time, revelations of control and abuse at home. Now Sahar recounted the catalogue of abuses that had driven her to consider suicide. Since the previous October, her family had shunned her as punishment for her perceived misbehaviour. She felt emotionally rejected by her parents. Her brother

Hamed had hit her shoulder and had assaulted her by throwing a pair of scissors across a table so that they struck her hand. He often berated her over her immodesty and her refusal to follow family rules.

Her mother had told her she must begin wearing a hijab, a traditional headscarf that would conceal her hair and her neck. Sahar told her mother she did not want to wear a scarf. She did not want to stand out from her friends. She wanted to dress like everyone else.

Although Sahar had cried in front of her teacher before, this time was different. She had never before talked of wanting to die. Enea thought Sahar looked tired and very sad. Until now, Enea had been a sounding board and confidante who helped to wipe away Sahar's tears, but Sahar had always footnoted her stories with the proviso that she did not want Enea to tell anyone else. She did not want her to do anything but listen. Now, for the first time, Sahar asked Enea to *do something,* though the girl did not fully understand the ramifications of her request. Enea contacted the vice-principal, Josée Fortin.

Fortin met privately with Sahar, who repeated her allegations. She told the administrator she had "had enough" and wanted to die. She had been assaulted by her brother, alienated by her parents and ordered to wear a hijab. Fortin contacted Batshaw, the anglophone youth protection agency. She told the agency that a teenaged girl was suicidal and was complaining of physical and psychological abuse at home. The file was marked Code 1, the most urgent status.

Jeanne Rowe, a small, middle-aged Haitian woman with a soft voice and more than twenty years' experience investigating child abuse complaints, arrived at St-Ex around three that afternoon and was taken to a small private room where Sahar was waiting. Rowe could see that the girl had been crying, and she was still crying softly. She looked very sad. Before Rowe could ask any questions or explain her role, Sahar quizzed her.

"Are you going to tell my parents?" Sahar demanded, sobbing.

"Yes, I will," Rowe replied. "We always meet with the child, and the parents have to be notified because we have to hear what they have to say, too."

Sahar's face was now a mash of tears and anxiety.

She is scared, Rowe thought.

"But I don't want my parents to know!"

"I have no choice, I have to talk to your parents."

"I don't want my parents to know. I want to go home. I don't want to be placed. The stuff I said, it's not true."

"I'll be sure that you are safe and protected, so you don't have to worry."

Sahar seemed panicked.

"I don't want my parents to know. I don't want to be placed. I want to go home. I don't want to be placed with strangers."

"I'm not talking about placement," Rowe explained. "I just want to talk to you."

The investigator could see that Sahar was retreating, throwing up a shield of recantations and denials of what she had told others. Rowe told Sahar that regardless of what she now said, Rowe had to call her home. Still crying, Sahar asked to leave the room to see her teacher.

Rowe then met privately and alone with Tooba, who had arrived at the school for the daily pickup. The mother was calm, Rowe noted. She had an explanation for all of the allegations, as Rowe recounted them. Tooba had no difficulty communicating in English.

She said she knew nothing of Sahar swallowing medicine in a suicide bid.

She said there were some days that her daughter would not speak to anyone in the house, so she would not bother to speak to her and she didn't think there was anything wrong with this. Tooba said she and her husband never used physical discipline with their children and Hamed had never assaulted his sister. She said the family never kept Sahar out of school, but they had taken her on a vacation to Dubai. When they returned to Canada, Sahar was tired and asked to stay home from school for another two weeks.

Rowe also met privately with Zainab, who had come to the school with Tooba. Zainab repeated Tooba's explanations, but she added that she didn't understand why Sahar was upset about being told by her mother to wear a hijab, since it was part of their culture and religion, although she said

Sahar's resistance to wearing the headscarf was probably the reason for her sadness. The older sister told Rowe she didn't understand why Sahar was trying to make problems for the family.

After Rowe spoke to Tooba and Zainab, she telephoned a manager to discuss the situation. The decision was made to let Sahar return to her home that night, although the agency had not spoken to anyone else about the allegations.

Before Rowe could leave the school, Shafia and Hamed arrived, so she met with them together. The father appeared agitated and angry, and began questioning Rowe before she could put the allegations to him.

"Who make report?" Shafia asked her in English in a loud and aggressive tone. "Who tell these things?"

"I'm sorry sir, I can't tell you the source," Rowe explained.

"Lies, all lies," Shafia snapped. "Tell me, who make report?"

"Under Quebec law, the source must remain anonymous."

"I get lawyer," Shafia said, threateningly. "I talk lawyer. Who make report?"

"Sir, even if you get a lawyer, the source of the report must remain confidential," Rowe repeated.

"Family all happy," Shafia insisted. "All lies."

Shafia offered no explanations, only blanket denials for all the allegations that Rowe enumerated.

The following day, before Sahar came into the classroom, Enea made a brief announcement to the other students already in the room. She asked them to be sensitive to Sahar's unhappiness. Enea explained that Sahar was upset because her father wanted her to wear a hijab to school.

Herna was saddened by the revelation. She could see that Sahar had been crying when she came into the classroom wearing a simple black headscarf. It was not wrapped tight, like the hijabs she had seen on many young Muslim girls. It was loose and Sahar's bangs protruded from the top of the scarf. No one said anything to Sahar immediately.

At the first break, Herna tried to cheer her.

"Why are you so sad?" she asked Sahar. "You look nice."

Sahar acknowledged her friend, but she did not answer and her mood did not brighten.

A little bit more freedom is being taken from her, Herna thought.

THE NEXT DAY, two days after their first meeting, Rowe met with Sahar a second time. Rowe noted that Sahar's demeanour and appearance had changed dramatically. The tears were gone. She was smiling and calm. Rowe asked her how things were going at home.

"Things are better," Sahar said. "I want to stay at home."

Rowe again went over the allegations. Unlike in the first interview, Sahar acknowledged her initial complaints. Her brother had hit her twice, she said, though she discounted one of the incidents: "It wasn't hard." Another time, he had slid a pair of scissors across a table during an argument and they struck her hand. Her mother was talking to her now, she said.

"She told me, 'Whenever you feel sad or something is hurting you, bothering you, talk to me,'" Sahar said, recounting the conversation with Tooba.

Sahar told Rowe that she was happy that her mother was speaking to her again and she was happy to be at home. She believed things had changed. She wasn't going to be hit any more, she said. Sahar acknowledged there was conflict about the hijab. She explained to Rowe that she had asked her mother if she could put off wearing the scarf until after the end of the school year, because she worried about explaining to her schoolmates why she was suddenly wearing it. Her mother had refused the request and Sahar had acceded.

Rowe thought the girl still seemed guarded and appeared to be minimizing events at home, but she was insisting on remaining with her family.

Rowe followed Batshaw's standard protocol, interviewing the accuser, the accused and the person who relayed the complaint. Rowe did not interview any of Sahar's schoolmates or friends—Jake or Herna or Patrick or Ray or Benjamin—teenagers who could have told her that Sahar had confided stories of physical abuse, alienation and control. They might have related how they had often seen Sahar crying at school, complaining of being shunned and being forced to dress and behave in ways her parents dictated.

Rowe wrote, in her final report, that Sahar "appeared to be struggling with the values of her religion and culture and those of her host country." It was a bold conclusion, since Rowe had spent scant time investigating what would be acceptable in Sahar's religion or culture. She didn't know whether any of Sahar's friends were Muslim, or Afghan, or whether they were sympathetic to her predicament or might be able to support her.

The conclusion neatly chalked it up to a "struggle" between two sets of values. From the smorgasbord of allegations and denials that had been provided, Batshaw concluded that Sahar was not at "immediate risk." The conclusion seemed to overlook eight months of information gathered by Antonella Enea. The decision was made to do nothing further to protect Sahar, or to investigate further the danger she might have faced. The allegations were marked as "founded" but the file was closed. The agency did not interview the only other adult who might provide first-hand testimony about what was going on inside the Shafia home. She might have corroborated Sahar's accounts of abuse and alienation, and she might have exposed Sahar's tormentors as liars.

No one asked "Aunt Rona" what she had seen.

GEETI SEEMED TO FADE INTO THE BACKGROUND in the family's first year in Canada. Whatever insecurities and anxieties she faced in adapting to a new country and a new school were overshadowed by the drama that revolved around her older sisters. Joyce Gilbert, who worked at the elementary school Geeti and Fereshta attended, and who lived downstairs in the building where they lived on Bonnivet, thought Geeti was quiet and shy. She was a sweet girl who always said hello. Gilbert found it odd that although Geeti, then eleven, lived only a few blocks from the school, she was not permitted to walk alone. Her mother delivered and collected Geeti and her younger sister each day.

To Mary-Ann Devantro, a friendly upstairs neighbour, Geeti seemed quiet and sensitive. The girl enjoyed visiting Devantro and her twin sister, Margaret. During one of her visits, Geeti explained that her father was building a new house for the family and they would soon move to the suburbs.

"Oh, that's nice, but we're going to miss you a lot," Devantro said. She noticed that Geeti's eyes seemed to be glistening as the girl got up from the chair.

"What's wrong?" the woman asked.

"Nothing," Geeti answered softly. "I got something in my eye."

Devantro asked the girl if she was crying.

"Yes," Geeti conceded. "I'm going to miss both of you. I wish my father could build you a house next to ours so that we could stay close to you."

IF ANYONE *HAD* ASKED RONA what was going on inside the Shafia home, she could have related the abuse she suffered too. Sahar turned to youth protection authorities for help, while Rona found an adult confidante, Fahima Vorgetts.

Vorgetts wasn't prepared for the anguish that flooded through the telephone receiver. Sometimes, it was overwhelming and left her sobbing.

"*Ma ra laghat zad,*" Rona said, in Dari. "He kicks me with his feet."

She was crying, as she often did, weeping uncontrollably at times, to the point that Vorgetts could not understand her. She tried to calm her, as she had been doing in almost every call since they began. By early June 2009, Rona was calling Vorgetts at her home in Virginia two or three times a week, recounting in each call abuse and torment by her husband and his second wife.

"You cannot see the scars on my body, but if you cut my chest, you will see the scars in my heart," she said. There were occasional blows, kicks and slaps, but the emotional assaults were relentless.

Vorgetts knew that many Afghan women struggled for decent lives. She was fortunate. An Afghan refugee herself, she had left her birthplace at the age of twenty-two and now, in middle age, she was comfortable as an American citizen who frequently travelled to Afghanistan to oversee assistance programs.

She had seen much misery during two decades of helping women and children in roles with Women for Afghan Women and the Afghan Women's Fund. She had seen first-hand the joy that a new school, stocked with usable books, could have, or the empowering effect of a small co-operative equipped with sewing machines and bolts of fabric. Women learned a skill and felt the invigorating effect of seizing a bit of economic power.

It was a long and slow rebuilding effort from the crushing oppression of the fundamentalist Taliban period, when women were forbidden to attend school and were forced to cloak themselves in public. Women were banished from politics, jobs and social circles. Despite the efforts of Vorgetts's organizations and many others, and the billions of dollars poured into her homeland by the west, Afghanistan remained one of the worst places in the world to be a girl or a woman. Ninety-five of every hundred women in Afghanistan did not acquire post-secondary education. Two-thirds were unable to work outside the home. Many Afghan women fled the country in a desperate bid to rebalance their prospects.

Yet here was Rona Amir, who had left Afghanistan for one of the western world's most prosperous and liberal nations, telling Vorgetts that in her new country she endured oppression and misery and that she saw no way out. Most of the calls came from a pay phone. Rona explained that she wasn't permitted to use the home phone and had no privacy in the home. She saved the monthly allowance that her husband gave her, sometimes a hundred dollars, and used it to buy phone cards for cheap long-distance calls. One of Rona's relatives in Germany had given her Vorgetts's number in the spring of 2008, after Vorgetts had agreed to try to help. The women also were related, though they had never met. Vorgetts's uncle was married to Rona's sister.

Fear tinged everything that Rona told Vorgetts.

She said that she didn't understand her rights in Canada and, at any rate, could not strike out on her own without papers. Shafia and Tooba had taken her passport and other documents. Even wedding photos that could prove she was Shafia's wife had disappeared from her room.

Rona said her co-wife often humiliated her. When guests came to the house, Rona would greet them and Tooba would mock her for trying to join the social event. If guests came and Rona did not greet them, Tooba would chastise her for her impoliteness. When Rona challenged Tooba, Tooba would demean her: "You are not a wife; you are a slave here."

Vorgetts urged Rona to leave the home.

"Go to the police," she told her. "Tell the police what Shafia has done to you. They will help you. This isn't Afghanistan. Go to a shelter for women. There are many of them. They will help you and protect you."

"I can't," Rona pleaded. "Shafia told me I can't go to the police because I don't have any status here and they will kick me out of Canada and send me back to Afghanistan." Rona was terrified at the prospect of being shipped back there labelled as a rejected and discarded wife, or perhaps as a wife who had abandoned her duty. She would be considered *besharaf*—shameless—in the eyes of Shafia's family in Afghanistan. She was afraid of what they might do to her.

Vorgetts repeatedly told Rona that Canadian authorities would take her side.

"The police are there to protect you," she told her. "Once you tell the police that you are his wife, they will know that he violated the immigration law. He lied to immigration and to the police. He'll be in trouble, not you."

Rona seemed to understand, but said she was too afraid to flee and go to authorities. She loved the children, she said, and did not want to be separated from them. Shafia mistreated the girls also, Rona told Vorgetts. He was strict and often angry. The children had no freedom. "When he comes home, the girls are all scared," Rona said.

At least a few times, Vorgetts convinced her to leave the house and Rona would pledge to get away. The following day, Rona would call and tearfully explain that she could not do it. Her fear held her back. She feared the effect of fleeing more than the pain of staying and enduring abuse.

"If I go to the police, or anything, Shafia will kill me," Rona told Vorgetts.

PART THREE

Chaos

"They were afraid and terrorized."
—Constable Anne-Marie Choquette

6

The Palace

ARCHITECT NABI NEDA was finally able to convince Shafia, in the first week of April 2009, to sign off on the blueprints for the house in Brossard. The plans had been altered more than half a dozen times because of Shafia's tinkering. He added rooms, changed the layout and enlarged the house until it was roughly six thousand square feet, three times the size of the typical Canadian home. A sweeping spiral staircase led from the main floor to a grand upper level, where four of the six bedrooms were located. There were five bathrooms.

Shafia had fretted about the bedrooms. He had talked to Neda about where each person would sleep. The house was big enough that the woman Shafia had described as his cousin could live with them.

On the second floor, there was a spacious master bedroom and spa-like ensuite bathroom that featured a large corner tub, a separate shower and two sinks. At the opposite end of the second floor was an identical master suite. When Neda asked Shafia why he needed two master bedrooms, Shafia told him that his daughter Zainab might soon marry and perhaps she'd live with them.

While Neda worked on the plans, his wife continued to badger him to end his relationship with Shafia.

"You're making yourself sick from the stress and all the work," Nasrin complained. She reminded him that although Shafia was wealthy, he was cheap and had never paid Neda for the value of his work. When he had begun the house project in 2007, Shafia paid him $2,500 a month, a meagre salary for an experienced architect. Shafia kept adding to Neda's responsibilities, imposing additional duties without boosting his pay, while promising that it would all be worth it.

"Come with me and we'll do business together and you will be rich," Shafia had told him. "You will be very rich."

Shafia had many schemes to make money. He talked of acquiring property to open a car lot, and had already proven himself adept at buying damaged vehicles from the United States through online auctions. The vehicles were shipped to Dubai, repaired and resold. Shafia wanted Neda to help him expand his empire. Neda could speak French and some English, and he could help Shafia navigate Canadian bureaucracies. Most of all, Shafia trusted him because he was an Afghan.

Despite his wife's protestation that he wasn't a businessman, Neda had agreed to go with Shafia to the mammoth Canton trade fair in Guangzhou, China, in the fall of 2008, where Shafia looked for goods that he could buy cheaply and ship to Canada. Shafia found shoddily made athletic shoes that he could buy by the dozen for eight to ten dollars a pair. In Canada, he could resell them at a substantial profit. Shafia also looked for Chinese-made construction materials that would mimic fine finishes at lower cost. He had told Neda about his bigger plans: The house in Brossard was an experiment, a test case. Shafia wanted to see how cheaply he could build a big, ornate home. If the experiment went smoothly, he hoped to move into the homebuilding business, which he figured would make him much richer.

Neda told his wife that the more he came to know Shafia, the better he understood that their personalities were not a good fit. Shafia was a man obsessed with money. Despite the greater fortune Shafia saw on the horizon, Neda was struck by his tight-fistedness. He insisted on staying in budget hotels and eating cheap meals. During the China trip, Neda paid for a good restaurant meal for the two men because Shafia thought it was too expensive.

THERE WAS A MORE REASONABLE EXPLANATION for the design of a new house with two master bedrooms. Shafia was a man who felt bound by tradition. Custom dictated that as long as he had two wives, he must treat them equally. To do less would be shameful. When Neda later learned that Rona was Shafia's wife, he concluded that the second bedroom was for her.

Tooba had made clear, from the moment Rona arrived in Canada, that she wanted her co-wife out of the family. The house design would have undermined her plans, if she had seen it. But Tooba seemed certain that Rona would never recapture a position of spousal equality. She taunted Rona about the new house: "It's a palace and you are not going to enter and live there."

SHAFIA'S EAGERNESS TO BUILD HIS PALATIAL NEW HOME evaporated two weeks after the plans were finalized. A calamity that he should have foreseen plunged the household into chaos and set Shafia off on an angry crusade. On April 17, Zainab fled the house, leaving behind a note that explained she would not return, ever. She called her boyfriend, Ammar Wahid, on his cellphone, early that Friday morning.

"Ammar, I want to leave my house, now," Zainab said. She was home alone, and it was the perfect time to slip away unnoticed. It wasn't the first time she had told Ammar she wanted to escape her domineering father, who was trying to force her into an arranged marriage with a relative.

"Why do you want to leave now?" Ammar asked her.

"You know I don't have enough freedom and my parents are forcing me to get married to a guy I don't want to. I want to go to English school and they're sending me to a French school. I hardly go to the school 'cause I don't like French and I don't want to be in a French school. You come and take me, now."

"Listen, I'm not independent yet," he reminded her. "I don't have my own place."

"If you don't come, I'm gonna leave on my own."

Ammar was afraid for her, but he knew he wasn't equipped to support her. He didn't have a job and he hadn't completed his high school credits. He was still living at home with his parents. Zainab was an adult and entitled to do as she pleased, but she was naive and had led a sheltered life. She'd never make it on her own, he knew. But he could hear the desperation in her voice and feared she'd make good on the threat to strike out on her own.

"Okay, okay," Ammar told her. "Give me time to borrow a car and I'll get there as soon as I can."

THE PAIR HAD BEEN SEEING EACH OTHER secretly again for two months, despite their tearful breakup and the punishment Zainab had faced after they were caught in the house in March 2008. Banished to her room and removed from school, Zainab had endured months of isolation. Throughout that period, she'd continued to send Ammar occasional emails. She believed their romance could be rekindled. Whenever she could snatch a moment at a computer with no one around, she would send him a message. She dispatched brief and unremarkable updates on her life that always included the paean that she missed him deeply and the pledge that she would find a way to see him again. He replied that he wanted to see her again too.

In December 2008 Ammar received a message with the subject line "muuuaaah . . . kisses":

> hey jaan i go to the skool my sisters go. . . . .i want to see u to.
> i wanna call u one day but i don't know how i will try soon i
> wanna hear u voice i miss u bad

The email explained that her brother was again shadowing her at school and she was wearing a hijab at night "coz i go to a coarse at nite with him sux." Zainab explained that she had found a new way to wear the head covering with style:

> well i changed the way i wear hijab its even more better than
> be4
> i take out a bit of ma hair and i tie the hijab at back and put
> on some big cirlce earings
> i will try sending u a pic like that i m sure u will like it

She referred longingly to March 14, 2008—evey tym I rem. . that I cry—the day that Ammar had returned to the family's Saint-Léonard house for their final farewell. Despite the email, the pair did not talk on the phone and they did not meet.

That month, December, Ammar travelled to Pakistan with his family, who were trying to push him into an arranged marriage with a woman in their home country. He refused and the family returned to Canada in late January 2009. Within weeks of returning, Ammar got a call from Zainab. She told Ammar she was happier. Her parents were beginning to trust her again and had allowed her to return to school, though she'd been forced to go to St-Ex, the high school near their home. She was taking French classes at night. All the Shafia sisters except Fereshta, who remained in elementary school, now attended St-Ex. Geeti had begun Grade 9 there in September 2008.

After a few minutes of catching up, Zainab and Ammar sensed that the connection between them was still strong. Zainab said she really wanted to see him, so they arranged a date for the following week at a spot where they had secretly met before, the public library near St-Ex. The pair began meeting weekly, often at the library or in a café at a nearby cultural centre.

ON APRIL 17, Ammar picked Zainab up and took her to a community health centre where a social worker listened to her complaints about life at home.

She was referred to Passages, a women's shelter. Ammar dropped her at Passages and told her he'd return the following day.

At the Shafia home, Tooba was panicked when she returned to find an empty house and Zainab's note. She knew that Shafia would be enraged when he learned of Zainab's shameful disobedience. Hamed placed an emergency 9-1-1 call to report that his sister was missing. He explained that the family had found a note in which Zainab had written that she wanted to live her own life. The operator took a description of Zainab and said police would be dispatched. Impatient that officers didn't arrive within minutes, Hamed called a second time.

Police did show up at the home hours after Hamed's calls, but not because of the missing person complaint. Just after 4:00 p.m., Constable Anne-Marie Choquette and a partner arrived at the apartment on Bonnivet. Sahar, Geeti, Mina and Zafar, who had been walking home from school, were with the officers. Tooba was at home with Hamed, Fereshta and Rona, who was introduced to the officers as a friend of the family. Shafia was not home but was due to return later.

The police officers had met the four Shafia siblings on a street corner a few blocks from the apartment, after receiving a 9-1-1 dispatch about a group of children who had reported that they were afraid for their lives. The siblings had received a call from their mother, police were told, explaining that their older sister had run away from home. Tooba had told the children that she feared their father's reaction to the news about Zainab. They were so alarmed that they knocked on the door of a home and asked a stranger to call 9-1-1. The children told the officers that their mother feared for her life.

Choquette noted that the children seemed afraid and unnerved when she met them. At the home, she spoke first to Tooba and Hamed, who explained that they were concerned about Zainab's disappearance. Tooba told Choquette, oddly, that Zainab was twenty-one years old, though her identification documents stated she was nineteen and Hamed had said she was nineteen when he called 9-1-1 earlier that day. Choquette took some notes about the missing girl and moved on to the real reason police had visited the Shafia home. She and her partner began interviewing the children separately, outside.

Three of them related a disturbing story of a violent outburst by their father and their older brother a week earlier.

Zafar told Choquette that he and the girls, the same group who had just called the police, had returned home late from a trip to the mall. They had arrived at the house around nine, contrary to a home-before-dark curfew. The late arrival enraged their father and Hamed. Zafar said his brother pulled his hair and hit him on the face. His father also hit him on the face and threatened him.

"He said, 'I'll tear you apart,'" Zafar told the officer. He believed it was a death threat. Zafar said his father often threatened to kill them.

Mina corroborated Zafar's account that their father and older brother were furious over their lateness a week ago. She told the officer that her father grabbed her by the shoulder and shook her, and Hamed punched her in the right eye with his fist. Choquette saw a mark near Mina's right eye.

When Geeti was interviewed privately, she told the officers that Hamed had punched her in her left eye with his fist the night of the shopping centre incident. She said her father pulled her hair and hit her on the face.

Sahar told Choquette that her father didn't abuse her but that her brother Hamed had slapped her and she had seen her siblings being abused.

All four children said their father abused Zainab. They told the officers that he pulled her hair and struck her and he was angry that she had a boyfriend. Zainab had run away so she could "live freely," Choquette was told.

The officer concluded that all the children wanted to leave the home to escape violence. She contacted a supervising sergeant, who contacted youth protection authorities, as required by the provincial protocol for cases involving children. The Centre jeunesse de Montréal dispatched an investigator, but he was sent to the house without critical information. The investigator from the French-language agency did not have details of the youth protection investigation conducted eleven months earlier, by the anglophone agency Batshaw, into Sahar's complaints of abuse and alienation.

Before the youth protection investigator arrived at the apartment on Bonnivet and while police were talking to the children outside, Mohammad Shafia returned home. Choquette noted an immediate change in the demeanour of the siblings. They stopped talking and they appeared frightened. Some of them and Tooba began to cry. Choquette would say later that she thought the children "closed up" when their father arrived.

"They were afraid and terrorized," Choquette would say. She felt that the father intimidated his children without saying anything to them. "He just looked at them."

As soon as Shafia arrived, Mina recanted what she had said earlier and told police that her initial accusations were lies.

Youth protection investigator Norman Osadchuck arrived at 9:00 p.m. Whereas the police officers had interviewed family members individually, Osadchuck sat them down in one room together and began to go over the complaints. Like the police, Osadchuck did not attempt to get an interpreter, although the accused parents spoke limited English and no French, and Osadchuck could not speak their first language, Dari. The children making the complaints were recruited as interpreters. Osadchuck spoke in English and sometimes in French, and the children translated his comments into Dari for their father and mother. Osadchuck had no way of knowing what the children were saying in Dari.

Choquette and her sergeant, who had arrived at the house, watched the group meeting. The children were quiet, except Mina, who repeated that what she had said earlier was not true. She told Osadchuck there was no violence in the home and she wasn't subjected to abuse. She said that she didn't want to leave. The other children remained silent.

Osadchuck decided that none of the children would be removed from the home that night. Osadchuck warned Shafia and Hamed about physical punishment of the children and explained that there would be follow-up interviews: the investigation was not complete. Tooba was not cautioned because the children had not alleged any abuse by their mother, though it wasn't clear, from their accounts, whether she had tried to protect them.

Osadchuck, like police, did not interview the only other adult in the home, Rona. No one arranged to take photos of the injury near Mina's eye. None of the interviews were recorded. The youth protection official and three police officers left the Bonnivet apartment just after 11:00 p.m. They had been at the home for seven hours. Choquette thought the children looked terrified.

"They were afraid that police would leave and all the repercussions," she would say later.

The children, who had told police that they were punched, slapped, pulled by the hair, shaken by the shoulder and often threatened with death, remained at home with their father and big brother, alone, for the entire weekend following the revelations. Police and youth protection authorities did not return to the apartment on April 18 or 19, even though an official at Centre jeunesse de Montréal later wrote in a report that the children "appeared to live under a regime of terror."

Three months later, Mina would tell another police officer that she had been taught that police would help you if you needed protection. "I didn't see the help," she would say. "I really didn't see the help."

As soon as the police and youth protection workers left that Friday night, Shafia and Hamed began hunting for Zainab. Within days, they found Ammar's phone number.

AMMAR RECOGNIZED THE VOICE when he answered his cellphone.

"It's Hamed. Where's Zainab?"

His tone was pleasant, but direct.

Ammar muted the call and turned to Zainab, who was standing beside him.

"Your brother's on the phone. What do you want me to say?"

Zainab had a look of panic.

"Tell him you're not with me," she said. "Just deny it. If you tell them, they're going to keep bugging you, and if they find out what happened, then they're going to come after you. I don't want that."

Ammar returned to the call.

"I don't know where she is," he told Hamed.

"I'm sure she's with you, Ammar," Hamed said. "You were the last guy to have any relationship with her."

"Yeah, but that was a year ago," Ammar responded, trying to sound disinterested.

"Where is she?" Hamed insisted weakly.

"Listen, Hamed, I went to my country for a month after we broke up and had no contact with Zainab after that," Ammar responded, growing more confident in the deception. He switched the call to speaker so that Zainab could clearly hear the conversation.

Ammar could hear Shafia in the background. He was speaking Dari to Hamed, so Ammar understood only scattered words. Eventually, Shafia came on the phone and quizzed Ammar about Zainab's disappearance. The conversation was a mix of English and Urdu, Ammar's first language. Shafia spoke enough Urdu to converse easily.

The young man repeated his lie that he didn't know anything about Zainab's whereabouts.

"Look, if you know where she is or if she's with you, and you guys love each other, let us know and we'll get you guys married," Shafia said. "Bring her back home and we'll get you guys married."

Zainab whispered to Ammar, "Don't believe that."

Ammar insisted he had not seen her.

When the marriage ruse failed, Shafia tried another approach. "Then you know what, I'm going to have to make a report to the police, so before I make the report, if you know where she is or if she's with you, tell me," Shafia said.

"You should," Ammar said, calling his bluff.

A POLICE OFFICER WHO REACHED AMMAR on his cellphone later that evening said that Zainab's parents had reported that she had been kidnapped.

Ammar acknowledged that she was staying at a shelter, was fine and that she had left home on her own accord. There was no urgency in the officer's tone, and she didn't want to talk to Zainab. Police did not seem to have drawn any sinister connection among the multiple incidents involving the Shafia family. The officer told Ammar to take Zainab to a police station in Saint-Léonard where she could speak to a detective.

The pair went to the station as soon as Ammar could reach a friend with a car. He was with Zainab when she met the detective, who asked if anyone had forced her to leave her home. She explained that she left on her own because she wanted more freedom. The officer said he understood that, but he was just doing his duty because the family had filed a complaint. He was soon satisfied that Zainab had not been kidnapped.

"We know that you're over eighteen, and you have the right in Canada, after you're eighteen, to do whatever you want," the detective said. "Wherever you want to live, nobody can bother you."

ON MONDAY, APRIL 20, Detective Sergeant Laurie Ann Lefebvre, a veteran child abuse investigator with Montreal police, and Daniel Gauvin, another worker from Centre jeunesse de Montréal, met at St-Ex with Sahar, Geeti and Mina. They didn't talk to Zafar because he was not at school that day, and they did not track him down. Norman Osadchuck, the youth protection worker who had conducted the initial investigation three days earlier, did not take part in the follow-up.

Before Lefebvre went to the school, she read the contradictory youth protection and police reports. Osadchuck had noted that he did not hear the allegations of abuse that the children had made to the first police officers who responded. Only one child spoke to Osadchuck, Mina, and that was only to take back the accusations of abuse she had initially offered.

First, Lefebvre and Gauvin met privately with Geeti. The officer thought the thirteen-year-old girl was dressed like a young boy. Geeti slumped across a chair nonchalantly, wearing jeans and a T-shirt, no makeup and no jewellery. She did not look anxious or afraid. As soon as Gauvin explained his role as an official charged with ensuring the well-being of children, Geeti asked to be placed in a foster family. Gauvin asked why.

"I want to have freedom, like my friends," Geeti answered. "They can do whatever they want."

Gauvin explained that this wasn't reason enough to remove a child from a family. Lefebvre asked Geeti to explain again what had happened Friday. Geeti said that she and her three siblings had been afraid of their father's reaction to the news that their sister Zainab had run away, so they called police. She related the events from the night the four children came home late from the mall. She said that their brother Hamed began yelling at them and Sahar talked back to him. Hamed slapped Sahar. Geeti did not tell Lefebvre the same story she had offered Choquette three days earlier, that she was punched and her hair was pulled. She told Lefebvre she *wasn't* hit. The officer asked Geeti if she was afraid of anyone in her family and she said no.

After twenty minutes with the girl, the police officer concluded there was no criminal case. Lefebvre was content to let the youth protection agency intervene.

The police didn't hear about other troubling signs of problems in Geeti's life. She was failing every one of her school subjects. Her attendance was abysmal, well on her way to a record of more than fifty missed classes for the year. That month, she had been caught stealing a muffin from the school cafeteria, a mischievous act intended to ingratiate herself with a group of girls at St-Ex who fancied themselves young rebels. Geeti wanted to belong. When she had been caught and taken to meet the school official who meted out punishment, Geeti cried effusively. She knit her fingers together in supplication and begged the official not to call her parents. She cried so hard that she could barely speak. She said if he called her home, it would be "difficult" for her.

The school had been so alarmed about Geeti's attendance and performance problems that a meeting was scheduled two months earlier with Shafia, Tooba and Geeti. When Shafia showed up at the appointed time with Mina, vice-principal Nathalie Laramée refused to meet with him. She didn't want to disclose what she had heard about Geeti in front of her sister. The meeting was eventually rescheduled several weeks later. Teachers had been telling Laramée for months that they were concerned about Geeti's poor grades and attitude. They feared she was being mistreated at home.

Lefebvre and Gauvin met next with Sahar. Her appearance surprised the officer. Sahar was wearing tight-fitting jeans, makeup and jewellery. She did not look like a girl who came from a strict and conservative home. When Lefebvre asked, Sahar explained that she changed her clothes and applied makeup after she got to school.

Sahar said she wasn't afraid of anyone at home. She repeated what she had said on April 17, that her brother Hamed had slapped her the night she and three siblings came home after curfew. She explained that Hamed acted in their father's place when he was away. Hamed's rules were strict, she said. Sahar said her father did not hit the children but sometimes he threatened to take them back to Dubai. The girl said she had a plan: just like her sister Zainab, she would leave home as soon as she turned eighteen.

Mina was polite when she met with Lefebvre and Gauvin. She parroted the account of the curfew incident her sisters had provided: only Sahar was hit. It was a slap delivered by Hamed because Sahar talked back. Mina said she didn't feel threatened at home and she was going to respect the rules. She also said that Hamed was in charge when her father was absent. The investigators asked her why the children had called police on Friday. Mina said they were afraid of their father's reaction, because it was a dishonour that Zainab had run away, showing a lack of respect for the family.

Lefebvre determined that no crime had been committed, except perhaps the slap delivered by Hamed. She filed a report that was passed on to the office of the Crown attorney, where a decision would be made about charges. No action was taken.

Gauvin met with Shafia, Tooba and Hamed two days later and warned them again that the use of violence against the children could lead to criminal charges. He wrote a note, "understands the situation." Gauvin concluded that the safety and development of the children was not at risk, and the file was closed. The agency's observation, days earlier in a written report, that the children "appeared to live under a regime of terror," seemed forgotten.

THE POLICE DEPARTMENT and youth protection agency had closed their files on the Shafia family by late April, but teachers and administrators at Antoine-de-St-Exupéry school knew there were continuing problems in the household. Geeti missed most of her classes during the last week of April, the same week that Daniel Gauvin of Centre jeunesse de Montréal was delivering a stern lecture to Shafia and Hamed about hitting the children. The school staff were growing frustrated and felt increasingly powerless to help the girls. They saw signs that did not seem to matter to police and youth protection workers. Geeti had begun to dress provocatively, as if she were mimicking her big sister Sahar.

Sahar told vice-principal Nathalie Laramée that there was violence at home, and Geeti told the administrator that she did not want to come to school. She wanted to be removed from her home and placed with another family. So Laramée called the Shafia family to a meeting on April 28, a week after Detective Lefebvre had been at the school interviewing the children. Shafia, Tooba, Geeti, Sahar and Zafar appeared in her office. Mina wasn't included because her behaviour and grades were acceptable. Although Zafar was passing his courses and was considered a good student, teachers complained sporadically about his behaviour and his refusal to complete homework.

Laramée thought that the father appeared agitated, perhaps nervous and angry. He immediately began speaking in a loud voice and repeating, "Policia, policia!" In broken English, Shafia told Laramée that he did not know what to do. Laramée, who did not know about the events of April 17 when the children had called police, didn't understand and asked what Shafia was talking about. The children, who acted as translators, explained that there had been a situation at home and authorities had come to the apartment.

Laramée explained that the school was concerned about Sahar and Geeti missing so many classes and often arriving late. In Geeti's case, Laramée pointed out, Quebec law required school attendance until the age of sixteen. She also cited concern about Zafar's occasionally problematic behaviour. Sahar translated some of what Laramée said into Dari for her parents. Only Shafia spoke, and Sahar translated his comments for Laramée. The administrator noted that Tooba was passive and quiet throughout the meeting. When Laramée had finished speaking with the parents and they were leaving, she asked the children to stay behind.

She asked Zafar why his father had been nervous during the meeting.

"Since the police came to our house, it's going much better," he told her, before he left the office. The two girls stayed. As soon as Zafar was gone, they told Laramée that what Zafar had told her was not true. They said things were not good at home when their father was around.

"Madame Laramée, I did not repeat and translate everything that my father was saying because there were a lot of lies," Sahar told the administrator.

Two days later, Antonella Enea, the teacher who had gained Sahar's trust in her first year at St-Ex, spoke to Laramée about Sahar. It was one of many conversations about the girl. The teacher said that Sahar had confided that Zafar had threatened to tell their father that she was hanging around with boys and behaving inappropriately, and that he was going to tell their father that Sahar was a prostitute. Sahar had told Enea that she feared her father would hit her once her brother passed on the lie.

Sahar had begun to wear heavy makeup at school and dress provocatively. Her schoolmates noticed the change and attributed it, in part, to the influence of Samia, a new girlfriend with whom Sahar had grown close. Everyone knew Samia as a boy-crazy extrovert.

But Sahar was most worried that her father would discover her bigger secret, the one she had been concealing for months. She had told Erma Medina that if her father knew it, she would be "a dead woman." Medina was the aunt of Angel Ricardo Ruano Sanchez. He was Sahar's twenty-one-year-old, Spanish-speaking, Catholic boyfriend.

Sahar had made it clear that she wanted a boyfriend. Sahar had met Ammar and had even joined her sister and her boyfriend when they met secretly at a burger joint.

"Awww, you guys are so cute," she gushed, when Zainab and Ammar kissed and hugged.

Ricardo was studying French at night at St-Ex with Zainab. She introduced Ricardo to her younger sister, who seemed to have a thing for Spanish-speaking boys.

Ricardo began visiting St-Ex at lunch hour so that he and Sahar could slip away to a nearby restaurant or park, where they hoped Mina and Zafar wouldn't see them. Ricardo had arrived in Canada from his native Honduras the previous year. He spoke limited English and was just beginning to pick up French. Sahar spoke a few words of Spanish. Despite the language barrier, the pair connected.

The couples—Sahar and Ricardo and Zainab and Ammar—met a few times. Ricardo did not have the smooth style and physique of Jake, Sahar's first Spanish crush, but the soft-spoken Honduran boy wooed her with sweet love texts that he penned in Spanish.

> I love you with all my heart and I can't love anybody more beautiful than you because you are like the air that I breathe every morning, the sun that warms me up. Every day you are like the moon that lights up my night. How could I deny you my love and my heart. I want only you to be the owner of my heart.

Within months of meeting, Sahar and Ricardo began plotting to run away together. Sahar had seen her sister do it. Ricardo said they could go to his country, where he still had family. They could get married there. They would be safe there. Sahar was intoxicated by teenage love, but her poetry hinted at her sober reality. She wrote to Ricardo in clumsy Spanish, carefully printing the words on a scrap of lined paper, with a bright red heart beside the six lines:

Te amo . . .
Por siempre
Para todo
la vida
Incluso Despues
De muerta

I love you . . .
forever
for all
life
even after
of dead

FIVE DAYS AFTER ZAINAB LEFT HOME, Ammar typed a notable if truncated sentence into the appointment log in his cellphone. He did not want to forget the date, April 22, 2009: "Enged wit ma angel."

He and Zainab had decided that they would marry. If necessary, they'd simply go to city hall for a quick civil union. Their families would not be happy, but at least the couple would be legally joined, and then no one could keep them apart.

Zainab had settled into life at the shelter. The rules were clear and the conditions were spartan. She shared a room with another girl. Curfew was 1:00 a.m. on weekdays. Phones and sharp objects weren't permitted inside the rooms, though she sneaked in the cell that Ammar had given her and hid it under her pillow. For the first time in her life, Zainab had freedom to come and go on a whim. She could talk to whomever she pleased and she was free to leave the shelter each day and meet her boyfriend, the boyfriend she had chosen.

She and Ammar were spending virtually every day together. They often strolled through Old Port, a two-and-a-half-kilometre strip of downtown waterfront walking trails, green space and restored historic buildings, close to the shelter. They lounged on park benches, munching on fast food. They gabbed endlessly about their plans and about the future they imagined together.

They strolled hand in hand. Ammar had to keep reminding her that it was okay. He had not forgotten the startling statement Zainab had made when they first started dating fourteen months ago: "If my family finds out about us, my father will *kill* me." He had scoffed. He knew she had led a sheltered life in Dubai and he was her first serious boyfriend, but he didn't *really* believe she'd be in danger.

"Even if they do find out, he's just going to get mad at you a bit and eventually he'll get over it," he had told her.

Now the police were involved. They knew Zainab had fled her house because she was being controlled and had been kept out of school. They knew how Zainab's family had behaved. When Ammar had taken Zainab to the police station to prove he had not kidnapped her, the officer had promised to tell Zainab's family to stop bothering Ammar, to stop calling his cellphone incessantly. The calls had stopped.

After she arrived at the shelter, Zainab realized she had left behind all of her identification, her permanent resident card, health card and other documents. The shelter arranged to have the police meet her at the apartment on Bonnivet so she could retrieve the papers because Zainab told them she didn't feel safe going there alone. Hamed said he didn't know where the documents were. Zainab knew he was lying, but the officers said there was nothing else they could do. Shelter staff helped Zainab start the process of declaring all her documents lost so that she could replace them.

Zainab and Ammar talked about Shafia's wealth. He probably thought he could do anything he wanted. But this wasn't Dubai or Afghanistan. Shafia could not buy the police, they figured. Ammar thought that even if he couldn't protect Zainab, certainly the authorities could.

The more time they spent together and the more they talked, the more Ammar grew to believe that they were fated to be together. They had overcome so many obstacles. Ripped apart in 2008, when Hamed caught them at the Bonnivet apartment, they had not given up on the relationship. They had pined for each other. Zainab had sent him a dozen emails during their year apart. In every message, she told him that she missed him and she had meant it. He had longed to see her nearly perpetual smile and had ached to put his arms around her again. He truly loved her.

He knew that she felt the same way. In the days after Zainab's flight from home, she clung to him. She began to talk about a life together forever and about commitment, trust and true love. She might have believed her words, or perhaps they were simply part of a story told convincingly that permitted her to imagine that she was a different girl living a different life.

She had been waiting for the right man, she told him. She gave herself to him.

7

The Other One

ZAINAB FOUND BLISS IN HER NEW FREEDOM, but Rona stumbled into horror.

Inside the Shafia household, there was anger and panic over Zainab's disappearance. Rona eavesdropped on a conversation that left her terrified. She didn't know what to do, although she considered herself the protector of the children. She was their "shield against evil," she had once told her brother Wali. But speaking openly about these family problems might cause more harm than good. Tooba and Shafia had often warned her and the children that family business was not to be shared outside the home. If Shafia knew she was talking about this, he would be furious, but he had left Canada for roughly six weeks on another of his many business trips.

Rona hoped that Fahima Vorgetts would know what to do, but Vorgetts was in Afghanistan for a month, so her answering machine took Rona's call. Next, she called her younger sister Diba in France, with whom she was close. She trusted Diba with family secrets.

"Please, swear on my children's head, you will not tell anyone else this," Rona said in a hushed tone. "Zainab has flown away. She left the house and she is on welfare. You cannot tell anybody. I want to keep the reputation of the family. If they know I have told you, my life would be in danger."

Rona explained that Shafia was so angry that he had made a terrible threat. She told Diba that she had overheard him talking to Tooba and Hamed in the house one evening, after the children had gone to sleep, in the days after Zainab disappeared on April 17. Shafia said that he would soon go to Afghanistan and Dubai to sell some property.

"He said, 'When I return, I will kill Zainab,'" Rona told Diba, recounting the conversation. She said that one of the others asked Shafia, "What about the *other* one?"

"He said, 'I will kill the other one too,'" Rona recalled. "When they say that *other* person, certainly it will be me."

Diba scoffed, "Sister, it's Canada, not Afghanistan or Dubai. Nothing will happen."

ZAINAB WAS HOMESICK after a week in the shelter. She had freedom, but she had never been separated from her family like this before. With Ammar's encouragement, she called home and talked to her mother, to tell her that she was safe. She knew that her father would soon leave Canada on another business trip.

Tooba wept throughout the call and pleaded with Zainab to return home. Zainab was happy to hear her mother's voice and to talk to her siblings, but she told Ammar she was not going home.

"I don't trust my father or Hamed," she said to him after the call. But she agreed to see her mother face to face. Zainab, Ammar and Tooba met near the shelter. Tooba began to cry as soon as she saw her daughter.

"If you guys love each other, I'll get you guys married," she said, tears streaming down her cheeks. Tooba reminded Zainab that her father was leaving the country.

"There's no way that I'm coming home," Zainab said, shaking her head.

"Look, I'll take you and your sisters and we'll get a different apartment. We'll live together, get you married to Ammar and then you move out."

"No," Zainab repeated.

Tooba turned toward Ammar.

"I'll get you guys married," she promised, hoping he could influence her obstinate daughter. "Tell her to come back home."

"Even if I tell her, in the end, it's her decision," Ammar said. "I can't force her to do things. I can give her my advice but if she doesn't want to listen, she doesn't want to listen."

Zainab wasn't swayed by her mother's plea. She told Ammar that she didn't trust her father. She returned to the shelter.

Tooba did not give up. She continued calling Zainab, pleading with her to come home. She insisted that she would arrange the marriage. Ammar told Zainab that he thought her mother was sincere. All those tears, the emotion. He could see how upset she was. Maybe she really wanted to help them, Ammar told Zainab. She's a mother, after all.

The tears, the pleading and Ammar's advice wore Zainab down. She agreed to return to the house, even though Hamed was still there. She had told the shelter workers when she arrived there that she had been subjected to psychological and physical abuse by her brother. He spied on her at school. He was the primary disciplinarian when her father wasn't around; it was Hamed who yanked her out of school and ordered her to stay in her room when she was caught with Ammar in 2008. In keeping with the shelter's mandate, however, its staff did not suggest she go to police and they did not try to stop her when she said she was going to return home. Zainab believed her mother. She wanted to marry Ammar and get away, for good.

On May 1, she returned to the apartment on rue Bonnivet dragging behind her the big blue Diesel suitcase stuffed with designer clothes that she had taken with her to the shelter. Her father had left Canada one day earlier.

ZAINAB'S RETURN HOME SPARKED A SERIES OF PHONE CALLS that left Latif Hyderi, Tooba's uncle, deeply troubled. Hyderi was surprised to get a call from Shafia; although they were not enemies, they were not close. Hyderi had been offended by Shafia's refusal to bring his family to the wedding of Hyderi's daughter two summers earlier, but he wasn't holding a grudge. He rarely saw the man. Shafia was often travelling on business. When Tooba visited Hyderi at his home, she usually came with one or two of her children.

Shafia's call followed a call from Tooba, ten minutes earlier.

"Uncle, I have a problem and I would like to talk to you about it," Tooba had said. "I want to come to your home to talk to you." She offered no details. As soon as Hyderi agreed to help, Tooba said she would come over and she hung up.

Shafia said he was calling from Dubai, and he sounded angry.

"Latif, do you know that Zainab has caused a problem for us?" Shafia said. "She wants to dishonour me. She is a whore. She is a dirty curse to me. She is a dirty woman." Shafia spat the words.

Hyderi was shocked by the foul insults, thinking that a father should not say such obscene things about his child.

Shafia's angry tirade in Dari continued: "O yak fahesha hast"—"She is a prostitute."

Stung by the venom, Hyderi didn't know what to say.

"Tooba will come and talk to you," Shafia said. "In the past, you asked for my daughter's hand and she didn't agree then. I don't know why she went to this Pakistani guy. Maybe she'll trust you. Just talk to her."

Hyderi agreed to talk to Zainab. It was an unusual reversal. Hyderi had suggested, soon after the Shafias arrived in Canada, that Hyderi's son Hussain would make a good match for Zainab. Tooba and Shafia had dismissed the idea, telling Hyderi that Zainab was too young. Now, Shafia was recruiting Hyderi to help him restore his reputation.

"For this dirty girl, just call a mullah and give her hand to that Pakistani guy to get her out of the house," Shafia said.

Hyderi agreed to talk to Zainab. While he was still on the phone with Shafia, Tooba, Mina and Fereshta arrived at his home. Tooba spoke briefly to her husband and hung up.

Hyderi could see that Tooba was crying.

"What should I do?" Tooba sputtered. "Why did this happen? Why did this day come to me?"

"My sweet niece, if you make this opportunity, I'll talk to the girl to find out what her problem is."

Tooba left and returned in fifteen minutes with Zainab. The group drove to a nearby McDonald's. Tooba went into the restaurant and left her sombre daughter with Hyderi in the minivan.

"Why are you doing this?" Hyderi asked gently. "What's the reason that you are marrying this Pakistani boy?"

Zainab had her head down, crying softly.

"We Asians have a good culture and we have to preserve our culture and the way that children are raised," Hyderi continued.

Zainab continued to cry and did not speak. Hyderi was persistent but he did not raise his voice.

"If you agree and if my son Hussain agrees, and if he's interested, we can ask for your hand," Hyderi said, trying a different tactic to dissuade her from marrying Ammar. "If you agree, we can ask for your hand in marriage to my son because you are a very good girl and it's better if you accept my son."

The suggestion did not break Zainab's silence. Tooba took her home.

The next day, Tooba called Hyderi and told him that Zainab had rejected his advice. She was insisting on marrying Ammar. Tooba asked Hyderi to help arrange it. She would take care of the celebration, but she asked Hyderi to find a mullah to preside over the *nikah*, the Islamic marriage ceremony. Tooba and Shafia didn't know a mullah, since they didn't attend mosque. Hyderi agreed to help.

On May 2, Zainab texted Ammar, explaining that she was optimistic that her family would follow through on the promise to arrange their wedding: "Evry thing is goin gud nw n dey r serious bout us." Hamed had given Zainab her own cellphone again, an apparent reward for returning home from the shelter.

GEETI NOTICED that though Zainab had returned home, she seemed to have won freedom. Plans were in motion to arrange Zainab's marriage to

Ammar. At thirteen, Geeti didn't fantasize about running away to marry, but she also wanted freedom. Youth protection workers had rejected her appeals to be moved out of her home. She had also told police and school officials of her wish to leave home. She was envious of the romantic dream worlds her two big sisters had discovered. She had met the boys who had transported Sahar and Zainab. She'd gone to the mall with Zainab and Ammar. She had giggled and mocked their public displays of affection. She had talked to Ricardo and had heard Sahar talk rapturously about how he would whisk her to another country where they could marry. The sisters shared a room and they shared their secrets. Geeti told Sahar she wanted to go with them.

Geeti scrawled a love note to her big sister. Clumps of blue block letters were splattered across the page in an explosion of emotion, some outlined in cloudlike red ink bubbles. Red hearts were drawn around some of the sentences and some of the *i*'s were dotted with smaller hearts.

> DEAR SAHAR
> I REALLY LOVE YOU.....
> i WISH 2 GOD DAT TILL iM ALIVE i'LL NEVER SEE U
> SAD!
> i HOPE WE'LL NEVER BE SEPARTED
> S + G 4LYFE
> I CANT LIVE, BREATH WHEN UR NOT THERE
> UR MY WHOLE LYFE 4 ME
> i CANT EXPRESS HOW MUCH I LOVE YOU
> I PROMISE BEFORE DYING iLL MAKE ALL UR WISHES
> CUM TRUE ONE BY ONE

Geeti feared that Sahar would leave her behind. At the bottom of the page, she wrote:

> i DON'T KNOW
> iF ONE DAY YOU

LEAVE THIS HOUSE
WHAT AM I GONNA DO????

Beneath each of the four question marks were four small red hearts, each split in half. Inside six of the capital Os, she drew tiny sad faces.

Sahar wondered if it was possible for her and Geeti to leave home together. At school, she asked her math teacher, Fathia Boualia, if she would be able to take Geeti with her if she moved out to live on her own.

"Why Geeti?" Boualia asked her.

"Because I'm very close to Geeti," Sahar answered. "We share the same room. We're always together."

"Sahar, the fact is, moving into an apartment is quite a responsibility and taking Geeti, she's just thirteen, that's the responsibility of adults," Boualia told Sahar.

Two weeks after Boualia's conversation with Sahar, on May 11, Geeti angrily stormed out of Boualia's class. She was angry because she had been denied the chance to go on a class outing, but she was also furious with Boualia, who wrote a formal expulsion note and sent Geeti to meet with vice-principal Nathalie Laramée.

Boualia had never seen the girl so angry. Geeti was still fuming by the time the meeting was held. She complained bitterly about Boualia.

"She's not a nice lady," Geeti told Laramée. "She told Sahar not to take me with her."

SHAFIA WASN'T CONCERNED only about the behaviour of his daughters. He believed that Rona was turning her back on Afghan customs and Islamic traditions. He had called Wali Abdali, Rona's brother who lived in France.

"Your sister has removed her head covering and she is using nail polish on her hands and feet," Shafia said. His tone was accusatory.

Abdali laughed. "It's okay, there are two women in the house and she is trying to look nice," he said. "Maybe there's a little jealousy. If this is a problem, you solve it by separating them."

Shafia didn't want either wife to suffer because of the dispute.

"Let them be women then," Abdali said, laughing again. "Keep out of the way."

Abdali knew there was friction between Tooba and his sister, particularly now that most of the children were grown and didn't need constant attention. Even Tooba had told him this. In one phone conversation, she suggested Abdali arrange to have Rona live with him in France. Tooba didn't want Rona with the family any longer. Rona called her brother regularly and related her troubles. Abdali had even suggested to Shafia that he give Rona a separate house so she could remain near the children.

"She is my wife, I cannot leave her," Shafia had said.

Abdali thought that Shafia was trying to treat his wives equally, a requirement of the polygamous culture in which they were raised, and to smooth over the tensions. Shafia did not tell Abdali that in Canada, Rona had been passed off as a cousin and a housekeeper.

LIKE RONA, TOOBA ALSO REACHED OUT TO SIBLINGS FOR ADVICE.

Fazil Jawid had not seen his sister in twenty years and had talked on the phone with her only sporadically since their family scattered across the globe during the great exodus from Afghanistan in the early 1990s. He ended up in Oxelösund, a small city on the Baltic coast of Sweden. His medical training in Afghanistan a distant memory, Jawid ran a small store and pizza shop.

The phone calls with Tooba accelerated dramatically in January 2009, to the point that she was calling him two or three times a week. She asked for his help with her family problems. She complained that life at home was not good. There was much conflict and unhappiness. Tooba told Jawid that her husband didn't want his daughters dressing like other Canadian girls. Shafia ordered the girls to stay at home when they weren't at school. They weren't permitted to go to the library or to social events or to meet friends outside school hours.

The children, particularly Zainab, had rebelled, she explained. Zainab had taken up with a Pakistani boyfriend and wanted to marry him. Tooba asked Jawid to speak to Zainab and try to convince her to continue her education.

In a phone call and an online video chat, Zainab told her uncle that she was under constant pressure from her father about the way she wore her hair, her clothes and whom she could talk to. Sometimes she wasn't allowed to go to school. She couldn't go out with friends. Her father wanted her to marry one of his nephews or cousins, someone she had never met, perhaps even someone in Afghanistan. He had promised her a house, a car, whatever she wanted, if she accepted an arranged marriage. She rejected it. She told Jawid she was fed up.

"I really hate my father," she told her uncle. "I just want to leave this house. I don't care what happens in the future, good or bad. I just want to leave."

She said that once she left for good, she'd tell authorities about the cruelty in the home, to help her siblings and her mother.

Jawid found her revelations heartbreaking but he told her she shouldn't rush into marriage. She was young and should continue her education, he said, but he could not change her mind. Jawid told Tooba that he wanted to speak to Shafia about the situation. He wanted to tell his brother-in-law to endorse Zainab's marriage to Ammar. Even if it turned out to be a mistake, it was her choice to make. She was in a different environment, where she could see the freedom that other girls enjoyed. It was only natural that Zainab would feel this way, Jawid wanted to tell him.

Jawid reached Shafia in Dubai in early May. Shafia was cool on the phone. He did not want to talk about Jawid's proposal to act as mediator in their family problems; Shafia already had a solution in mind.

"The girl is a whore," Shafia said. He repeated the curse that Latif Hyderi had heard: "O yak fahesha hast."

"This disobedient girl doesn't listen to us," Shafia continued. "She has chosen a Pakistani. If they get married tomorrow, after one day, she will be on the streets begging because this Pakistani guy has no life, no money, no house."

Shafia said Zainab was visiting the library, using computers and talking to boys, all things that offended his strict notion of cultural modesty. He said he wanted Jawid to invite Zainab and Tooba to Sweden. Fereshta would have to go too because she was always with her mother.

"There is water there, everywhere," Shafia said. "When they come there, you call me and I'll come there too. We'll go to the side of the river and do picnic. We'll do kabob and after that we'll push this girl into the water so she can get drowned."

Jawid was horrified.

"I can do this in Dubai," Shafia said. "It's easy. That's why she doesn't come here. But it's easier in Sweden and nobody would suspect me if it happens in Sweden."

Jawid swore at Shafia, hung up and called his brother Jawed Jawad in Montreal. It took several days to reach him. He told his brother that Shafia had said he wanted to kill Zainab, and he believed Shafia was serious. He asked Jawad to be alert to the family's activities. He feared that Shafia would try to take the family out of Canada to a country where he could follow through on his threat. He told his brother to warn Tooba, and also tried to call her directly. Again, it took him several days to reach Tooba. He told her what Shafia had said, that he wanted to drown Zainab. Jawid urged his sister to call the police if Shafia tried to take the family on a trip.

Tooba thanked Jawid for the warning. She said she'd be alert. But she did not ask for any more details of Shafia's scheme, nor did she ask her brother for advice about how to protect her daughter.

IN A SPAN OF A FEW WEEKS, at least three people—Rona, Tooba and Fazil Jawid—had heard of Shafia's desire to kill Zainab. If Zainab knew of her father's intentions, either she wasn't troubled by them or she had decided to conceal her concern. She seemed happier and more optimistic, Ammar thought. The rules at home seemed to have relaxed after she returned from the shelter. Her father wasn't around and Hamed was not telling her what to do. She could leave the house whenever she wanted and met regularly with Ammar. They were going on real dates, to the movies, to restaurants. She was staying out until ten or eleven at night. It was a remarkable change. Her family was moving ahead with the wedding plans.

Hamed talked to Ammar and explained that they were trying to arrange a *nikah* with an Islamic scholar, followed by a reception where the families would meet and celebrate. Ammar told Hamed that his family would not participate. They weren't happy about his decision to get married, believing he needed to finish his education and get a good job, so they were refusing to come to the wedding. Hamed said it would be disrespectful if no one were there to represent Ammar, and asked him to find someone who would pretend to be a family member and come to the reception. When Ammar failed to find anyone, Hamed said he'd try to find a stand-in.

Hamed also failed and, on May 17, Ammar got a phone call from Hamed telling him that the *nikah* would be performed the next day. Ammar complained about the short notice, but Hamed said it had to be tomorrow. Zainab also talked to Ammar and told him he had to come.

Though Hamed was helping to plan the marriage, he had continued to try to poison the relationship.

"You know, man, she doesn't really want to marry you," Hamed told Ammar. "She's just playing around with you."

"Why would you say that?" Ammar asked him.

"I know that 'cause in the past we got her engaged to someone and she broke the engagement after."

Ammar knew that in the year that he and Zainab had been separated, she had resisted her father's pressure to agree to an arranged marriage with a relative she had never met. Hamed made it sound as if Zainab had jilted a lover.

"She broke that engagement after a couple of months," Hamed continued. "She's gonna do that with you too. I don't know why you're wasting your time with her."

Ammar didn't believe him but thanked him politely for passing on the information. That night, Ammar talked to Zainab on the phone. She quizzed him about his conversation with Hamed.

"What did you tell Hamed about me?" she asked Ammar. "He told me that you said, 'I don't want to be with your sister. She's running after me and she won't let me go. I'm stuck with her.'"

Before Ammar could explain that Hamed was playing them against each other, Zafar grabbed the phone. He had heard his sister's half of the conversation.

"Don't believe Hamed," Zafar said. "He's trying to break you guys up."

Ammar liked Zafar and treated him like a younger brother. They had played soccer together, hung out and talked. Zafar said he didn't like his father and he knew the secrets that Zainab kept from her parents. Zafar had told Ammar, "You seem like a good guy and my sister is happy. It would be best if you guys just get away from here."

ZAFAR'S TOLERANCE FOR SIBLING ROMANCE didn't seem to extend to Sahar, however. He wasn't certain she had a boyfriend but he suspected something was going on. In mid-May, at the same time he was encouraging Zainab and Ammar to marry, he discovered Sahar and Ricardo together at the café near St-Ex. Sahar's schoolmate Samia was with them.

Sahar and Ricardo were embracing when she spotted Zafar coming into the restaurant.

"Here comes my brother, we have to stay away from each other!" Sahar told Ricardo. They quickly moved apart. Zafar came directly to their table and began to question Ricardo.

"How did you meet my sister?" he asked. "Are you her boyfriend?"

Ricardo was afraid to tell him the truth.

"No, no, we're just friends," Ricardo said.

"No, you're her boyfriend," Zafar insisted. "Tell me the truth."

Ricardo said he had just met Sahar through Samia. *She* was his girl-friend, he told Zafar.

By now, Ricardo and Samia had stood up and begun walking out of the restaurant to get away from their inquisitor. Zafar followed them.

"If she's your girlfriend, prove it," he demanded.

Samia knew that Sahar would be in trouble if her relationship with Ricardo was exposed. She and Ricardo knew what they had to do: they embraced and kissed.

AMMAR DIDN'T HAVE A CAR, so Hamed picked him up in downtown Montreal in the Shafia minivan on the evening of May 18. They drove to the apartment on Bonnivet and picked up Zainab, and then drove to the nearby home of Latif Hyderi, where Hyderi and his adult son Reza got in.

The group drove to the Azzahra Mosque, where Sheikh Ali Falih Altaie was waiting. The soft-spoken Iraqi immigrant knew the Hyderis but had never met anyone in the Shafia family. They weren't members of the Azzahra community, but he was happy to help any Muslim family. The quintet gathered in Altaie's small office at the front of the mosque. Altaie explained the process to the betrothed couple. They seemed subdued, perhaps nervous, he thought. Their religious differences, tied to a fourteen-hundred-year-old schism in Islam, did not bar them from marrying.

Zainab was a Shia Muslim and Ammar was Sunni. The couple had never talked about who should have been the Prophet's rightful successor after his death. Ammar believed there was only one God. Everything else was a construct of man and organized religion, designed to make money. Ammar believed that to be pious, a person needed only a good heart.

The couple stood between the fat, brown leather couches that lined three walls of the office. On the fourth wall, behind Altaie's cluttered desk, was a framed mirror. At the centre of the glass was a silver relief of Al-Masjid al-Haram, the great mosque at Mecca in Saudi Arabia, Islam's holiest shrine. In the corner of the room two flags hung from two-metre poles, the crimson Maple Leaf and the azure Quebec banner. Altaie began to read verses from the Qur'an:

And of His signs is that He created for you from yourselves mates that you may find tranquility in them; and He placed between you affection and mercy. Indeed in that are signs for a people who give thought.

When Altaie had completed reading the verses, he asked Zainab three times if she accepted Ammar as her husband. He asked Ammar three times if he accepted Zainab as his wife. They agreed without hesitation and the *nikah* was concluded. The newlyweds signed two copies of a marriage certificate, a letter-sized sheet that bore a gold seal and an elaborate border of blue scrollwork. Altaie handed the certificates to Ammar but Hamed plucked them away. He told Ammar that he would take care of registering the marriage with provincial authorities. He did not make good on this pledge.

THE DAY AFTER THE *NIKAH*, Zainab was transformed. She looked like a Bollywood starlet.

Her flat-ironed hair cascaded to the middle of her back. It looked darker, like shining patent leather against the light pink and blue Indian bodice that hugged her torso. At her midriff, the sleeveless top was cut in an upside-down V so that a small triangle of skin peeked out at the waistline of the matching skirt. Blue and white beadwork rimmed the plunging neckline. A strip of sheer pink fabric was wrapped over her left shoulder.

Her face was a smooth mask of foundation and powder. Mascara and eyeliner highlighted her eyes. She would be a striking bride at her wedding reception, but not because of her mother's help.

"You decided to leave the house and now you want clothes?" Tooba had snapped when Zainab asked her mother for a wedding outfit. "Don't expect anything from me." She refused to take Zainab shopping for a dress. She did not offer to take her to the hairdresser. Those tasks were left to the family of Tooba's uncle, Latif Hyderi. Tooba did one thing to help Zainab:

she protected her from her brother. The night before the reception, after the *nikah* was completed, Tooba told Hyderi that Zainab should stay at his home.

"Hamed is very angry and I don't want him to hit her," Tooba told her uncle. Zainab slept at the Hyderi home. The next morning, Hyderi's daughter Azita took Zainab to a salon so that she could have her hair and makeup done. She also loaned Zainab the beautiful pink and blue outfit.

Zainab had little other family support on her big day. Her older siblings were forbidden from attending the reception. The sister to whom she was closest, Sahar, skipped school and spent the day at an amusement park with Ricardo. Shafia made no effort to return to Canada from Dubai for the first marriage of one of his children, and he did not call to congratulate his daughter or wish her well. During the reception, he would talk to Hamed.

When Ammar arrived at the reception, at an Iranian restaurant in the city's west end, more than a dozen people were milling around, munching on Persian food from a small buffet and making small talk. They were cousins, aunts and uncles of the Shafia family, all eager to meet the Wahid family.

Quiet chatter had begun among the guests, who were wondering why no one from the bridegroom's family was at the party. People were gossiping, asking why Zainab would make such a foolish decision. "What's going on?" Tooba could hear whispers of outrage. She began to cry.

Almost as soon as Ammar arrived, Tooba cornered him. Hamed was with her.

"I told you to bring some of your family members!" Tooba said.

"Listen, I told you guys that nobody's coming from my side," Ammar said. "Even Hamed tried getting someone to pretend they're, like, my parents or uncle or whatever. I don't understand why you guys are doing this."

Hamed interrupted. "Just let it go," he said to his mother. "Let them go."

Tooba, more agitated, persisted. "What are my family members going to think about me that I'm letting my daughter go with a guy who doesn't have a family or anything?" she asked.

"You should have thought of that before, 'cause I told you nobody's coming from my family," Ammar said.

By now, Zainab had joined the group.

"You can't back out now," she told her mother. "We have to do this."

"Your uncles and your cousins and aunts, what am I going to tell them?" Tooba said. "It's going to look bad on us."

Hamed seemed to want the drama to end, but he supported his mother.

"What are we going to tell our family?" he added. "It's a culture thing. They won't understand."

Tooba, Hamed and Zainab walked away, around a corner, out of Ammar's view and earshot.

Hyderi and Tooba's brother, Jawed Jawad, who also lived in Montreal, joined the threesome after a few minutes. Jawad could not contain his anxiety.

"Why this cruelty, for God's sake?" Jawad asked. "Who is this guy? Why is she marrying him?"

Zainab began to cry. Tooba collapsed onto a chair. Zainab threw herself onto her mother's chest and cried out, "If you don't agree, I will reject this boy."

Zainab was yelling now, telling her mother that she didn't want to upset her. "What should I do? What should I do? I'll just ask him to leave. I don't want to marry him."

Zainab found Ammar fifteen minutes after she had disappeared with her family. She was crying like a little girl, he thought. Big tears streamed down her cheeks and her chest was heaving.

"I can't do this," she sputtered. "This can't happen."

Ammar was bewildered.

"Why? What happened?"

"My family's not going to accept this and I can't ruin my family's reputation."

Ammar wanted to be strong in the face of the ruinous events unfolding, but he felt overwhelmed. They had grown so close, so quickly. They had overcome so many obstacles and now they were being ripped apart again.

Zainab lowered her voice and explained the other, frightening reason she would not go through with the marriage.

"Hamed said if I leave with you, he's going to *kill* everyone here and then he's going to kill himself," Zainab said. She was sobbing and she looked terrified.

"He's not going to do it," Ammar said, without hesitation.

"I'm sorry, I can't do it, I don't want anybody to get hurt."

"He's not going to do it," Ammar repeated. "But it's still your choice whether you want to come with me."

Ammar felt crushed by the words, all the tears, Tooba's accusing questions. His heart was pounding in his chest, but he was not angry; he was heartbroken. He told Zainab he loved her and left the restaurant.

AFTER THE DISASTROUS WEDDING RECEPTION, Tooba, Zainab and her relatives retreated to Latif Hyderi's home. Hyderi felt that everyone's heart was bleeding. He put on music and asked the young people in the room to dance in a bid to dissipate the dark mood.

His son Hussain came in.

"You're a dishonourable person," Tooba said. "You should have started a relationship with Zainab before she became involved with the Pakistani boy."

Hyderi seized on Tooba's anguished accusation to suggest again, as he had several times before, that Hussain and Zainab should be engaged. It was a perfect match. They were distant cousins. A good Afghan boy and a good Afghan girl. Hussain said he wanted to talk to Zainab himself first, to clear up some things, before making any commitment.

The next day, Hyderi took Hussain to the Shafia apartment on Bonnivet, and the families left the pair alone in a room to talk. Hussain asked Zainab why she wanted to marry Ammar. She told him that she was fed up with the restrictive life that her father had imposed. She wanted to get away and she wanted to shame her father in the process. She wanted "revenge" on him, she told Hussain.

They talked for half an hour and Hussain was convinced that Zainab didn't love Ammar. She was available. He suggested they talk some more, to get to know each other. Just four days later, Hussain revealed his feelings for her, in a text message sent May 24: "if i tell u that i am madly in love with u from first that i saw u do u believe me."

HYDERI CALLED SHAFIA OVERSEAS to discuss the possible match between their children. He began to talk about the dissolution of Zainab's marriage to Ammar, but Shafia already knew what had happened. Hyderi said he was asking for Zainab's hand in marriage for his son Hussain. Shafia's tone was angry, but he said the match could be a good thing. He made it clear, however, that he wanted to oversee the arrangements.

"Don't let that girl have any contact with your son until I come and then we'll figure this out," Shafia said. Hyderi said he was arranging the marriage for the sake of the honour of Shafia and his family and not out of some desire to get Shafia's money. The match between two good Afghans would erase all memories of the terrible episode with the Pakistani boy, he suggested. "I just want to clear this bad spot from the skirt of Zainab."

Shafia was still seething over Zainab's relationship with Ammar. He believed that she had shamed him.

"She is a dishonourable person," he said. "If this thing happened and I was there I would have killed her. I wouldn't let her live."

Hyderi tried to calm him.

"Why do you want to do that?" he said. "She's your daughter. She's your child. Children can make mistakes."

Hyderi told him the matter was solved and people would forget. His honour was intact.

"God gave you such good children, why are you talking like this?" Hyderi asked. "Leave it alone." He thought Shafia sounded arrogant and vengeful.

"I'm not happy and she didn't do a good thing. If I would have been there, I would have killed her," Shafia repeated.

Hyderi arranged to meet with Tooba to talk about Shafia's threatening tirade and to ask why the family had not completed the annulment of Zainab's marriage. On the day of the reception, Ammar had been called back to the restaurant and the mullah who had conducted the *nikah* the day before had instructed Ammar to say "divorce" three times. Zainab was too distraught to complete the process. The mullah said she could come to see him at the mosque the next day to fulfill her part of the dissolution, but her family did not take her.

Hyderi asked to speak to Tooba alone because he believed Hamed acted as a spy who fed information to his father. But Tooba arrived at her brother Jawed's house with Hamed, and the group met on the porch. Hyderi asked Tooba why they had not completed the annulment and she said they had simply been too busy. He told Tooba and Hamed about the troubling phone conversation in which Shafia said he wanted to kill Zainab.

"He is a very serious and emotional person," Hyderi told them. "I am afraid he will come here and make a problem."

Hyderi said Hamed had a duty to talk sense into his father.

"You are a young man," he said. "We old people are every emotional. If God unwilling, that your father comes here . . ."

"But how can I disrespect my father?" Hamed interjected.

"I didn't tell you to disrespect him, but you have to be careful. It is not Afghanistan. It is Canada. It is a different environment. The girls are going to school and they see their classmates and they learn from them. Make your father aware of this and convince him to allow his daughters to make their own decisions."

"But what should I do, fight my father?" Hamed asked.

"No, you must respect your father but he must understand the conditions in this country," Hyderi replied.

He told Hamed that his sisters were being treated like "political prisoners." It was completely against the rules of Canadian society.

"When these girls are under these pressures, one day it will implode," Hyderi said. The problems with Zainab would be repeated with all the girls, he predicted.

After more than an hour of conversation, Hyderi left. He had not been home long before the phone rang. Shafia was calling from Dubai. He sounded angrier than he had in their previous call.

"Why did you tell Tooba and Hamed that I'm very emotional and might do something?" Shafia demanded. "I thought you are a man, a real man. I told you my secret and you say this to other people!"

"Shafia, I didn't say this out of hypocrisy," Hyderi answered. "I didn't want you to come here and something happens, you beat someone and then a problem will be created for you. Whatever I did, I did it because of your children. They love me."

Shafia's anger was not assuaged.

"If this girl runs away, if she learns that I'm coming, do you know what will happen?" Shafia sneered.

Hyderi said he was certain that Zainab would not run away.

"Why do you think like this?" he asked.

"If I had come there and killed this girl, would you have informed the government?" Shafia asked.

"Shafia, God unwilling that something like this will happen. I'm a Muslim and as long as I'm alive, I would not be a partner in your crime with you. I will be the first one to call the police."

HUSSAIN MET WITH ZAINAB IN LATE MAY. They went to a park and then to a restaurant and spent a few hours together. Tooba told Hussain to be sure to return Zainab home before Hamed returned from school, since he would call his father in Dubai and Shafia would be angry that Hussain and Zainab were meeting.

A few days later, Shafia called from Dubai and spoke to Zainab. He told her that he wanted her to marry his nephew in Afghanistan. She said she was content to marry Hussain. Her father ordered her not to talk to Hussain or meet him until they were formally engaged. It would happen after he returned to Canada, Shafia told his daughter.

As she had done with Ammar before, Zainab ignored her father's edict. She and Hussain met often. They went to parks and restaurants and hung out, sometimes for hours. They talked and traded text messages every day.

"I don't care if Hamed or my dad finds out," Zainab told Hussain.

Although Zainab told her family she was moving on and was happy to marry Hussain, she had not forgotten Ammar. A week after their tearful separation at the wedding reception, Zainab secretly called him.

She told him that she had talked on the phone to her father, who had forgiven her. He was coming home in early June. Zainab planned to meet him at the airport and apologize for running away from home and for bringing shame on the family. She told Ammar that she believed things were getting better at home.

"I'm allowed to go out now," Zainab told him. "They're telling me I can go to the school that I want. I want to finish my education and then in the future I'll think about getting married, if I want to."

Ammar told her he was happy for her, happy that she might get the freedom that she wanted. It was easy for a family to blackmail a Muslim girl, he thought. He still felt deeply wounded. She did not tell him about her pending betrothal to Hussain.

"The best thing for both of us is to move on," Zainab said. "We weren't meant to be together."

ON SATURDAY, MAY 30, Sahar went to school for an extra help session designed to boost her failing grade in mathematics.

Early in the class, Sahar collapsed onto the floor and lapsed into unconsciousness. Classmates told the teacher, Fathia Boualia, that Sahar wasn't eating properly, and some thought she might be starving herself to lose weight. She seemed to have grown thin in the past few months. An ambulance was called and Boualia telephoned Sahar's home. The teacher could not reach anyone, so she jumped into her car and followed the ambulance to hospital. Once there, she called the Shafia home again. After several tries,

Geeti answered. Boualia told her that a parent must come to the hospital as soon as possible. She noted that Sahar's health card was expired.

Hours passed and none of Sahar's family members arrived at the hospital. At three o'clock, hospital officials said Sahar could leave. Doctors had not found anything seriously wrong with her, although she was still unsteady. Boualia still could not get in touch with Sahar's parents. Hospital staff said they could not release Sahar by herself and asked the teacher to drive the girl home. Boualia resisted at first, explaining that it wasn't appropriate for a teacher.

"Can I go with you to your home?" Sahar asked Boualia, who had an eighteen-year-old daughter.

"I can't host a student at my home like that," Boualia told her.

Sahar told her teacher that her life at home was stifling. Her family imposed rigid rules. She wasn't permitted to have contact with boys. It wasn't the first time that Sahar had confided in Boualia that her home life was unhappy. She had told the teacher before that she was afraid of her father and older brother, though she had never explained why she feared them.

"I would really like to know your daughter, as a Muslim woman," Sahar told Boualia.

"No, I'm your teacher," Boualia said. "I have to keep my distance. I can't take you home like that."

In the face of this refusal, Sahar suggested going to a friend's house because there was no one at her home. Boualia was uncomfortable with the idea but felt she had no choice. When they arrived at the house, she spoke to the grandmother of Sahar's friend. The woman explained that Sahar had stayed there before.

Hamed did not change his plans because of Sahar's hospital visit. The next day, Sunday, May 31, he jetted to Dubai to join his father. It wasn't clear why Hamed was making the ten-thousand-kilometre trip, for a two-week stay, at a time when the family appeared to be in crisis and already lacked its patriarch. Hamed took with him the laptop computer that he kept in his room at Bonnivet. Its hard drive was accumulating a puzzling series of documents and files. A text file created April 28 contained the phone number for a gynecologist in Montreal and three words: "Antifreeze (Ethylene Glycol)." A separate text file created two days later included the website address of Dante Sports, a business that touted itself as "the oldest and most experienced gun shop in greater Montreal."

No one in the Shafia household was a hunter.

HAMED'S DEPARTURE EMBOLDENED ZAINAB to talk to Ammar about meeting secretly. She was still in regular email contact with him. He invited her to come to watch him play hockey but she said she could not sneak away.

On June 2, Zainab emailed Ammar to tell him that she was sorry she could not make it to the game but "seriously i m mising u toooooooo." She wrote that there was one thing she was really happy about:

> it was my dream to marry u n i dit it once soooo nw even one day if sum thing happens to us like dead i wnt die with out my dream being full filled i love u much n thnx 4 loving me the same way

She explained that she was going to Toronto to the wedding of a cousin, but she quickly returned to the subject that preoccupied her.

> we had an amazing love story 2gether i m gonna write it down in a boy with alll mine u r pictures on it if u don't mind can u send me sum of our pistures 2gether onthis email ... ... i will always keep that book and on top of it i will write a true love story ... ... n may b one day if we meet wen we r all old then i will give it too u to seee loveu take care ... ... i miiiiiiiiiiiiiiiissssssssssssssssssss ssssssssssssssssssssssssssssssssssssssssssssssssssssssssssssssssssss ssssss uuuuuuuuuuuuuuuuuuuuuuuuuuuuuuuuuuuuuuuuuuuuu

uuuuuuuuuuuuuuu toooooo

even ever i listen to maahi i rem u coz u hated m listening to
that song i uesd to love it

. . . .

ur wife . . . .

and best friend zainab

While Zainab reminisced about lost love with Ammar, she was again texting regularly with Zubaida Siddique, the best friend she had left behind in Dubai. She had told Zubaida that her relationship with Ammar had ended and that there was a new man in her life. Zubaida asked Zainab to send her photos, so she could be the judge of whether Hussain would be a good match. It was a ritual the close friends had always followed. As she had done with Ammar, Zubaida began referring to Hussain using the affectionate Pakistani term for brother-in-law, *jeju*.

The same day that Zainab emailed Ammar about their "amazing love story 2gether," Zubaida texted Zainab about Hussain: "howz my new jeju ;-) h0pe u w0nt leve diz 1."

INVISIBLE ROUTINES INSIDE HAMED'S LAPTOP COMPUTER recorded its new connection to the Internet, beginning June 1, via a wireless network in Dubai named "SAMI99." Usually, the machine was connected to a router inside the Shafia apartment on Bonnivet with the ID "MShafiaa63580."

On June 3, someone began using the laptop to scour the Internet for unusual information. Every keystroke of these searches was preserved on the hard drive and, although they would later be purged from the search history, they remained in a hidden corner of the computer's memory, among hundreds of thousands of website records that would be accessible to an expert who knew how to recover them. The saved data included information that revealed that the searches were performed on google.ae, the version of the search engine available to web surfers in the United Arab

Emirates. Anyone in Dubai who typed "Google" into an Internet address bar would be routed to google.ae.

The peculiar searches began just after 2:30 p.m. Dubai time. The first words typed into Google were "Montreal Jail."

Three minutes later, another search: "Can a prisoner have control over his real estate."

Twenty seconds later another search: "Montreal Jail."

A second later: "Can a prisoner have control over their real estate."

Five seconds later: "Can a Prisoner have control over his real estate."

A minute later: "can prisoners have rights to sell his real estate."

All of the searches were entered in English with virtually no errors by the typist. Mohammad Shafia was barely able to read or write in his first language, Dari, and he was wholly computer illiterate.

8

Whore

A FEW DAYS AFTER SAHAR'S HOSPITAL STAY, she confided in Antonella Enea, her teacher, that she was afraid because her father would soon be returning to Canada.

"Why are you afraid?" Enea asked.

"Because my brother Zafar will tell my father that I'm a whore," Sahar answered, repeating the claim she had made a month earlier.

Enea was alarmed and, the next day, called youth protection authorities. Sahar had told Enea that she had had previous contact with the Centre jeunesse de Montréal and a social worker there should be familiar with her. It had been only seven weeks since the agency had sent an agent to the Shafia home to investigate complaints that the children feared for their lives.

Enea relayed Sahar's fears to the agency. It was the third complaint to youth protection authorities in the past fourteen months involving the girl.

The woman who took Enea's call said there was no social worker assigned to Sahar. She told the teacher that the agency could not provide service to the girl, at any rate, since she would turn eighteen in October. Enea was disappointed. The people she thought were best equipped to help this lost child said she wasn't their problem. The youth protection agency told Enea to refer Sahar to community shelters, though it did not provide information about any such shelters.

The teacher didn't know anything about shelters for young girls, so she contacted Frédérique Normand, the psychologist at St-Ex. Normand made a series of phone calls and gave Enea contact information for two shelters. By then, Sahar had told her teacher that she would go to the home of a close friend for the weekend. She felt safe there and her parents didn't know where the friend lived. The school staff scheduled a meeting for Sahar with a school social worker on the following Monday. The staff also arranged for Sahar to get into the school through an alternative entrance, in the event that she feared her parents would show up at the school's main doors.

A PLEASANT, SMILING TEENAGER appeared in social worker Stephanie Benjamin's office on Monday, June 8. Benjamin knew that Sahar had told school staff that she feared being beaten by her father. She hoped to gain Sahar's trust, so that the girl would expose her scars and reveal family secrets.

Sahar told the social worker that she was no longer afraid. Her father and mother had separated and were living apart, Sahar said, offering a lie. Benjamin asked why Sahar had been afraid of being beaten. The girl told her that it had happened before, though she did not provide any details and Benjamin did not press for more.

Benjamin asked Sahar how she got along with her family. Sahar explained that her relationship with her older brother was strained and that he was closely allied with their father. When their father wasn't home, Hamed took his place and exercised control over her, telling her whom she could have as friends. Sahar told Benjamin that she also had conflict with her younger sister Mina. She said she was close to her mother and to her sister Geeti.

As Sahar recounted her difficulties at home and her fears, she continued to smile. She was constantly smiling, Benjamin noted. She wondered if the smile was a cultural mannerism or a mask. It did not seem natural.

Sahar would not share any intimate details of life at home. She told Benjamin that she wanted to get a job and earn money so that she could move away from home as soon as she turned eighteen. Sahar said she dreamed of becoming a gynecologist because she was touched by the poor health of women in Afghanistan. The social worker gave her samples of resumés and reference sheets and pointed her to job referral agencies. Benjamin scheduled another meeting for the following day, hoping that Sahar would drop her mask.

Benjamin saw Sahar the next day, but the girl remained distant. She would not open up. She reiterated that she simply wanted help getting a job so she could save money and get a place of her own. Benjamin did not see her again.

ZAINAB AND AMMAR MET SECRETLY on the afternoon of Friday, June 12. Ammar was waiting for her at the subway station. They embraced, kissed and walked to a nearby park and found a bench.

Zainab told Ammar that he should move on and make something of his life, maybe go back to school. She played cheerleader as she had done before, telling him he had great potential and that she'd be proud of him when he did something big one day. Ammar's response betrayed his heart. He did not want to move on.

"I don't know if you're gonna get married or not later in the future but if we're not together, I recommend you to get married to someone nice who will take care of you, who would understand you. At least you could be away from all that disaster in your life," he said.

"I'll never get married," she said. "Never, 'cause I already got married and marriage doesn't mean anything now."

"I'm not saying you have to get married right now, but with time, everything heals up," he said. "So, if we're not meant to be together, then we're not meant to, but if we are meant to be together, then no matter what, even after ten years, we'll get together."

They were both crying.

"No matter what happens, wherever you live, wherever I live, you always will be in my heart," he continued. "If ever you need anything, you always can call me and I'm always there for you, whether it's your good times or bad times."

Zainab did not talk about Hussain. She did not mention the series of fawning messages she had received the evening before during an exchange of texts.

Hussain had written, "I wonder what is especial about u that i cant think of anything nor anyone But u."

Nine minutes later: "I am so much in love With u jokes apart i been in love before too But never loved anyone as much i love u."

Thirteen minutes later: "I promise u you will never regret of ur decision and the love that u see in my eyes 4 ur self it will remaine 4 ever."

Eleven minutes later: "Yes definitely i miss u so much u made me crazy about ur self the more i see u the more i want to be With u."

Zainab shared Hussain's messages with Zubaida. She confided that his daily romantic missives were overwhelming. On June 12, the day that Zainab met Ammar, Zubaida sent a teasing text to her friend, telling her that her new beau seemed "desperate" so she should be cautious: "Hey!OMG, y is ds jeju actin s0 desp0.bt c0m dnt hve sex b4 ur wedin."

Zainab had not told her friend that she had been intimate with Ammar. She replied to her friend with a believable lie: "LOL dnt wry im vrgn."

THE DAY AFTER ZAINAB AND AMMAR'S MEETING, Shafia and Hamed returned to Canada. Zainab apologized to her father again for her shameful behaviour. She feared his reaction. To her surprise, he kissed her on the forehead and told her that what she had done was not good but he did not berate her.

"Be careful in future, don't do stupidity," he said.

All seemed to be forgiven. She expected that she and Hussain would soon be officially engaged. But Tooba told Hussain's family they should not push to formalize the wedding plan immediately. Shafia was tired after his extended business trip and the long journey home. He needed some time to relax.

Whoever was using Hamed's laptop to conduct a detailed online search for isolated locations near bodies of water did not take a break. The searches, which had begun while the computer was with Hamed and Shafia in Dubai, accelerated once they returned to Canada. Over the next few weeks, thousands of maps, web pages and photos would be viewed.

On June 14, more than two dozen searches were conducted using Google, Google Maps, Google Earth and Wikipedia. Locales within a day's drive from Montreal where there was water, mountains, rivers, bridges or islands were studied. There was a Google search for "mountains on water in quebec" and Wikipedia searches of "Mount Babel" and "Mont Wright." Directions were mapped from the postal code for the Shafia home on rue Bonnivet to Mont Brome, Mont Saint-Bruno and several imprecise destinations including "mountain with water" and "mountains." In addition to the searches, the researcher began browsing photos of the locations through a web-based service called Panoramio.

The searches didn't appear to relate to any business idea that Shafia had explained to Nabi Neda. Neda knew that Shafia was looking for property around Montreal to build houses and to open a car lot. Shafia had never said he was on the hunt for isolated waterfront land or vacation properties.

The next day, June 15, the Google Maps searches continued. The searcher viewed dozens of maps and then dragged and zoomed to inspect locations. Just after three o'clock that Monday afternoon, the map was centred on a point in the northeast end of the city of Kingston, Ontario. The isolated area was known as Kingston Mills.

As the mapping and searches continued, the laptop continued to collect and store a detailed electronic trail. Because the machine was reasonably modern and was using an up-to-date Microsoft operating system, it was continually saving snapshots of the contents of the hard drive. The average computer user would not understand that the invisible shadow copy operation was preserving files on the machine, including Internet search histories, text and images. Purged histories and deleted files would be retrievable, months later.

Early on June 16, the first in a string of sinister searches occurred: at 1:26 a.m., someone typed, "facts documentaries on murders." Later that day, the searches for locales close to water shifted to searches about going out on the water. How "to rent a boat in Montreal" was searched. Maps for boat rental outlets in the area were perused.

The next day, June 17, there were new, peculiar searches: "Metal boxes," "Iron Boxes in Montreal," "treasure boxes in montreal," "Huge boxes in montreal." There were dozens more searches for boat rentals near Saint-Léonard, for yachting, houseboats, and websites of retail outlets that sold boats, and "requirements for renting a boat in montreal."

No one in the Shafia family was a boater. None of the children could swim. Despite this, the computer research being conducted on Hamed's laptop focused again on secluded destinations near water. On June 19, dozens of Panoramio photos of rivers, lakes and fast-moving water were viewed, along with searches using Google Maps and Google Earth. Many rugged wilderness locales were studied.

The driving route to Réservoir Dozois, a remote lake more than four hundred kilometres northwest of Montreal on the Trans-Canada Highway, was mapped. Panoramio photos were scanned of Lac Pythonga, a lake located in an isolated wilderness area three hundred kilometres northwest of Montreal. Photos were viewed and directions charted for a trip to Grand-Remous, a tiny town more than 250 kilometres north-west of Montreal, where the Trans-Canada Highway crosses the churning Gatineau River.

Zainab had not heard anything about a wilderness getaway. She told Hussain, whom she was secretly meeting every day, that things were remarkably calm at home. It didn't seem to matter to Hamed that she was disobeying her father's edict to stay away from Hussain until they were for-mally engaged. Zainab said she didn't care anyway that Hamed knew that the two were talking and meeting.

But one thing upset her. Six days after Zainab's father and Hamed returned to Canada, her cellphone was cancelled. It was her lifeline to the outside world. It had allowed her to talk easily to her old Top Girls pals in the Middle East and to her boyfriends. She told Hussain she didn't know why the phone service was suddenly terminated. Hussain told her not to worry. Everything was going to work out. They would be engaged soon and she'd be able to leave the house.

The day after Zainab's cellphone service was cancelled, her brother Hamed went out for the entire day. He wasn't out of contact. Just after noon, he made a cellphone call to the apartment on Bonnivet. The call was routed through a cellphone transmission tower near Grand-Remous. Roughly three hours later, he received a call from home that was routed through a cellphone tower near Mont-Laurier, about thirty-five kilometres east of Grand-Remous. Just after seven, Hamed placed another call home, which was routed through a cellphone tower in Montreal, five kilometres from the apartment on Bonnivet.

Roughly an hour later, the unusual computer research that had been underway on the Shafia laptop throughout June resumed.

At 8:20 p.m., "where to commit a murder" was typed into a Google search.

The next day, June 21, Zainab told Hussain that the entire ten-member family was going on an end-of-school-year trip to Niagara Falls, Ontario. Zainab didn't really want to go, but she would not be permitted to stay behind. She didn't know how long they'd be gone, but she told Hussain that their engagement would be formalized as soon as the family returned.

ON JUNE 22, SHAFIA BOUGHT A THIRD VEHICLE to add to the family's fleet, which already included a Lexus SUV and a Pontiac Montana minivan. Shafia would tell people later that he bought the small, black car for his daughter to drive, although he also planned to use it for the vacation trip. Only Shafia, Tooba and Hamed had driver's licences.

Shafia paid $5,000 to a used car dealer in Montreal for a 2004 Nissan Sentra with 113,000 kilometres on the odometer. The compact, four-door sedan was in good shape, but it had a feeble 1.8-litre engine and a small passenger compartment. It seemed an unlikely car for a family of ten planning a thirteen-hundred-kilometre round trip across two provinces, particularly given that they already owned two vehicles that could each seat at least seven people in comfort. The Sentra had seat belts for five, but three adults in the back was a tight fit. It seemed an even more peculiar choice when Shafia told his family that they would continue on to Vancouver, British Columbia, a further four thousand kilometres west of Niagara Falls.

The same day that Shafia purchased the Sentra and the family prepared for the cross-country adventure, Ricardo texted Sahar. A week or more apart would be a long separation for the affectionate couple accustomed to daily contact. Ricardo wanted to give her a going-away gift of poetry, a reminder of his devotion:

> the only thing I would wish in this world, is to have you
> every day of my life, the world is very large and it's so large
> that one day I could even lose you, but in this world, as large
> as it is, there's a small heart, and you can never get lost in
> that heart, because it's only for you, my love

That afternoon, the Hyderi family was shopping at Sami Fruits, a large fruit and vegetable warehouse near their home in Saint-Léonard, when they bumped into the Shafias. Hyderi was in the parking lot when he heard someone calling out, using the Dari word for uncle: "*Kaka, kaka!*"

Hyderi turned and saw Zafar near the Lexus, waving to him and calling out. Tooba, Rona and the other Shafia children were there and they walked over to say hello. Zafar said his father and Hamed were in the store. The children told Hyderi that they were getting food for a trip to Niagara Falls and Vancouver. Hyderi was surprised and said that if he had known about it, he would have suggested his family join them.

"You have to bring Zainab back safe and sound," Hyderi told Tooba. She told him not to worry, she wouldn't let anything happen to her daughter.

Hyderi thought Tooba seemed suddenly anxious, eager to end the conversation and get away from him. She was glancing around nervously. Zafar announced that his father was coming out of the store. The children, Tooba and Rona returned to their vehicle as Shafia arrived and greeted Hyderi.

It was an uncomfortable encounter, the first time the men had spoken or seen each other since their telephone conversation in May, when Shafia had chastised Hyderi for revealing his "secret." Hyderi asked Shafia why he had not called him since he returned to Canada from Dubai. Shafia said he had been busy with his children and planning their vacation.

Shafia reached out his hands and clasped Hyderi's hand in a customary Afghan greeting between men. He held Hyderi's hand firmly.

"You said that a girl is the asset or property of other people," Shafia said, recalling Hyderi's conversation on the veranda of Jawad's house with Hamed and Tooba, while Shafia was in Dubai. Hyderi had talked about the traditional belief that a daughter belongs to her future husband, and not to her own family.

Shafia squeezed Hyderi's hand tightly, more tightly than Hyderi thought reasonable and in a way that delivered a message—*just watch what happens now.* Then Shafia left with his family. Hyderi was unnerved.

JOYCE GILBERT, THE SHAFIAS' DOWNSTAIRS NEIGHBOUR, didn't know they were leaving until she saw them piling bags and food into two vehicles, the Lexus and the small black car she had never seen before. They told her they were going on a twelve-day vacation. She watched them pull away at 2:30 p.m. on Tuesday, June 23.

Although Shafia had told family members they were going to Niagara Falls, the caravan of two vehicles headed northwest on the Trans-Canada Highway, rather than southwest toward the Ontario border. The route would take them into the rugged and isolated Quebec interior. It was a course that a traveller headed for British Columbia might follow, but each family member had packed only a few pieces of clothing.

Nearly twelve hours after the convoy set out from Montreal, at 2:00 a.m., it was in Grand-Remous. But the family didn't stay there. The group reversed direction and drove thirty-five kilometres east along the route they had just travelled, back to Mont-Laurier, where they rented motel rooms for the night. The next day, June 24, they headed south on a winding, rural highway. They crossed the Ontario border at Hull just after six in the evening and continued south until they reached Highway 401, the major expressway that would take them west to Niagara Falls.

Shortly after six, Zainab texted Hussain in Montreal using Sahar's cellphone. She explained that she hadn't been able to contact him the day before, during the first day of their trek, but she offered a surprising revelation:

> salam hw r u evryone rlly missng u the thng is i cldnt call u
> last nite n 2day cuz they wer plnng 2 go 2 vancvr n thy went
> half way and chgd ther mind n nw we r on wy bck 2 tor

Zainab related that her father's accommodating attitude had disappeared on the first day of the trip when he learned she had bought a phone card. Zainab told Hussain that after the family stopped at the motel, she and Rona had gone to a store to buy a card so they could make cheap calls. When Tooba asked where they had been, Shafia overheard the answer. He was furious, Zainab said, because he believed that she was talking to Hussain.

"If I find out you talk with Hussain before the engagement, no one can be worse than me," Shafia told Zainab. She lied and told her father that she wanted the card to call a girlfriend. He didn't believe her.

Zainab told Hussain that she was upset by her father's angry outburst: "he gt rlly mad at me n i didt eat whole day n i ws cryng whole tym n he came up 2 me n kissd me n said nakhro nako." Hussain knew that the two Dari words at the end of the sentence meant "don't overreact," but it didn't ease his growing anxiety.

He thought that Zainab's father was acting *weird*. He had told his family they were going to Vancouver, then changed his mind one day into the trip. He had been kind to Zainab, and then controlling and angry on the day they left Montreal. Hussain wondered what was going on. He feared that

1. A snapshot of Rona Amir and Mohammad Shafia on their wedding day in 1978. Rona and Shafia were married in a lavish ceremony at the Intercontinental Hotel in Kabul, Afghanistan.

2. Tooba (*left*), Shafia (*centre*) and Rona at Tooba and Shafia's wedding in 1988. As he had done for his wedding ten years earlier, Shafia booked Kabul's most impressive venue—the Intercontinental Hotel.

3. A snapshot of the pre-wedding celebration in 1988. Shafia sits between his two wives, Tooba (*left, in green*) and Rona.

4. A Shafia family snapshot taken in 2003, while they were living in Dubai. *From left*: Hamed, Rona, Geeti, Mohammad Shafia, Zainab, Sahar, Tooba. Images of the remaining Shafia children have been removed. Tooba's defence lawyer, David Crowe, submitted this photo as evidence at trial that Zainab, Sahar and Geeti had not been forced to wear hijabs.

5. Zainab (*far right*) with other Top Girls inside Dubai's Al Sadiq Islamic English School in 2007. At left is Fatma Kassim and second from left is Zubaida Siddique, girls whom Zainab considered "like sisters." She cherished their friendship and stayed in touch after her family moved to Canada.

6. The Al Yasmeen apartment building in Deira, an older section of the city of Dubai. The Shafia family lived at Al Yasmeen for most of their ten years in the UAE, and it was here that Zainab said her tearful goodbyes to Fatma and Zubaida when the family left for Canada in 2007.

7. The flat on rue Bonnivet in Saint-Léonard, Montreal, where the Shafia family lived from their arrival in Canada in June 2007 until the arrests in July 2009. It was here that Hamed exchanged the Lexus for the Pontiac minivan on the morning of June 30, 2009, just hours after the victims were killed.

8. A photo of Rona believed to have been taken inside the Shafia apartment in Montreal, likely in early 2008. The photo is one in a set of about two dozen in which she posed in different outfits, wearing makeup—activities Shafia considered shameful.

9. A photo of Geeti from the Antoine-de-St-Exupéry high school yearbook, probably taken in September 2008.

10. Zainab and Ammar Wahid, in a self-portrait believed to have been taken in April 2009, when Zainab had left the family home to live in a women's shelter. They were married four weeks later in a religious ceremony, but the marriage lasted only one day.

11. Sahar and her boyfriend, Ricardo Sanchez, in a photo believed to have been taken in May 2009. Police recovered the image from Sahar's cellphone and also found a print in a suitcase during their search of the Shafia home. Investigators believe this photo and several dozen others were seen by Shafia in Dubai as evidence of his daughter's immodesty and misconduct. Shafia and Tooba both claimed he did not see the photos until after the deaths. He said the pictures enraged him and were among the reasons for the curses heard on wiretaps.

12. Sahar and Ricardo in a photo believed to have been taken on May 19, 2009, the day that the celebration was held for Zainab's wedding to Ammar Wahid. Sahar was not permitted to attend the celebration and instead skipped school to go to an amusement park.

48. Sahar - exif 22 May 09

13. Sahar, in a photo believed to have been taken by a schoolmate inside a classroom at St-Ex in May 2009. Contrary to her father's wishes, at school Sahar often wore makeup and what Shafia considered revealing clothes.

14. Zainab and Hussain Hyderi, Latif Hyderi's son, who planned to formalize their engagement after the Shafia family's trip to Niagara Falls in June 2009.

15. A self-portrait of Sahar and Zainab, believed to have been taken on June 25, 2009, in a hotel room in Niagara Falls.

16. A self-portrait of Sahar believed to have been taken on June 26, 2009, in a hotel room in Niagara Falls. This is one of several photos of Sahar that Shafia claimed he did not see until after his daughter's death, but which enraged him as evidence of her immodest behaviour.

17. Another example of the "bra and underwear" photos that infuriated Shafia, this photo features Zainab and is believed to have been taken on June 27, 2009.

18. Geeti, photographed on June 23, 2009, while the Shafia family was en route to Niagara Falls.

19. A snapshot of Rona and Sahar, believed to have been taken on June 26, 2009, while the family was in Niagara Falls. Sahar and Rona were particularly close because Tooba gave Sahar to Rona to raise as her own daughter.

Shafia was scheming to whisk the family away to an Islamic country, like Dubai or Afghanistan.

Hussain texted a stream of questions to Zainab, who didn't seem to share his concern.

"baby why r u so wrrd," she replied.

Hussain explained his fear and warned Zainab to be wary of a trip to an airport. She promised to stay in touch every day.

More than nine hours after the convoy had left Mont-Laurier, it stopped. Several among the group needed a washroom break and a chance to stretch their legs. They had found a secluded and peaceful spot just north of the highway. Most travellers on Highway 401 never saw the small signs that pointed the way to the tiny, scenic hamlet at the junction of the Cataraqui River and Colonel By Lake. Only boaters, fishers and history buffs were well acquainted with Kingston Mills.

The group spent forty minutes there. By 9:30 p.m., the two vehicles were leaving Kingston as they continued west along Highway 401. The convoy passed through the Toronto area around midnight and arrived in Niagara Falls around 2:00 a.m. on June 25. They booked into the Days Inn on Lundy's Lane, at the outer fringe of the tourist zone, where the room rates were cheaper. A major expressway and a large cemetery were near the hotel. It was a long walk, five kilometres or more, to the neon-lit museum and novelty strip or to the area overlooking the falls.

The travellers were divided into two groups. Zainab, Sahar, Geeti and Rona stayed together in one room and the other six family members were in another room.

ZAINAB CLOSED THE HEAVY HOTEL BATHROOM DOOR and locked it. There was no chance of being discovered. She stretched a white cotton towel across the tiled floor and stepped onto it. She yanked off her top, unbuttoned her jeans and slid them from her legs. She stared at herself, stripped to her bra and underwear, in the full-length mirror secured to the back of the door.

She draped her ponytail along her left shoulder and arm, admiring the reflected image of her supple, five-foot-five frame. Her skin was smooth and firm. Her 125 pounds gave her curves. She knew that her blossoming form was a lure.

Two months ago, when she had been strolling the mall with Ammar, a modelling scout had shoved a business card at her. He'd said she was beautiful and had a unique look. She could make it in the business, he had suggested. She had not been able to contain her smile.

Zubi had been right when she texted three weeks ago that obviously the Top Girls were "hot guls" and boys got "mad bout us." Zainab had laughed, but not dismissively.

She selected the black and white filter on the cellphone camera and held it up with her right hand. Her left hand clutched her left hip softly, fingers pointing inward. She flexed her right knee, raising the leg in front of her left slightly so that her body appeared to flow toward the floor as a slender, symmetrical column of curves and shadows.

The first frame captured all of her. She lowered herself. Kneeling, legs straight back, she snapped again. The perspective flatteringly captured her leanness. In this pose, her thighs did not touch, even though she had brought her legs tightly together.

She pivoted her body so that her left side faced the mirror. She raised her left knee off the towel until her thigh was parallel to the floor, at the same time swinging her calf back so that her leg, from hip to toe, formed the first two strokes of a Z. With her left hand positioned on her thigh, near her knee, the thin strap of her underwear was concealed from the camera. She looked naked, save for her bra.

Two days earlier, Sahar had taken similar pictures of herself in the same bathroom mirror.

The girls did not delete the photos from the cellphone.

ZAINAB STAYED IN REGULAR CONTACT WITH HUSSAIN. She had had an hour-long conversation with him on June 27, the day she locked herself in the bathroom with the camera. She told Hussain that she had not had any more angry encounters with her father, in part because he wasn't around. Zainab told Hussain that her father and Hamed had left in the Lexus early that morning. At 8:30 p.m., when Zainab and Hussain's conversation began, Shafia and Hamed still hadn't returned.

SAHAR RECEIVED ANOTHER SYRUPY TEXT MESSAGE from Ricardo, written in Spanish, on June 28, five days into the family vacation:

> if I had the moon, the sun, the sky or the sea, or the stars, at
> this moment,
> I would give you all of it—all of it to you, my love
> the only thing at this moment that I have is the love in my
> heart,
> and many kisses to give you, forever, my love

Zainab talked to Hussain twice on June 29, around noon and again just before six. In the second call, she said the entire family was planning to go somewhere around six, perhaps out for supper. The couple talked about their budding relationship and the possibility of a life together. Zainab did not mention anything about a plan to leave Niagara Falls that night.

By 6:45, however, the group had checked out of the hotel. Roughly an hour and a half later the two-vehicle convoy was on the highway heading back toward Toronto. The twelve-day vacation had been halved.

Rather than bypass Toronto on the 401, the caravan detoured into the city for a look at the skyscrapers and bright lights of Canada's biggest city. Sahar used her cellphone camera to snap photos of the domed stadium and the nearby CN Tower as the car whizzed past the landmarks just after 9:30.

An hour later, both Shafia vehicles stopped for a washroom and drink break in Ajax, a small community forty kilometres east of Toronto. The stop lasted about half an hour. Around the same time as the pit stop, Sahar texted Ricardo that her father had announced they would stop for the night at a hotel because everyone was tired. She told Ricardo they were a few hours away from Montreal. She also wrote that she thought the division of people between the two vehicles was strange, though she didn't explain why she felt this way. The four family members who had caused Shafia the most problems since the family moved to Canada two years earlier, Zainab, Sahar, Geeti and Rona, were crammed into the small Nissan with Tooba.

Once the cars were back on the road after the break in Ajax, Sahar's friend Samia called and the girls talked for a little over half an hour as the convoy continued east. When the call ended, so did the nearly constant stream of texts and calls between Sahar and her friends.

Sahar had texted with Samia and Ricardo hundreds of times during the five-day Niagara trip. But when the call with Samia ended at 11:31 p.m., Sahar stopped sending texts or answering calls on her cellphone. Samia called Sahar's cell five times in the following two hours, but Sahar did not answer.

At 1:36 a.m. on June 30, something happened to Sahar's cellphone.

A text message arrived at that time, routed through a cellphone tower located on Station Road, a short, two-lane stretch of asphalt just north of Highway 401 and one kilometre east of Kingston Mills. The text was the last transmission the phone received. After that time, the phone did not accept texts and voice calls were forwarded. There were only four possible explanations: the phone had been turned off, its battery had died, it had moved into an area where transmissions could not be received, or it had been damaged or disabled.

9

Splash-Crash

A DRY THROAT WOKE EIGHT-YEAR-OLD DYLAN a few hours after he dozed off. He clambered out of bed, careful not to rattle the bells attached to doors throughout the house. He wasn't sleepwalking this time. He walked to the kitchen and poured a glass of water, but he did not look out the window that afforded a view across the bay.

Dylan's home, on a small spit of land that protruded into swampy Colonel By Lake, had a good view of the upper lock at Kingston Mills, one of four that lifts boats fifteen metres up from the Cataraqui River, the southern access point to the Rideau Canal on Lake Ontario, to the level of Colonel By. The canal is a remarkable two-hundred-kilometre inland waterway connecting Kingston to Ottawa. Planned by British engineers, it was carved through mosquito-infested forests and glacial rock more than one hundred and seventy-five years ago.

Every summer day, Dylan could watch dozens of boats pass through the flight of locks, fancy twelve-metre cruisers that cost as much as a nice house, small aluminum fishing boats piled with gear, and shiny speedboats. Not now. The locks had closed for the day five hours earlier.

Dylan looked at the digital clock on the stove. It was 1:40 a.m. He took his glass of water to the front door and stepped out onto the porch. He left the door open. As he sipped, he heard a strange noise, a splash-crash, followed by a short beep, like a car horn cut short. The noises sounded as if they had come from the locks.

Dylan hurried back to the kitchen and ducked out through the patio doors onto the rear deck. He could see directly across the bay toward the upper lock, two hundred metres away. Because the lock property and the road that snakes around it were unlit and isolated, the panorama was black, save for two thin, horizontal shafts of light. After a moment of staring at the scene, Dylan realized he was looking at the outline of a car, without any lights on. The shafts of light, the headlights of another vehicle, illuminated it.

The vehicle without lights appeared to be on the grass on the east side of the upper, northernmost lock. The vehicle with its headlights on appeared to be on Kingston Mills Road, where the two-lane asphalt curved sharply near an old blockhouse, a squat, stone building that once quartered British soldiers charged with defending the locks.

There must have been an accident, but it couldn't be too serious, Dylan figured. He didn't hear anyone yelling for help and he didn't see any people moving about. He saw only the beams of light and the two vehicles.

Fatigue and boredom soon took hold. After a minute or two squinting into the darkness at the puzzling scene, Dylan returned to bed without telling anyone what he had seen and heard.

THE EARLY MORNING DISTURBANCE WASN'T UNUSUAL. Robert Miller was growing accustomed to being awakened at odd hours by weary travellers. Highway 401 was half a kilometre north of his establishment, the Kingston Motel East. Each day thousands of drivers took the Highway 15 exit that funnelled traffic south toward the city and past his motel, the second along the route. Inevitably some stopped, looking for a comfortable place to rest their heads. Miller took pride in the place, though he'd been on the job for just two weeks. The tidy, treed grounds included two single-storey buildings arranged in an L-shape, though not connected. There were twenty simple, clean rooms and a kiddie playground.

The buzzer in Miller's bedroom was sounding. Someone at the front door of the motel had pushed the button on the wall-mounted intercom.

Miller looked at his bedside alarm clock. It was 2:00 a.m. He answered the phone, which rang in unison with the buzzer, and a young man's voice said "we" need rooms. Miller told the caller he needed a few minutes to get dressed, then he'd be out.

The residence where he and his wife lived was attached to the rear of the living-room-sized motel office, which commanded a view of the driveway and grounds through big windows on three sides. Four bright fluorescent fixtures on the canopy ceiling bathed the main entrance in light.

The relationship between the lanky young man with dark, curly hair and the shorter, older man at the motel counter wasn't obvious to Miller. He couldn't place the unusual accent and didn't ask. They didn't seem threatening and said they'd pay cash for the rooms. Miller noticed a big, light-coloured SUV parked next to the pillar under the entrance canopy, facing toward the rear of the motel complex. Since the men said they wanted two rooms, he assumed there were other people in the SUV. He did not see anyone in the vehicle, nor did he see another vehicle.

"How many people?" Miller asked.

The two men looked at each other without answering.

"How many?" Miller repeated. "Our pricing is based on the number of people."

The younger man said there would be nine guests.

"Six," said the older man.

Some guests lied about the size of their group to drive the price down. If this was their scheme, they didn't seem to have rehearsed the appropriate answers, or they had forgotten their lines.

"Are there going to be six?" Miller asked.

The men finally agreed. They were a group of six.

"Are there going to be three for each room?" Miller inquired.

The men looked at each other and signalled their agreement without speaking. They just needed the rooms for one night, they told the proprietor. Miller handed them the keys to Rooms 18 and 19 as they were completing the registration forms. The older man left the office immediately with the keys.

As promised, the young man produced cash, $206.80 for the two rooms. He signed the registration form "Hamed Mohammad Shafia" and indicated he was from Saint-Léonard, Quebec. He pushed the paperwork back to Miller and left the office.

Miller looked to his left, through a side window in the office, and saw that the SUV was already parked in front of the rooms. A few minutes later, before Miller had finished filing the forms and closing the office, he noticed the SUV backing out of its parking spot. The vehicle began to drive out of the motel complex. That was unusual, Miller thought, so he stopped what he was doing and paid attention.

As the SUV passed the office, Miller thought he could see the younger man behind the wheel and the older man in the front passenger seat. He couldn't see anyone else. The motel manager was puzzled as he watched the vehicle turn left, heading north on Highway 15. It was well after two in the morning and there was nothing open in that direction. A right turn would take a traveller south into the city, where there were twenty-four-hour fast food joints, coffee shops and convenience stores. The route north from the motel led to the highway interchange and then, just a few hundred metres farther, to Station Road, a shortcut to the scenic Kingston Mills locks.

Miller decided not to head straight back to bed. He stayed up another half-hour, wondering where the SUV might have gone and watching for its return. There was no sign of it by the time he locked up and returned to bed around 2:30 a.m. He did not see the black Nissan Sentra that Shafia, Tooba and Hamed would later insist had arrived at the motel minutes after the Lexus.

HUSSAIN HYDERI WAS TICKED OFF AT FIRST when he didn't hear back from Zainab on the evening of June 29. She had promised to call or text him by midnight. His upset turned to worry when she didn't respond to text messages the following day, or on Wednesday. He spoke to Tooba's brother in Montreal, but Jawed Jawad also had no news of the family.

By Thursday, Hussain and his father, Latif, were alarmed.

Latif Hyderi visited Jawad at work and while he was there, Jawad received a phone call from Hamed. He had terrible news: there had been an accident and four members of the family were dead. Hyderi was horrified and disbelieving. He recalled the terrible things that Shafia had said about Zainab and the terrible thing he had said he wanted to do.

Hussain wasn't the only person who was concerned about Zainab's whereabouts and her welfare at the end of June.

Zainab had stayed in regular contact in the past month with Zubaida, her friend in Dubai. But as the month ended, the communication ceased. Zubaida called the Shafia home in early July, asking about Zainab. The family members who answered told her curtly that Zainab wasn't at home and then hung up without providing any explanation. Zubaida had Hussain's cellphone number, given to her weeks earlier by Zainab. Zubaida reached Hussain and he conveyed the horrible news that Zainab, Sahar, Geeti and Rona were dead.

"You won't believe it," Hussain told her. "It's a murder, a murder mystery."

PART FOUR

The Investigation

"Although it's a coroner's investigation, we're treating it as suspicious."
—Staff Sergeant Chris Scott, July 1, 2009

10

Deliberate Acts

A FEW HOURS AFTER THE NISSAN SENTRA, with Zainab, Sahar, Geeti and Rona inside, slipped beneath the surface and settled on the bottom of the canal at Kingston Mills, the Lexus SUV plowed into a pole in a parking lot in Montreal.

Two police officers, working in separate cities three hundred kilometres apart, were dispatched that morning to seemingly run-of-the-mill matters involving automobiles owned by Mohammad Shafia. Constable Brent White in Kingston and Constable Nathalie Ledoux in Montreal soon suspected something was amiss.

HAMED USED HIS CELLPHONE to dial 9-1-1 at 7:55 a.m. on June 30.

"Ah, hello, had an accident on St. Leonard," he said.

"*In* St. Leonard?" the operator asked.

"Yes."

Hamed was not calling about the Sentra.

"Okay, where, sir?"

"Ah, the street, Langelier," Hamed answered.

He explained that the accident had happened close to 8655 boulevard Langelier. This information placed him in Montreal, a few blocks from the empty Shafia home on rue Bonnivet. His mother, father and three siblings were in the Kingston Motel East, a three-and-a-half-hour drive west. Zainab, Sahar, Geeti and Rona were undiscovered at Kingston Mills.

Hamed had been with his family six hours earlier.

He told the 9-1-1 operator that he was not injured, it was just "car damage," a minor, single-vehicle collision "with a pole." The operator took Hamed's contact information and said that an officer would be dispatched. Hamed did not tell the operator that he was in a hurry, even though his father had called him about an emergency in Kingston an hour earlier.

Constable Ledoux arrived minutes later to find Hamed behind the wheel of a silver Lexus in the vacant parking lot of L'Intermarché grocery store on busy boulevard Langelier. She could see damage to the front left corner of the Lexus and what appeared to be corresponding marks on a steel guardrail that protected a garbage enclosure at the side of the store. The officer saw silver and yellow debris on the ground. The Lexus was stopped at an angle, with its nose close to the guardrail.

Ledoux asked how the collision happened. Hamed explained that he was backing up to park and turning at the same time when the front left corner struck the guardrail.

Ledoux wondered why Hamed had tried to park in this spot when the large lot, with spaces for more than fifty cars, was virtually empty. It would have been much simpler to put the big SUV in another nearby space. She figured he worked at the grocery store and this was where employees were instructed to park. To her surprise, he said he didn't work there. Ledoux didn't ask for any further explanation. It was a minor incident; her report was necessary only for insurance purposes. She looked at Hamed's licence, insurance and registration documents and completed the paperwork. Hamed was sitting calmly behind the wheel of the Lexus when she finished her report and handed back his documents.

"Can I get my vehicle repaired immediately?" Hamed asked her.

TWO HOURS AFTER HAMED'S CALL TO POLICE in Montreal, Kingston constable Brent White received a computer dispatch in his patrol car instructing him to check out a report of a car in the water at Kingston Mills. It was a low-priority message. The ten-year veteran officer had been to many such calls. They were almost always the work of pranksters who would steal a vehicle, joyride it around town and then dump it into one of the many lakes and rivers in the Kingston area. Annoying and time-consuming, these calls rarely led to arrests or anything more than insurance claims. White sent a computer reply explaining that he would respond as soon as he was done with a downtown traffic stop.

It took White ten minutes to drive from downtown to Kingston Mills. Although locals considered Highway 401 the informal boundary between the city's urban core and its rural north, the Mills was within the city limits and under the jurisdiction of the municipal police force.

When White drove over the northernmost of the four locks on the Kingston Mills Road swing bridge, just before 10:30, he was immediately flagged down by lock worker John Bruce, who motioned for White to pull his cruiser through an open gate and onto a grassy triangle. Bruce had opened the gate to allow White's cruiser onto the Parks Canada property. White drove down the gently sloping lawn beside the stone ledge along the east wall of the lock and parked.

After White climbed out of his car, Bruce explained that he had dis-covered what appeared to be a submerged car just beyond the gates of the northernmost lock. He had first spotted oil on the water as boats began moving through the locks that morning. He then realized a car was block-ing the swinging gates of the upper lock, preventing staff from moving boats through. White peered down from the stone ledge where he stood, about two metres above the water. It was a warm, grey morning with a light drizzle falling, but the constable could discern the outline of a car just beneath the surface. He could not see inside the car. Near his feet, White spotted what seemed to be fresh gouge marks in the lip of the ledge. They were white and chalky. *Kids*, White thought immediately.

He was struck by the timing. Tomorrow was Canada Day, always a busy day at the lockstation as vacationing boaters plied the Rideau Canal. The pranksters probably considered themselves hotshots who had succeeded in shutting down a vital lockstation at an important time.

"I was here until about eight last night, and there was nothing in the water when I left," Bruce told the officer. The swing-arm gate that controlled access to the east side of the property, where White had entered, was locked overnight, Bruce said. He explained that it was always kept locked.

White noticed two small plastic silver letters, an *S* and an *E*, sitting on a wood beam at the side of the canal. He did not learn until later that parks staff had found them on the ground near the edge.

White thought this seemed a strange spot for joyriders to dump a car. There was a large pond adjacent to the road and accessible in a straight line once a vehicle hopped the low curb. To get to *this* spot, the driver had threaded the needle, squeezing the vehicle between an ancient steel apparatus used to open the underwater lock valves and the wooden steps that protruded from the end of the swinging lock gate mechanism. The car had been steered along the narrow, elevated stone ledge on the east side of the canal, next to the northernmost of the four locks.

It couldn't be an accident, White was thinking. This seemed *deliberate*. Whoever put this car here wanted it to be found. They must have known that it would be discovered this morning as soon as the locks began operating. But how did the car get to the ledge?

White wasn't sure if this was a crime scene, but he followed standard procedure, calling for an underwater search and recovery unit. He radioed to the dispatcher to request one from the Ontario Provincial Police. Kingston Police did not have a dive unit.

A diver happened to be at Kingston Mills, with his gear, and willing to go into the water. Canadian navy diver John Moore was trying to get home to Manotick, a small community near Ottawa, after a four-day boating and camping trip in the Kingston area. Moore and two companions were partway through the four locks in their small aluminum boat when they were told they could not continue on. He figured that, at the least, he could get the plate number for police so they could trace the car.

White began to walk around the large expanse of grass east of the canal, looking for clues to the car's path to the water. He walked past a large rock outcropping toward Kingston Mills Road, which curved around the east side of the property. Near the road, in the grass, he found two triangular pieces of clear plastic, each about three inches long. He picked them up and turned them over in his hands, but didn't see any connection. He put them back down in the grass where he'd found them and continued walking. At the road, he saw what appeared to be black tire marks across the concrete curb and faint tire tracks on the sandy ground next to the curb. He wondered if this was the spot, about thirty metres east of the canal, where the car had left the road and driven onto the grass toward the water.

White circled back to the stone ledge to find that John Moore had donned his scuba gear and gone into the water. Moore surfaced after a few minutes underwater, pushed back his mask and told White what he had seen.

"There's at least two females in there, maybe more," the diver said.

White told Moore not to touch anything and to get out of the water immediately. The officer's mind was swirling. He needed help and he knew he needed to protect the scene and control access to the area. He radioed to dispatch that the major crime unit, identification officers and senior staff were required. Within minutes, a patrol sergeant was racing to the Mills, and detectives were notified that a seemingly routine stolen-car prank was a major incident. Half a dozen police vehicles converged on Kingston Mills, and senior officers ordered the road blocked and all boats in the area inspected.

Moore also gave White the plate information, a Quebec licence reading 699 ZCD. A computer check showed that the vehicle was registered to a man in Montreal named Mohammad Shafia.

AS OFFICERS STRUNG HUNDREDS of metres of yellow tape at Kingston Mills, staff at the Kingston Motel East, two kilometres south of the scene, noticed something odd. The older man in Room 19 kept drawing the curtain back just enough to peer out into the parking lot. He seemed to be watching for something, but didn't want to be observed himself. Every time Christine Bolarinho got close to the window, the man yanked the curtain shut. The motel housekeeper wondered if it was just her imagination, so she walked past the room several times. On each pass, the window peeper appeared and then quickly concealed himself. Bolarinho also crossed paths with a middle-aged woman who had come out of the room.

"Good morning, do you need towels, or your garbage taken out?" Bolarinho asked.

"No, my son sleeping," the woman said, in less than perfect English. "Maybe after he wake up, will need towels."

The woman was pleasant but not talkative.

When Robert Miller returned from some morning errands, Bolarinho told him about her encounters with the people in Room 19. She explained that they'd given no indication they were checking out. Miller went to the room shortly after eleven.

Shafia, to whom Miller had sold a phone card early that morning in the motel office, answered his knock. While the door to the room was open, Miller could see a middle-aged woman lying sideways across the bed closest to the door. Shafia stepped out of the room and closed the door behind him.

"I just wanted to remind you that checkout time is eleven, so if you're not checking out, you'll have to pay for another day," Miller told him.

Shafia glanced at his watch.

"Son coming to pick up in half-hour," he told Miller. "Can wait?"

Miller said he could give them leeway, and he returned to his daily chores around the complex.

About half an hour later, near noon, Miller noticed an unfamiliar greenish-blue minivan parked outside Rooms 18 and 19. There was no sign of the SUV he had seen when the two men checked in. Half an hour after that, Miller was in the office when Shafia and Hamed appeared and asked to book the two rooms for a second night.

Shafia asked for a deal, but Miller said they'd have to pay the full rate again.

The men signed the paperwork. They did not ask for directions or for any help. Miller didn't notice anything unusual in their behaviour. He did not see them pull away in the van shortly after noon.

HAMED STEERED INTO THE VISITOR PARKING AREA at the front of the Kingston Police station with his parents in the family's Pontiac minivan just after 12:30, around the same time that Detective Constable Geoff Dempster was parking in the rear employee lot. Dempster wasn't supposed to start until 2:00, but he had been called in early to help with the unfolding events at Kingston Mills.

Dempster had dreamed of being a policeman since he was a young boy growing up in Napanee, a town of five thousand people just west of Kingston that was known as the home of a big Goodyear tire plant and Quinte, an infamously overcrowded provincial detention centre. Everyone arrested in Kingston and awaiting a court date was locked up at Quinte.

Unlike many officers, Dempster didn't have any family working in corrections or policing as role models. He had begun reading crime books as a youth, excited by the intrigue and action that swirled around the imaginary lawmen in the stories. At the age of twenty-four, he joined the country's biggest municipal police force as a rookie constable, but he left Toronto just three years later when he had the chance to move closer to home. He spent his first five years on the Kingston force as a uniformed constable. He quickly established himself as an officer who was articulate and confident in interviews with witnesses and criminals. His boyish good looks, brown eyes and sandy blond hair were disarming. He was promoted to the position of detective constable in the department's sexual assault unit, a squad where interviewing skills were critical to success. The unit solved 90 percent of its cases by gently coaxing detailed statements from victims— women who had been assaulted and children who had been molested—

and through clever interrogation of perpetrators. Dempster proved himself a skilful interviewer and, in 2008, he was transferred to the major crime unit, the elite squad of officers who investigate robberies and murders.

The team of four officers, led by a sergeant, was Kingston's equivalent of a big-city homicide squad. The medium-sized city recorded just two or three murders annually, so there was no need to maintain a full-time team of dedicated homicide investigators. If the major crime unit was overtaxed, other experienced officers working in the fraud, sexual assault and general investigative teams could be shifted. Dempster had worked on three homicides while he was in the sexual assault unit.

HAMED, SHAFIA AND TOOBA APPROACHED BARBARA WEBB, a short woman with a broad smile who sat inside the fishbowl-like bulletproof glass enclosure in the lobby of the police station. Hamed spoke into the metal grille and told Webb, a civilian employee, that he and his parents, who were standing behind him, wanted to file a report because his two sisters and the family's Nissan Sentra were missing.

Years of experience on the front desk had taught Webb to ensure that her face did not betray her feelings. She knew that a Nissan Sentra with Quebec plates had been found underwater at Kingston Mills with bodies inside. Her blinking computer screen indicated that half a dozen officers and vehicles, including senior staff, were already at the Mills, with more on their way. Webb asked the Shafias to take a seat for a moment.

She went to see Rick Hough, the sergeant in charge of the patrol shift, who was working in a nearby office. She told Hough that there were three people at the front desk who appeared to have information related to the discovery at Kingston Mills. Hough asked her to go back and collect more information but be careful not to reveal that police had already found a vehicle and bodies. Webb returned to the front desk and asked the threesome to come forward. Hamed spoke up. His father stood beside him, while Tooba remained an arm's length behind them. Hamed revised his first account.

"My *three* sisters and a woman are missing," he told Webb. Shafia began to speak softly to Hamed, so that Webb could not hear the conversation. Hamed turned back to Webb and explained that the "woman" was his father's cousin. "She's about fifty years old."

Hamed could provide only the first three digits of the licence plate. He said the car was black. The family was staying at a motel on Highway 15 and had woken up that morning to discover that the four people and the car were gone. Webb again asked the trio to take a seat while she passed the information to officers.

Dempster, who had initially been told to go to Kingston Mills to help take statements, was now assigned to interview the people at the front desk. The orders had been relayed from Staff Sergeant Chris Scott, the senior officer in command of twenty-five investigators and four sergeants in the criminal investigation division. Scott was at Kingston Mills. He had gone to the scene, in part, because the sergeant in charge of the major crime unit, who would typically have taken a lead role in the incident, was hundreds of kilometres away, attending a training course at the Ontario Police College. Scott was confident: in Dempster, he had an adept interviewer for the three people who should be able to help police unravel the mystery.

AFTER WEBB RELATED TO DEMPSTER WHAT SHE'D BEEN TOLD in the two conversations, he met the trio in the lobby and asked them to follow him. He took them through the security doors, past a fountain that trickled down a wall of dark stone, and around a corner to a three-by-four-metre room appointed with a modern brown leather couch, matching armchair and coffee table. The victim–witness lounge was a comfortable, living-room-like space where investigators met with people who were not suspected criminals.

Dempster asked Hamed to repeat the information he had given Webb. Hamed explained that his family was from Afghanistan. His father did not understand or speak English, he told the officer. His mother could understand English but could not speak it. Their first language was Farsi, a variant of Persian, he said, inaccurately. During the small talk, Dempster was steeling himself for his solemn duty. He had made death notifications to families many times before, but never in a situation like this, never for four victims.

Dempster told Hamed, and asked him to translate to his parents, that police had found a car underwater nearby and that there were bodies inside, probably the bodies of their family members. Dempster said the police could not confirm the identity of the people in the car until a dive team arrived, but they were almost certain that the victims were members of the Shafia family.

Shafia and Tooba began to cry. Hamed appeared choked with emotion. Dempster thought it seemed a cruel double blow to ask an eighteen-year-old to serve as translator and communicator of this grim news, while coping himself with the revelation that three of his sisters were dead. The officer resolved to get an interpreter. He realized that they could not rely on translations provided by Hamed because it was vital that he interview the family members individually as soon as possible. He left them to grieve.

The private firm that provided professional language services to the police department was contacted and, based on Hamed's statement about their language, plans were made to send a Farsi interpreter to the police station as quickly as possible. Farsi and Dari are regional dialects of Persian, so their speakers can communicate easily, but there are subtle differences, akin to the differences between Canadian and British English. Dari, which is spoken in Afghanistan, is less common in Canada than Farsi, which is spoken in Iran.

Some information was trickling back to the station from the investigators at Kingston Mills. Dempster learned that officers had not found any signs of violence at the scene. No bullet shells, no blood and no weapons had been found. There was nothing to suggest a crime had been committed. For now, the case was being treated as a sudden death investigation in which the regional coroner and police would work together to determine how the victims had died. Dempster would treat the Shafias gently.

DETECTIVE BRIAN PETE REMAINED WITH HAMED AND TOOBA while Dempster took Shafia and the newly arrived interpreter to a small interview room on the second floor of the building where his conversation with police could be recorded. The spartan, bathroom-sized interview room was nothing like the comfy victim–witness lounge. It was outfitted only with a small rectangular table and three chairs. Shafia sat in a stiff wooden chair at the end of the table and glanced up at a small video camera mounted near the ceiling. A microphone was concealed in the soundproofing that covered the wall.

IN THE VICTIM–WITNESS LOUNGE, Pete asked Hamed for the name of the motel where the family had stayed overnight in Kingston. It was critical that officers get there as soon as possible, to the spot where the four missing people reportedly were last seen. Hamed said he didn't know the name of the motel, but there was a receipt in their vehicle. Pete followed Hamed out of the building to the visitor parking lot, where he retrieved a slip of paper from a green Pontiac minivan and handed it to Pete. The receipt from the Kingston Motel East showed a booking for two rooms on June 30. Officers were dispatched to the motel to take control of the rooms.

DEMPSTER'S INTERVIEW OF SHAFIA began at 3:45 p.m., a little more than two hours after the officer had informed him that police believed his missing family members were dead inside a submerged car. Shafia seemed calm. He was not crying, distracted or struggling to compose himself. This interview was the first opportunity for police to get meaningful information that would help them understand how the Nissan had ended up in the canal and how the victims had died.

"So what I am going to ask you to do is to tell me as much as you can . . .

about this," Dempster said. "You can start anywhere you want. Start at the beginning and if you can, give me *as much detail* as possible."

Shafia explained that the family had gone to Niagara Falls on vacation, because they had enjoyed a visit to the falls the previous year. He said that his daughter Zainab wanted to get engaged and she was anxious to get home to Montreal. Shafia said that he had returned to Canada from a business trip on June 13.

"My main base is in Dubai," Shafia said, drawing the officer's attention to his globe-trotting business life. Shafia explained that he was selling off investments and moving assets to Canada. "In Laval I have bought a shopping centre, in Laval, for two million dollars. I have paid for it."

This was a detail, but not one that would help Dempster determine how the Nissan got into the water. Dempster steered the conversation back to the Niagara Falls trip.

Shafia said that after five nights in Niagara Falls, they had set out for home, but "the distance was far" so they could not drive it all in one night.

Dempster asked about the daughter who wanted to get married.

"She wanted to get engaged," Shafia said. "It wasn't for sure yet. She liked a boy and wanted to get engaged to him."

On this topic, he offered detail: "And that too was a tribal relationship. And it wasn't confirmed for sure. We were talking between ourselves. It wasn't a hundred percent. We were happy. The boy was a nice boy. We were happy but he was of her liking. If he wasn't, then nothing."

The interview progressed haltingly. Dempster had to wait for his questions to be translated into Farsi by the interpreter, and he often had to wait again as the interpreter went back and forth with Shafia to ensure she understood his awkward answers before she translated them back to Dempster.

"It's a rule between Muslims that they first come, and if the girl is accepting, then they will ask and give," Shafia said, explaining Zainab's marriage plans. "They had not yet come. There were no such things going on. We were talking between ourselves."

Shafia did not say that the suitor was Hussain Hyderi.

Dempster continued to ask about the trip.

Shafia explained that ten people had travelled in two vehicles. He described them as a Toyota Land Cruiser and a Nissan, though he later corrected himself and told Dempster that the Toyota was a Lexus. Shafia said they owned another vehicle, a Pontiac. He omitted a detail: he did not tell Dempster that the Nissan had been purchased the day before the trip to Niagara Falls.

Shafia said that only he, Tooba and Hamed had driver's licences, but several of his children "would turn on the car and take it away" if he wasn't around. He pointed the finger at his younger son and his oldest daughter. "The car keys would be at home and they would sneak it out," Shafia said.

When the discussion returned to the events of June 29, Shafia explained that they had toured through downtown Toronto on the way home from Niagara Falls, but they had not stopped there. They had made a washroom and drink pit stop at a spot about an hour west of Kingston. Shafia said he bought water and juice for everyone. When they arrived in Kingston, they stopped to book a motel, but the first establishment was full so they moved on to a second. Shafia said his wife told him she was "dizzy" and could not drive any longer, so they needed to stop.

Once again, Shafia offered detail, but it was not something that would help police: "We got here and this motel was *expensive* too," he said.

A moment later, he expanded on the story of Tooba's fatigue. "The second one. She said, 'It's okay, I am tired.' She said, 'Even though we have taken this hotel for a very *expensive* price, like one hundred two, one hundred three dollars.'"

Dempster and his interpreter did not say anything.

"The motel is very *expensive* because we got tired and could no longer drive," Shafia said.

When the interpreter said the family took rooms at the second motel for $102, Shafia interjected, "Three dollars," in English, concerned that Dempster knew precisely how much they had paid.

Shafia said that when the family arrived at the motel, Tooba was driving with Zainab, Sahar, Geeti and Rona in the Nissan. The four passengers went to Room 18, and the other six family members went to Room 19. Shafia did not explain why the family didn't split into groups of five. Shafia said that soon after they arrived at the motel, Hamed announced that he was going to drive to Montreal by himself, while the rest of the family remained in Kingston.

"Hamed?" Dempster asked, with puzzlement.

"Yeah, said, 'I'm going to Montreal,'" Shafia answered.

"*Last* night?"

"Yeah."

Shafia had delivered the first in a string of incongruities that set Dempster's antennae vibrating. The family had made a tiring six-hour drive from Niagara Falls to Kingston, and yet Hamed had been eager to drive for another three to four hours, at 2:00 a.m., to get to Montreal. Dempster asked Shafia about this point several times, to be sure he understood it.

"He was going alone because he had work and we didn't want to go," Shafia said. "We wanted to stay for two or three nights, right."

Dempster did not press Shafia about this peculiar new detail. Nine family members were prepared to spend several days in Kingston with one compact car, the Nissan, that could barely accommodate five people, while Hamed took the big SUV, with seats for eight, back to Quebec.

The officer wanted to know what happened after Hamed left for Montreal.

"Then, I woke up in the morning, uh, I did what, I saw that the car is not there," Shafia said. "Uh, because I don't know the language, I went to make a call via the phone and was told that the phone could not make a call to Montreal. So I bought a card."

Shafia said he bought a phone card at the motel office and called Sahar's cellphone. He got no answer.

"Then I called Hamed at around 7:30 a.m. and I told Hamed, 'It's not here and the car is not here, do something and return back here. I don't know what happened. We should go to the police and make a report to find out where they are.'"

The list of implausibilities grew longer.

Shafia was so concerned about his missing family members that he wanted to alert police, yet he did not suggest that Hamed, who spoke fluent English, simply call police in Kingston. Instead he told his son to make the three-to-four-hour drive back to Kingston so they could go to the police station. Dempster didn't yet know that Hamed was intimately familiar with the 9-1-1 telephone system. The young man had placed a call that morning and he had called twice ten weeks earlier, on the day that Zainab ran away from home.

Shafia obliged Dempster's request for details, sprinkling tidbits as the officer asked him to go back over the events. Shafia added that when he awoke that morning, he first washed his face and then went outside. When he saw the Nissan was missing, he checked the door of Room 18, where Zainab, Sahar, Geeti and Rona were supposed to be sleeping. Shafia said he pushed the door and it swung open because it was not latched. The television was on and he saw a bag of clothes and a Thermos. No one was inside.

Shafia said he was worried. His worry stemmed from other events that morning, events that he had omitted in his earlier account. Now, he recalled them. He said that when the family had first arrived at the motel, his wife gave the keys to the Nissan to Zainab and Sahar because the girls said they needed to retrieve clothes from the vehicle. They did not return the keys, Shafia told Dempster.

A few moments later, Dempster told Shafia he needed to step out of the room for a few minutes. Dempster went straight to the monitor room, where Detective Brian Pete was observing a video feed of the interview.

"Did he just tell you that Hamed drove back to Montreal *in the Lexus*?" Pete asked Dempster. "Because I just went out to the parking lot with Hamed and they're driving a Pontiac minivan."

Dempster was startled by the revelation but uncertain of its significance. He was not privy to the discoveries unfolding at Kingston Mills, where officers were documenting and collecting broken shards of plastic that appeared to be from a vehicle. But Dempster knew the Lexus was now significant. When he returned to the interview room, he did not tell Shafia about his conversation with Pete.

As soon as the officer sat down, Shafia clarified that the SUV was a Lexus, not a Land Cruiser. Dempster saw an opening. His manner was still soft. His voice was gentle.

"Is that what Hamed took back to Montreal?" he asked.

"Yeah," Shafia answered.

Dempster asked him if his Pontiac was a car.

Shafia said it was big, like the Lexus.

Dempster did not jump directly to the important question he planned to pose. Instead, he asked Shafia to repeat his account of the trip from Niagara Falls to Kingston, including the detour through Toronto, the washroom and drink break, the arrival at the motel and several driver changes along the way. The two men spent the next half-hour going over these events, and then Dempster finally asked the question he had been saving.

"What car did Hamed drive back from Montreal today?" the officer asked.

Shafia explained, matter-of-factly, that Hamed had returned to Kingston in the Pontiac minivan.

"Why not the Toyota Lexus?" Dempster asked.

"I don't know," Shafia said.

"Did he say why?"

"No."

Dempster thought it implausible that Shafia's eighteen-year-old son had left the family's luxurious SUV in Montreal and swapped it for a bland minivan without explanation or questioning from his father. Shafia's answer suggested this was precisely what had happened.

11

Picking Up the Pieces

WHILE DEMPSTER PLODDED THROUGH INTERVIEWS at the station, officers swarmed Kingston Mills.

Staff Sergeant Chris Scott and Detective Steve Koopman arrived at eleven thirty, an hour after White. A uniformed sergeant, Darren Keuhl, had joined White at eleven, to help secure the scene. Scott performed the same ritual as the officers who preceded him. He did a mental inventory of the scene. There were only two significant buildings: a blockhouse that overlooked the upper lock, and a visitor centre with public washrooms that was located across the road about 150 metres southwest of where he stood. The locks were part of a canal that cut through the centre of the property, and a turning basin jutted out from the canal at the second lock. There was a separate pond on the property's northeast side. Scott walked out onto the stonework at the edge of the canal and peered down at the water.

How could this car get here? Scott wondered. He looked to his left, toward the swing-arm steel gate about nine metres south of where he was standing. If the gate were open, a car could turn from Kingston Mills Road onto the grass and travel directly to the ledge in a straight line. But canal workers said the gate was always kept locked, and they were certain it had been locked when they left the previous night. There was no indication that the lock or the gate had been tampered with overnight.

Scott had investigated hundreds of collisions during the ten years he had worked as a uniformed constable. In many single-vehicle collisions, the car's path and the reason for the crash were soon obvious. Nothing was obvious here.

The officer scanned the rest of the property. The only other route to this ledge was circuitous and littered with obstacles, including a large rock outcropping, a tree and a picnic table. Once the driver dodged those hazards, in the dark, she would have had to steer the car up a grass incline, make a hairpin right turn onto the eight-metre-wide stone ledge, and then travel several car lengths before turning sharply left through a gap between obstacles on the ledge to fall into the water. The gap was less than a metre wider than the car. None of the obstacles that the car would have passed along this route showed obvious damage, suggesting that the vehicle wasn't barrelling out of control at high speed toward the water. Like White, Scott noted the large pond close to Kingston Mills Road and just northeast of the canal. Someone who intended to drive the car into water would have a much simpler path to get to that pond.

It just doesn't make any sense, thought Scott.

A small, lean man with a shaved head and a frequent grin, the twenty-year veteran was analytical, intense and virtually ego-less. A local boy who grew up in the small nearby city of Brockville, he was respected by his colleagues as a leader who had earned his stripes coming up through the ranks. In Toronto, Scott had worked in 14 Division, the busiest police precinct in the country, home to the ethnically diverse Chinatown and Little Italy districts, at a time when ruthless Vietnamese gangs peddled drugs and routinely assassinated rivals.

Scott was a keen observer and a fast learner during his decade in the trenches. His leadership skills were quickly recognized when he came to Kingston in 1998. One year later, Scott was promoted to sergeant and, two years later, to staff sergeant. He was placed in charge of thirty officers in the department's drug unit, intelligence team and penitentiary squad. Under his guidance, the drug squad became an independent unit that no longer required the assistance of other departments. Scott also oversaw the formation of Kingston's first street crime unit, and he secured training that gave the department full-time surveillance capabilities. He prided himself on getting more from others than most people thought possible and he pushed himself, expanding his skills whenever possible. Two years earlier, he had been the first Kingston officer invited to attend the prestigious fifteen-week FBI training program in Quantico, Virginia, for law enforcement leaders from around the world.

Scott had been at the helm of the criminal investigation division for just six months when the Nissan was discovered, but everything he'd done since he first began carrying a badge seemed to have prepared him for this. Skilled at marshalling talent around him, he was the perfect Kingston cop to lead the investigation.

Within an hour of his arrival at the locks, Scott was told about the report filed by the Shafias at the station. The civilian diver had reported seeing at least two bodies inside the submerged car, but it now seemed possible there could be four bodies underwater, or two dead and two missing. The scale of the investigation was expanding rapidly, and key decisions needed to be made quickly.

Scott assumed command, in the absence of the major crime unit sergeant. He radioed the station and asked an officer to contact the Ontario Provincial Police again to explain that the dive team was urgently needed. Scott assigned Koopman to interview John Moore, the civilian diver, and to canvass the small residential neighbourhood nearby, half a dozen homes on a spit of land just west of the locks. Scott asked Sergeant Carolyn Rice, who headed the sexual assault unit and who had remained at the station, to mobilize more officers.

Koopman soon brought Scott a valuable new piece of information. During his door-knocking trip along Daylan Avenue, the short street west of the canal, he had found an eyewitness. Dylan told Koopman what he had seen and heard early that morning. The young boy's account seemed to coincide with evidence police had found, the broken pieces of plastic and the scuff marks on the curb near the blockhouse, the small building at the eastern edge of the property. Dylan had seen the headlights of a vehicle near the blockhouse.

Constable Julia Moore arrived at Kingston Mills around noon, half an hour after Scott, in a panel van packed with gear. To her colleagues she was known as "ident," a forensic identification officer specially trained to photograph, collect and examine evidence such as fingerprints, footwear impressions and DNA. Moore was as close as it came in a small-town Ontario police force to a cop on the television show *CSI*. White explained to Moore that he had seen gouge marks on the stone ledge near the sunken car, found shards of plastic in the grass a substantial distance east of the water, and seen tire marks on the curb that separated the grassed area from Kingston Mills Road. White accompanied Moore, who was toting a large camera, as she began to walk the property. He guided her to the spot about thirty metres east of the canal where he had left the two pieces of clear plastic lying in the grass. Moore placed a small yellow sandwich-board-style plastic marker numbered "1" between the two shards. She carefully positioned a fifteen-centimetre ruler near one of the pieces and snapped several photos so that the evidence marker and ruler were visible in the frame. She took close-ups, repositioning the ruler next to the second piece of plastic. Each piece was roughly eight centimetres at its longest edge. Moore walked twenty paces north of the marker and snapped more photos that showed the perspective looking south, with the canal distant on the right side of the frame.

Once Moore was confident she had documented the pieces from several perspectives, she put them into a paper bag that she sealed and numbered. The officer didn't know that she was gathering the pieces of a jigsaw puzzle. There were fifteen more pieces to collect and assemble before a telling picture would come into focus.

MOORE HAD FINISHED PHOTOGRAPHING and collecting evidence when the Ontario Provincial Police underwater search and recovery unit arrived at Kingston Mills, shortly after four.

Constable Glenn Newell planned two dives to the submerged car. During the first, he would carry a video camera to document the scene. He would remove the bodies during the second dive. Newell went into the water for the first time shortly after five. He did not have far to swim.

As he stood on the bottom, only a metre of water separated the top of his head from the surface. Rays of sunlight cut through the turbidity, past the floating bits of dirt, rotting leaves and weeds, and struck the smooth metal and glass of the submerged vehicle beside him, a machine in an alien landscape. The beams of light danced on the shiny surfaces.

Newell considered the visibility good because he could see more than a metre ahead. It was not cold or dark or dangerous in the shallow canal, the way it had been for most of the hundreds of dives he had completed in twenty-four years of searching for bodies in lakes and rivers across Ontario. In many cases, he groped through weeds or along a silty bottom beyond the light's reach. Often, he could not see anything; he would inch through black water until he could feel a submerged apparatus or until he pressed up against the unmistakable softness of a body. He had brought more than 250 people back to the surface, but never so many at one time.

Never *four* bodies.

Here, Newell did not have to search or grope or anticipate in darkness an awful discovery. He could see it plainly, though he could not understand it. It was very strange, he thought. The bodies, suspended like specimens inside the car, seemed to be piled on top of each other.

The car was almost in Colonel By Lake. At Kingston Mills, the lake was connected to the Cataraqui River by four large stone lock chambers, each as wide as a tractor trailer and as long as three rigs. Boats entered the locks through thirty-centimetre-thick oak gates that swung open like saloon doors. The car had come to rest on the bottom just outside the northern-most lock, with its right rear bumper nudged up against the lock gates. The vehicle's nose was close to the stone wall of the canal. It appeared to have plunged backwards off the wall, which was two metres above the water's surface.

Dressed in his neoprene suit, fins, gloves and a full face mask equipped with headphones and a microphone, Newell was tethered to the surface by a cable as thick as his thumb. The camera he carried had no viewfinder. The surface crew told him where to point the lens as a recorder captured the footage. His camera lingered first over the car's front end, peering down at the silver badge: "Nissan." On the edge of the hood above the badge, there was a softball-sized dent and a scrape. Newell moved around the driver's side and discovered a large scrape as long as his forearm on the top of the left front fender. He documented more gashes along the rocker panel beneath the driver's door. When he peered beneath the car, he could see why the vehicle was tilted, nose down. The rear wheels were suspended off the bottom because the right corner of the rear bumper was snagged on a protrusion on the wooden lock gate. The front wheels were turned to the left.

When Newell moved to the rear of the car, he saw that the driver's-side tail light was smashed and missing pieces of its red and clear plastic housing. The bumper and fender beneath it were significantly dented and scraped. The silver S and E from the "Sentra" nameplate were missing. Newell moved around to the passenger side. The tires were fully inflated and this side of the car was mostly devoid of gashes and dents. He made his way to the front and swam up and over the hood until the camera could peer down through the windshield into the passenger compartment. The glass was undamaged.

Newell had been underwater for ten minutes at this point. For the first time, the half-dozen police officers huddling around the video monitor on the surface saw what the car contained. Through the front windshield, beyond the steering wheel, slender legs in tight-fitting pants came into view. The feet, missing socks or shoes, were starkly white in the drab underwater environment, where everything seemed drained of colour.

When Newell moved around to the driver's side, he could see a thick mat of dark hair next to the pillar between the front and rear side windows. The manual crank driver's window was completely rolled down, so he had an unobstructed view of the head of a young woman. It was tilted to the left. Knots of hair wafted lazily around her, obscuring her face. Her body was strangely positioned. She seemed to be hugging the driver's seat from behind so that her torso was in the rear passenger compartment, but her legs extended between the front bucket seats into the centre console. Her right hand was wrapped around the driver's headrest while her left arm dangled toward the rear footwell. Geeti was not trapped or entangled in any part of the car.

Newell could see that the slender legs and shoeless feet he had seen through the windshield belonged to another young woman who was facing the rear of the car. She was floating with her arched back up against the roof so that her head, arms and upper body were draped over the front passenger seat, dangling into the back seat. Long dark hair swirled around her face. Her toes rested on the front edge of the driver's seat. It was as if Zainab had been slung over the seat, face down.

No one was sitting in the front driver or passenger seats. Newell was surprised. In 90 percent of the underwater recoveries he performed on vehicles, he found a body in or near the driver's seat. Often, panicked drivers became entangled in the steering wheel or seat belt of a sinking car and were found dead in or near the spot they'd been when they were piloting the vehicle. Newell could not tell who, if anyone, had been driving this car when it went into the water.

The officer reached into the car with the video camera, through the open driver's window, to document the controls. The shift lever on the floor-mounted console was in first gear and the keys were in the ignition. The two front seat belts were unfastened. A cellphone lay on the driver's seat.

Newell moved on to the rear of the car, where the driver's-side rear window was rolled down an inch. A screen of objects—a large black and white purse, a blanket and a plastic bag—were pressed up against the glass, mostly obscuring the view into the back seat. In the lower right corner of the window, a smooth, bare back was visible near the glass. The person was wearing black pants and a black crop top. Pink underwear peeked from the waistband. Sahar's upper torso and head were turned toward the centre of the car and were concealed by the blanket. To the left of her torso, a clenched hand with manicured nails protruded through the debris, beneath the plastic bag. Rona's hand rested on the front edge of the rear seat.

Newell swam up and hovered over the rear window. A blue teddy bear, wedged under the glass, grinned up at him. Near the bear, a pair of heads were butted together, face down. Only a tangle of hair was visible. He swam over the vehicle to the passenger side and found a splash of colour, a fuchsia top with thick straps, clinging to the torso of the barefoot girl he had first seen through the windshield. A mound of hair that had fallen around her head as she drooped over the passenger seat back concealed Zainab's face.

Newell had now seen all of it, every corner of the gouged and scraped vehicle that contained four contorted bodies and a few bits of debris. He was more perplexed. The water was shallow, the damage to the car was superficial and there were no signs that any of the victims had become ensnared, if they had struggled to escape the sinking car. The open driver's window was large enough that a person could easily pass through. Newell could have swum through the opening, even with the air tank on his back, though the procedures he followed forbade it. He saw no evidence that anyone had tried to get out through the window, although he believed it would have been an easy path to freedom.

The position of the bodies was puzzling. In small sinking vehicles, frantic occupants seeking to flee would bump into each other, Newell knew from experience. Often, they would end up falling back into the spots they sought to escape. Two of the victims in the Nissan Sentra were awkwardly draped around and over the seats. There were no signs that the other two had struggled to flee.

His reconnaissance complete, Newell swam to the surface.

He told the Kingston officers that there were four female bodies in the car and he saw no obvious signs of trauma, although his view of three of the victims was obscured. Newell said it didn't look as if any of the victims had made any effort to escape the car.

"Have you ever seen four people drowned in a vehicle?" Chris Scott shouted from shore.

"I've never come across that," Newell answered.

It would be a fairly simple process to remove the victims, one at a time. Newell would swim the bodies to shore and pass them up. On his next dive, Newell opened the left rear door of the Sentra and reached in to grab Sahar. Unrestrained by a seat belt, she was easiest to reach and to remove. He slid her out of the vehicle and swam her to the surface. He passed the girl to officers and repeated the process three times. Rona. Geeti. Zainab.

Scott helped lift the limp bodies out of the cool water. The sodden girls and Rona, all fully dressed, were gently placed into white body bags on the flat expanse of grass next to the water. The bags were left open so that Julia Moore could photograph them. They were beautiful and unblemished, but it was a ghastly, sad sight, Scott thought.

DETECTIVE CONSTABLE GEOFF DEMPSTER began his interview of Hamed at the station at 5:30 p.m., before the underwater recovery operation was complete at Kingston Mills. Dempster felt as if he were operating blind, conducting critical interviews without knowing what investigators had discovered at the scene. It wasn't ideal, but it was unavoidable. Still, he expected a flood of information from the family.

They'll feed you with a firehose.

He considered this a universal truth for investigations of sudden deaths—automobile crashes, industrial accidents or medical crises that lead to fatalities and typically don't involve crimes. Sudden death cases are a staple for patrol officers, who are a police department's first responders. The lowly constable who arrives first at a tragedy often inherits the task of talking to family members, to notify them of the death and also to gather clues about its cause. The quest for clues is an effort to ensure that a crime has not been committed.

Dempster had been through the process many times in the eight years he had spent in uniform. In every case, family members overwhelmed him with trivial details about the victim and his activities—what he had for breakfast that day, the car crash he had been in years earlier, his love of skateboarding a decade before his death. Dempster was struck by the dearth of information he had received from Mohammad Shafia. The officer had struggled to extract details from a man who had just lost three teenaged daughters and a cousin.

Dempster wondered if it was a problem of language and culture. The interview had been stilted and difficult. His ability to read the nuances of speech and body language was impaired because Shafia's answers were filtered through an interpreter. Dempster hoped that things would be different with Hamed, who spoke English.

A timeline was taking shape in Dempster's mind as he began to question Hamed. The witness from Daylan Avenue said he saw two vehicles at the canal between 1:30 and 2:00 a.m.; the Shafias arrived at the motel around 2:00; Hamed drove from Kingston to Montreal in the family's Lexus, overnight, soon after the family checked into the motel; and Hamed drove back to Kingston in a different vehicle by noon.

The officer didn't plan to pose key questions first. He would tread carefully and not press too aggressively. The investigation was still classified as a coroner's case. Because the Shafias were not considered suspects in any crimes, police had not cautioned them about their legal right to remain silent and their right to contact and confer with a lawyer. At any moment, they could stop answering questions and walk out of the police station. Dempster wanted to keep them talking.

The officer was cordial. His tone was sympathetic.

"It's an unfortunate incident that has brought us together here today," Dempster began. He appealed to Hamed to "tell me as much as you can" so that officers could provide his family with a complete understanding of what had happened. Hamed wasted no time. In a span of a few minutes, just minutes into the interview, he reconstructed the past twenty-four hours, highlighting the same events that his father had outlined.

The family was heading home to Montreal from Niagara Falls and stopped in Kingston to get motel rooms, Hamed explained. He suggested that the group in the Nissan—Tooba, Zainab, Sahar, Geeti and Rona—park and wait until he and his father found a motel. The three other children, who were with Hamed and Shafia in the Lexus, were left at the motel that they eventually found. Hamed and Shafia then drove back to the spot where the five family members were sitting in the parked Nissan and led them back to the motel. Hamed "really wanted to sleep," he told Dempster, so he lay down for a few minutes and, at that moment, he saw his sister Zainab come to the room.

"She asked, uh, my mom for the keys, for the keys for the Nissan," Hamed said.

"Yeah."

"She wanted to, um, take her clothes and everything, uh, I don't know what, to change or something, so after she got the key, um, I never saw her. I never saw her. That was the last time I saw her, ya know."

"Okay."

"Yeah, and the others, I saw, the last time I saw them, um, was, um, when I picked them up from the parking place."

What transpired after the family got to the motel seemed improbable. The young man who had just driven for roughly six hours, and who was so fatigued that he *really* wanted to sleep, got into the family's Lexus and drove three hundred kilometres.

"I needed something personal," Hamed offered, vaguely.

When Dempster pressed him, he explained that his father bought cars at online auctions, and in Niagara Falls he could not find an Internet café. For this reason, he had to drive to Montreal to get his laptop computer. He offered more when Dempster pressed on.

"You know, there are a lot reasons, you know, you, you go back to a place, uh, say if you don't feel like staying at one place with your parents, ya know," Hamed said. "You just want to drive somewhere else, ya know."

When Dempster asked Hamed if he thought that Zainab asked for the keys to the Nissan so she could secretly take it for a drive, the young man was full of detail.

During the Niagara Falls trip, Zainab, who did not have a driver's licence, suddenly expressed a strong interest in driving, Hamed said. He had seen her practising in a parking lot. "I saw her once or twice, like, she was really, uh, enthusiastic to really try driving," he said.

"Yes."

"So that, that's what scared me a lot, ya know. She, she's never been like that, uh, I'm not sure if you know it or no, but uh, she's, uh, you know engaged, to be engaged with someone."

"That's Zainab?" Dempster asked.

"Yeah, she's the eldest."

"Yeah."

"Yeah, so he must have taught, uh, her how to drive," Hamed offered.

"Oh yeah?"

"Yeah, so she, uh, she always keeps on asking, ya know, 'I want to drive, wanna drive, wanna drive.'"

Hamed's story was missing important details. He didn't know where the Nissan was parked while the five family members waited for a motel to be found. He wasn't sure what time they found the motel. He wasn't certain what time he got back to Montreal. He was unsure when precisely his father had telephoned him after he reached Montreal or when he had made the decision to return to Kingston.

Dempster asked Hamed what he thought had happened to his family members.

Hamed said that when his father first called him, when he was in Montreal, he figured the girls took the car and ran into something. "And they're scared to come back, ya know, maybe they crashed it somewhere and they don't want to come back, that's what I thought," he told Dempster.

His sister Zainab had run away from home more than a month ago, he added.

"Yeah, and she never even called to tell that where is she, ya know, so we kept on calling her and stuff like that and she came back after sixteen days," he said.

"Her boyfriend had a car," Hamed told Dempster about thirty minutes later.

"That's for . . . that's how she learned to drive, I guess."

Though Hamed had already told Dempster that Zainab's fiancé must have taught her to drive, he suggested that her former boyfriend must have given her the driving bug.

Dempster asked when Hamed's father had called him that morning and where Hamed was when he took the calls. Hamed said he was at home when he got the calls, though he had earlier told the officer that he had still been en route to Montreal.

The officer had been questioning Hamed for forty-five minutes when he suddenly switched subjects.

"How come you came back in the Pontiac?" he asked.

"I, 'cause, uh, he usually tells me but this time . . . he never told me that, um, 'cause that Lexus, uh, SUV, ya know, when you drive from, uh, Montreal to Kingston," Hamed stammered.

Dempster believed Hamed was withholding information. The detective was preparing to confront him but allowed him to stumble through his answer.

"Mhmm," the officer murmured.

"That's one of the reasons, I guess, no, no special reason 'cause, uh, takes more gas and fuel and stuff like that."

"Um, what is the Pontiac, is it a van? Is it a car?"

"It's a van."

"It's a van?"

"It's parked outside, yeah."

"Okay, who puts gas in the car?"

"Dad."

"Your dad does, so did he tell you to bring the van back to Kingston today or was that your choice?" Dempster asked.

"Uh no, he didn't tell me."

"That was your choice?"

"That was my choice yeah, I just, uh, thought I'd bring it."

Dempster moved on. He returned to the chronology, beginning with Hamed's drive back to Montreal and the phone calls from his father. The officer spent five minutes trying to pinpoint the times of the calls before suddenly changing the subject again.

"Hamed, do you know what happened to your sisters?" Dempster asked. He was looking down at the big pad of lined paper in front of him when he began to speak, but he quickly looked up and stared at Hamed.

The young man with the big mop of dark curls was sitting impassive and silent with his arms tucked tightly at his sides. Dempster did not look away. Nearly ten seconds elapsed before Hamed began to gently shake his head from side to side.

"No," he said softly.

"You don't?" Dempster asked.

"No."

"And your aunt?"

"No."

Dempster asked Hamed if he understood clearly what the officer had already explained, that the family's car was found underwater and that there were bodies inside.

"Yeah," Hamed answered.

Dempster revealed that police had spoken to a witness who heard a splash in the middle of the night. The officer leaned forward in his chair, resting his forearms on his thighs, so that he was much closer to his subject. Dempster's fingers were knit loosely together. He spoke very softly and slowly.

"And what if I told you that that same person also saw another vehicle," the officer said, pausing for a second. "But that other vehicle drove away and that it was a large vehicle."

Hamed seemed momentarily frozen.

"You mean someone pushed them in?" Hamed responded.

Dempster did not stop to consider the gravity or prescience of Hamed's remark. Dempster had not suggested that the Nissan was pushed into the water.

"No, but just that there was somebody else there," Dempster replied immediately. "That other person, that other car, probably knows what really happened but they're . . . they're very scared and afraid and maybe ashamed to, to say what they know."

If Hamed understood that he was "that other person," he refused to acknowledge it or confront the accusation directly.

"Who do you think the big car belongs to?" Hamed asked.

"Hamed, I think you know more than what you've told me here today," Dempster shot back, ignoring the question.

"I, I have no . . . I have no idea," Hamed sputtered.

"Hamed, my only job here is to find the truth and find out what happened last night."

Dempster emphasized a familiar theme: his purpose was to discover what happened so that he could give Hamed's parents the peace of mind of knowing the full story.

"Yeah, but uh, I'm uh, telling you the truth here," Hamed offered. "I don't know, uh, I seriously don't know what you're talking about."

Dempster suggested that someone had witnessed the Nissan's plunge into the water but he wasn't accusing that person of causing the tragedy.

"Accidents are accidents," Dempster said. "I'm not saying that that other person caused it. I'm not saying they did it on purpose, but there is somebody out there that, that knows really what happened and, and we need that person to speak up and we need that person to—"

Hamed interrupted. "Yeah, but uh, I, I seriously have uh, it's just like a shock to me that you're telling me this. That uh, that I must have witnessed something." He acknowledged that he understood he was "that other person." "If I would have witnessed something, I would be the first person to tell my mom and dad, don't you think?"

Dempster would not relent. He told Hamed there were "some discrepancies" in his recollection of times and telephone calls during his early morning trip to Montreal. Hamed offered to give the officer his cellphone invoice.

Dempster returned to the car swap.

"Okay and, and um, the reason for coming back in the Pontiac and not the Lexus was because it's better on gas?"

"Well, that's one of the reasons, ya know," Hamed said.

"Yeah, what would be another reason?"

"Uh, nothing, uh nothing big, ya know, nothing ya know that's worth telling."

"Okay, which is more fun to drive, the Lexus or the Pontiac?" Dempster asked.

"Well, the Lexus of course."

Dempster asked where the Lexus was, and Hamed explained that he had left it in the garage at their home in Saint-Léonard. Dempster asked if there was anything wrong with the Lexus.

"No," Hamed lied.

"So if we ask the Montreal Police to go and just have a quick look at it, there's—"

Hamed interrupted, "But if I had an accident with it, I would have it in Montreal, I wouldn't have it in Kingston, would I."

"Yeah."

"And I would have a police, um, what is it?"

"Report," Dempster said.

"Yeah."

"Is there anything else that I should know?" Dempster asked. "Is there something else like, like I was saying, it's not I'm saying that you are lying. I don't like to say people are lying but . . ."

"No, you could say that, if you think," Hamed said. "If you feel I'm lying or something, you can tell me right away."

Dempster asked again why the three girls and Rona would drive off in the middle of the night.

Hamed repeated what he had said earlier: Zainab wanted to drive. He refused to take up Dempster's invitation to speculate why a fifty-year-old woman would go with the three girls. He would not engage with Dempster as the officer speculated that Hamed had followed the Nissan in the Lexus, trying to stop the girls from taking off on a joyride that led them to a dark road "that had a lake at the end of it."

Hamed said nothing.

12

"Why Should I Lie?"

THERE WAS NO FIREHOSE OF INFORMATION.

Shafia and Hamed had not flooded Dempster, during their interviews, with details. The officer was frustrated by their inability to recall key facts or offer meaningful explanations for events. He felt sure that they were withholding information. Kingston officers had contacted police in Montreal and learned that Hamed had reported a collision with the Lexus that morning. Montreal officers were posted outside the Shafia home in Saint-Léonard and were watching the garage by the time Dempster sat down in the interview room with an interpreter and Tooba at 7:15 p.m.

The grieving mother seemed calm, but she began to pick at the ends of the long patterned scarf that was draped around her neck and knotted at her chest. The tears that had flowed freely hours earlier were gone. She appeared to be grinning, or smiling, perhaps nervously.

Dempster said there was one big question on everyone's mind: How did the Nissan Sentra get from the motel into the water?

"Can I say?" Tooba asked eagerly, in Dari, without waiting for the interpreter.

"Yes, please," Dempster answered, after he heard the translation.

The family was driving home from Niagara Falls and stopped to get motel rooms, she told him. She was sleepy and feeling sick. Moments after they checked in, Zainab came to Tooba's room and asked for the keys to the Nissan so that she could retrieve clothes from it. Tooba trusted her, so she gave her the keys.

Tooba said, after that, "Man nemifahmam"—"I don't know."

It was a tidy denouement. She didn't know what happened next because she slept. The next morning, when she awoke, her husband told her that the car and four family members were missing.

Although the interview would last an hour, Tooba had dispensed, in the first eight minutes, the only real information she would give Dempster. What followed were minor elaborations and many denials. The grieving mother drew the attention of investigators to the actions of her eldest daughter. She said everyone in the family was content to stop in Kingston, except Zainab, who wanted to get back to Montreal as soon as possible. Tooba did not use the word "motive," but she intimated that one existed to explain why Zainab would take the car. During the drive home from Niagara Falls, Zainab had made a request that her mother rebuffed.

"She told me couple times that, 'Give me the keys so I can drive, give me keys to drive,' but I didn't."

Dempster asked if Zainab had ever taken the car without permission. Tooba furrowed her brow as she considered the question.

"One time, um," she said, raising the first finger of right hand. "One, one time or twice in the hotel that we were in, Days Inn, in Niagara Falls." She raised her second finger. She said her younger son and Zainab had taken the car keys.

"There they drive around the parking twice," she said.

Dempster asked about Hamed's plans the previous night.

Tooba said she didn't know the details, but had heard Hamed speak to Shafia about the building that he owned in Montreal.

"And work for building came up and that's all I understood," she said. "I didn't ask what it was."

Tooba said she knew Hamed was going to drive back to Montreal, but she was asleep when he left. She said if she had been awake, she would have gone with him, because she worried about him driving alone. Tooba seemed to have a different attitude toward her eldest daughter. She told the officer that Zainab was a girl who "would do whatever she wanted to do."

Unlike Hamed, Tooba was happy to speculate when Dempster invited her to explain why the four family members took off in the car.

"Only desired, only desire to drive car. She desired a lot. I think she thought, 'My mom and dad are asleep, let's go for a drive and return.' That's it."

After half an hour, Dempster excused himself from the room for five minutes. He returned with a different agenda. He faced Tooba squarely as soon as he sat down.

"Were you there when the car went in the water?" the detective asked.

"No, no, I wasn't there," Tooba answered. "Me said key, they took from me, I didn't understand."

"If you were not there, my job is to find out what happened and tell you."

"Me, me to you my story told, is what my story is. There, I didn't have any work to do there. Just took the keys from me and they left, said give, we just want our clothes from the car. Since I was very tired, I went to sleep. Didn't know further."

"As a parent, one parent to another, if something happened to my child, I would want to know the truth," Dempster said, seeking a bond with her. "I would not, I would want to know what happened."

"Yes, true. Your saying is true. If understand, I would have told you everything but haven't seen anything. If I knew, I would have told you and you could have helped me."

It was a typical ploy for a police interrogator to feign empathy, but Dempster wasn't acting. He had two young children at home. His older son was eight, the same age as Tooba's youngest daughter. The officer had been heartbroken when he saw Fereshta burst into tears after she learned that three of her sisters were dead.

"I can only know the truth if people talk truthful to me," Dempster told Tooba, building toward an accusation.

"Yes, that's true but I don't know," Tooba answered. "If I knew, I would tell you everything. I just know that she took the keys from me and I didn't know. I was very tired and I went to bed."

She said that she did not hear or see the Nissan leave the motel.

Dempster asked Tooba, in a question that revealed a working theory of the night's events, if Hamed had chased the girls himself or if both Hamed and Shafia had gone after them.

Tooba dismissed the idea, saying simply that they didn't know the four were gone at that time. "Until next morning, we didn't know," she said.

"People have not been truthful with us today," Dempster said. He delivered the accusation gently, with the same soft voice.

"Yes, whatever it was I told you, I don't know further than this," Tooba insisted. "If I know anything, it's more difficult to me than you because my kids were there. I would have told you the whole truth."

Dempster sat silently for fifteen seconds before he delivered a bombshell.

"Your daughters' deaths and your husband's cousin might not have been an accident," he said.

"Meaning what?" Tooba asked.

Dempster, who had his hands in his lap, extended them quickly out to his sides, palms up, in a seeming gesture of uncertainty. He sat silently again for fifteen seconds before answering her.

"It would mean that something happened to cause it," he said.

"I don't know anything else," Tooba said.

"I think you know that Hamed went after the girls when they took the car."

"No, no, believe me, I don't know this, don't know since I was tired."

"My job is to find the truth. I don't stop until I find the truth."

"Right, I want you to find the truth," Tooba said.

"If the truth is, this was an accident, it wasn't supposed to happen, I need to know that, know now."

"If I don't know something, why should I lie? No. Whatever I knew, whatever I understood, from there till here, I told you."

BY THE TIME TOOBA'S INTERVIEW WAS COMPLETE, the four bodies had been taken from Kingston Mills to a downtown Kingston hospital. Police told the parents that they would have to go there to positively identify each person. Hamed did not accompany them. Police said they needed to talk to him again. Investigators were troubled by the inconsistencies in his first interview.

Dempster tiptoed for the first few minutes, then reminded Hamed that they had talked earlier about the question of an accident with the Lexus.

"You made a comment that if you had one, you would have reported it," Dempster said.

"Hmmm."

"Did you report one today?" Dempster asked.

"Yeah," Hamed answered, without hesitation.

"Yeah, why did you tell me you didn't?"

"I said if, uh, 'cause if, if, I would tell you then, uh—"

Dempster interrupted.

"Okay, why are you hiding that information from me, Hamed?"

"No, 'cause if I would tell you, you would go tell my dad, that's uh, that's the thing."

He was simply a frightened teenager who had crashed Dad's fancy SUV, and now he feared the consequences of the discovery of his driving escapade. Hamed told Dempster that he planned to tell his father about the collision when they returned to Montreal.

Dempster asked Hamed for "the whole story" of the crash.

"The accident, uh, when I got back, it was on a pole and, uh, in the shopping centre mall, uh, in a shopping centre parking. It was, uh, on a pole and I reported it and, um, that's it."

Dempster had grown accustomed to Hamed's ponderous, vague replies and refused to politely accept them any longer.

"No, details," he snapped.

"Uh, but what details?" Hamed asked.

Dempster said he wanted to know *everything* about the crash: "I love details." It took eight minutes to elicit a more meaningful account.

Hamed had driven first to the apartment on Bonnivet, where he sat for a few minutes. He was hungry, so he drove to L'Intermarché supermarket about two minutes away. He thought it opened at seven thirty. In the parking lot, he crashed the SUV into "a pole." He had parked perpendicular to the lines painted on the pavement, so, when he saw his error, he reversed, then drove ahead and the front left corner of the Lexus clipped the pole. He called police immediately after the crash and an officer came to the parking lot. When the officer left, he did not go into the supermarket.

"'Cause uh, after you have an accident, you don't feel like eating," Hamed said.

He drove home, put the Lexus in the garage, got a drink and, soon after, left in the Pontiac to drive back to Kingston.

"And you didn't tell me about that before," Dempster noted.

"Yeah, 'cause uh, first of all, it was nothing related to this," Hamed answered, as he folded his arms and leaned back in the chair.

"It's not?"

"It's not."

Dempster raised again the possibility that the girls had left the motel in the Nissan and were followed by Hamed in the Lexus. Perhaps the two vehicles collided because he was trying to stop them, Dempster suggested.

"Got into an accident with *me*?" Hamed asked.

"Yeah," Dempster said.

"How did they end up in water?" Hamed asked.

"Hmm," Dempster murmured, refusing to answer.

"How did they end up in water?" Hamed repeated.

"I don't know," Dempster replied. "That's, ya know, what I don't know. I keep going in circles here because—"

"But you know what," Hamed said, cutting him off and slapping his right hand on the table. "I'm telling you, and I'm already in, uh, a lot of mess."

"Yeah," Dempster said.

Hamed began shaking his left hand in the air and then slapped his open palm on the table several times.

"I don't know what you're doing, uh, if you want to blame it on me."

"I don't," Dempster said.

"I don't know, I don't know where you're going with this, honestly, uh, to be honest with you, man, I don't know where you're going with this, okay, this, I understand," Hamed said, tapping drawings he had made of his collision in Montreal.

"Then you're going in circles, you know. You're going straight, then you're making an illegal left turn or, you know, you're going back where you started. I don't understand this. I don't know, uh, to be honest with you man, uh, I, I, I didn't want them to go back to Montreal and, uh, I made an accident with them and, how did they end up in water? Seriously, I don't understand this. I, I'm just telling you straight up, man."

His baffling soliloquy complete, Hamed drummed the fingers of his right hand between his legs against the wooden chair. Dempster, leaning over the table with his right elbow on the surface and his chin in his hand, stared at Hamed for thirty seconds.

Dempster broke the silence by asking if Hamed's sister was angry that the family decided to stop in Kingston. Hamed said he thought his siblings were "okay with it." The question was the first in a series about the possible motives of Hamed's sisters to take the Nissan without permission. Hamed said he didn't think they were looking for a place to buy food. He said it was his best guess that "they wanted to take it for a test drive."

Dempster said police could not find anything to explain why the four family members were driving in that area or why the car ended up in the water.

For the first time, Hamed seemed frustrated with the persistent questioning, but he indicated he was ready to sacrifice himself.

"The . . . ya know, right now, uh, my brothers and sisters, my mom and dad, they're here, right?" he asked.

"Yes."

"You can let them go. I'll, I'll stay till morning with you."

Dempster didn't respond to the offer. He continued to ask about a motive to explain the actions of the victims. A few minutes later, Hamed made clear that he was not going to tell the officer anything more than he already had.

"Ya know, I could sit, uh, till morning with you and say the same thing, you know."

Dempster turned to a different subject. He asked Hamed to tell him about Rona.

She was "a nice person," and "good," he said, but despite being fifty years old, she was ready to do whatever the girls suggested. "I don't know but, uh, she was an aunt which used to hang around with the girls, twenty-four seven," Hamed said.

"Oh yeah?"

"Twenty-four seven, yeah."

Hamed said he had never seen Rona stay up past midnight.

He offered Dempster only one other significant piece of information before the interview ended. He told the officer that if he had been in Kingston and knew the family members were missing, he would have searched for them himself.

If he saw them underwater, he wouldn't be able to do anything, he said. "Like it's, obviously I would call 9-1-1, right."

AFTER HAMED'S SECOND INTERVIEW was completed that evening, the six surviving Shafia family members were taken to a Holiday Inn in Kingston, where they would spend the night at police expense. They were not permitted to return to the Kingston Motel East because police had not yet examined the rooms and collected evidence at the motel.

It was after 10:00 p.m. by the time Chris Scott convened a meeting at the station of twenty investigators. Everyone involved that day was present. Scott had assumed the role of major case manager. He had been at Kingston Mills throughout the day, until the Nissan Sentra was hoisted out of the water by a large crane and hauled to the police station on a flatbed truck. The sopping car was locked in a secure storage area in the basement of the station. Three cellphones had been found inside. In the trunk were four items—a small suitcase, two large purses and a large tote bag—stuffed with the apparatus of womanhood, disposable razors, tweezers, mascara, eyeliner, lip gloss, bikinis, bras and hair irons. In the suitcase, officers were surprised to find an assortment of expensive-looking gold jewellery. They would learn later that it was worth more than $20,000.

Scott made clear that everyone at the meeting would have a chance to speak and to relate what he or she had learned that day. The meeting was Scott's first opportunity to hear first-hand from Dempster what he had uncovered in his marathon six hours of interviews with Shafia, Tooba and Hamed. Dempster had collected a critical timeline of events: the trip to Niagara Falls, the drive to Kingston on the evening of June 29, check-in at the motel, and Hamed's early-morning trek to Montreal and back later that morning. Dempster told the group that he believed the adults were withholding information. Hamed had concealed his collision in Montreal and his vehicle exchange, and Dempster was suspicious of his explanations.

"We gotta get eyes on that Lexus," Dempster said.

Senior officers agreed. Hamed had told police that the Lexus was parked in the garage at the family's home in Montreal and that no one else had keys or access to it. But the officers didn't know if this was true. They were concerned that the vehicle could be moved or tampered with before they could determine whether it had played a role in the deaths. They wanted to see it for themselves. So far, they had only been able to keep watch over the apartment and garage in Montreal.

Detective Clint Wills, who had conducted a second interview of the eight-year-old boy who lived near the canal, said he found Dylan credible when he said that he saw two vehicles at the canal, in the dark. Investigators wondered if Dylan had seen the Lexus and the Nissan at the canal, together.

Some of the officers around the table heard, for the first time, puzzling details about the condition of the Nissan. When the car was found, the ignition was turned off, the headlights were off, and the dome light was switched off, so that it would not come on even when a door was opened. The centre-console-mounted gear shifter was in first gear and not Drive, the typical position. Both front seats were reclined to a steep angle.

Several officers had seen impressions in the grass that suggested a car had driven around a large rock outcropping at Kingston Mills. The ident officers had not been able to document any clear tire tracks or footprints.

The group heard that the three other Shafia children, who were at the station throughout the day, were interviewed individually. They did not provide any information that would help explain the deaths, but their accounts meshed with what the adults had told Dempster. The children said they were dropped off at the motel when the family arrived in Kingston, and when they awoke the next day, they learned from their parents that the four were missing.

A common theme developed during the meeting, which was articulated by Scott: "This just doesn't add up. How did that car get there?"

When the meeting ended, around midnight, a decision had been made to try to examine the Lexus. Detective Steve Koopman was assigned to meet with Mohammad Shafia early the next morning and ask for his consent to allow police into the garage of the family's Montreal home to inspect the SUV. Police knew securing Shafia's permission would be delicate. If he refused, police would probably not be able to get a warrant. For that, they needed reasonable and probable grounds to believe a crime had been committed and that the search would uncover evidence that could be used to prosecute the crime. For now, the investigators had only a suspicion that something wasn't right.

BY THE TIME CHRIS SCOTT PUT AWAY HIS NOTES and locked his office, it was after 1:00 a.m. He could not stop thinking about the implausibility of a young, inexperienced driver piloting a car into the water at that strange location in the dark, without colliding with any of the obstacles around the canal property. There was only one way to know for certain what it would have been like to drive around that property at one or two o'clock in the morning.

Scott turned north out of the police station parking lot and took the same route the Shafias would have followed if they drove directly from Highway 401 to Kingston Mills. Scott pulled onto the shoulder at the canal property, parked and turned off his vehicle and its lights. He was only a few metres from the area where the pieces of plastic had been found in the grass, but Scott could not see the ground. It was oppressively dark. There were no streetlights and no floodlights illuminating the isolated property.

Scott got out of his vehicle and walked across the grass, toward the water.

I can't believe how black it is, he thought. He was now more convinced that the explanations for the deaths that police had heard that day didn't add up, though he did not plan to tell anyone about his late-night visit to the scene. He would let his team of investigators follow the evidence.

13

Project Jigsaw

IT SOUNDED AS IF PEOPLE WERE WALKING AROUND in the apartment above Joyce Gilbert's ground-floor flat. *How could that be?* she wondered. The Shafia family had gone on vacation eight days ago. It was July 1, so they weren't due back for another four days. At around 6:30 p.m., Gilbert went outside to investigate and was surprised to find half a dozen police officers in the driveway of her building. They asked Gilbert to move her car because it was blocking the garage door. After Gilbert moved her car, a detective backed the Shafia family's silver Lexus SUV out of the garage. Gilbert could see that the front driver's-side corner was damaged. The headlight lens was shattered and the metal hood and fender around it were wrinkled. A chunk of reflector dangled from the broken socket.

Gilbert noticed her neighbour, Mohammad Shafia, standing across the street next to his minivan. She thought he looked sad and lost, so she walked over to him.

"What happened?" Gilbert asked. "What's wrong?"

He seemed to be choking back tears.

"Three of my daughters dead and my cousin is dead," Shafia told her. Gilbert burst into tears. As the pair talked, they watched a police officer walk around the Lexus, snapping photos.

"Son came with Lexus," Shafia continued, in broken English. "Have accident here and leave Lexus here and take van to Kingston."

Shafia walked away from Gilbert, over to the police officers by the Lexus.

Kingston detective Steve Koopman was taking photos of the damaged front end from a variety of angles. He asked Shafia if he knew where the small scrapes came from that were on the lower section of the front bumper. Shafia said he thought the damage was old. He said the small scratches on the right rear bumper happened in a parking lot about two years ago.

Koopman did not ask about the significant damage to the front corner, since Shafia had already told the officer he didn't know about Hamed's collision in Montreal on June 30. Koopman had asked Shafia about it during a videotaped conversation, through an interpreter, at the police station in Kingston early that morning, before Shafia, Koopman and his partner drove to Montreal. The primary purpose of the interview was to secure Shafia's permission for police to examine the Lexus, but Koopman put other questions to him. Investigators were anxious to ask again why Hamed had taken the Lexus to Montreal and returned to Kingston in the minivan.

"Well, he went in order to go to work the next day," Shafia told Koopman. "Meaning, if this incident hadn't happened, he would not have come."

Shafia explained that the nine people who had remained in Kingston had planned to stay for several days. When they were ready to go home to Montreal, Shafia said, he would have called Hamed to come back to Kingston to pick them up.

"From there, when he came back, me from him, he said, 'I just brought this because its consumption is less. I brought this.' So I just didn't ask him any more." Shafia said that if he had known about Hamed's collision, he would have told Dempster about it in his first interview.

Shafia said he didn't talk to Hamed about the vehicles the previous night, in the Holiday Inn. It was not a good night, he said. His wife was crying and he spent considerable time consoling her.

"We talked about this and nothing else."

When Koopman asked whether the Lexus had been in any other collisions, Shafia offered a new detail that bolstered the family's portrayal of Zainab as a rebellious girl who might take the Nissan for a joyride. He had omitted it during his interview with Dempster.

Shafia told Koopman that he saw his daughter back the Nissan into the

Lexus in the parking lot of the hotel where the family stayed in Niagara Falls. Shafia said he was watching from the window of his room and rushed out to the parking lot to snatch the keys from Zainab.

"I just looked at the Lexus," Shafia said. "I was so frustrated as to why she did what she did since she doesn't even have a driver's licence. If this happened to someone else's car, she would've created a problem for me."

Shafia said he was "very angry" and warned Zainab that she was not ever again to touch the keys to the car. He repeated what Tooba had told Dempster about Zainab: "Even on the highway she requested her mother to give her the car to drive. My wife stopped and told me and I said to her, 'You will get us all killed by her.'"

Shafia offered no resistance when Koopman sought permission to search the Lexus. The grieving father said he was willing to do whatever the police asked, even if it took five years to explain the deaths.

"What I want is to know is if my family member has been killed, has gone in the water, has been strangled, has been drugged," Shafia said. "What has happened? That's what I'd like to know. If he has taken drugs, if he has gone mad. This is not human behaviour."

Shafia said he didn't want to consult a lawyer, after Koopman explained that he had the right to get legal advice before agreeing to the search of the vehicle. The officer also emphasized that Shafia could withdraw his consent at any time.

"The car has to be fully checked," Shafia said.

He said he was certain that the Lexus was not connected to the deaths, but he understood police needed to investigate fully. Shafia had one unexpected request. He asked to go with police to Montreal so that he could retrieve fresh clothes for the family. He promised to stay out of their way. Although it had not been part of the plan, investigators decided to allow him to tag along. The Kingston officers drove in a police vehicle; Shafia followed in his minivan. At the apartment, they were met by four Montreal police officers.

When Koopman and his partner popped open the rear hatch of the Lexus, they spotted something interesting, in plain view. Three pieces of jagged plastic lay on top of a big blue plastic cooler. Koopman spied a fourth piece wedged into the gap where a hand would be inserted to flip up the cooler lid, and a fifth stuck in the weatherstripping around the edge of the hatch. In all, the officers found ten shards of plastic inside the rear cargo area of the Lexus. Four were black, two were silver, three were transparent and one was transparent and orange. It seemed that someone had collected the plastic that fell off the vehicle when the front left headlight was damaged and had placed the pieces in the back of the SUV. Shafia readily agreed when Koopman asked if they could take the pieces back to Kingston for examination.

The officers allowed Shafia to take tote bags and running shoes from the back of the Lexus, and then followed him into the house and watched as he collected a few more pieces of clothing.

The investigators weren't done with the Lexus. They drove the SUV to the nearby L'Intermarché parking lot, where Hamed had reported the collision with a guardrail. Koopman snapped photos while his partner drove the vehicle close to, but not touching, the steel barrier. Koopman figured that it would be easier to compare the damage on the Lexus to the height and shape of the guardrail with a visual record. It looked as if the rail could have hit the front corner of the SUV, the detective thought.

The officers returned the Lexus to the garage on Bonnivet and headed for Kingston with ten pieces to add to the jigsaw puzzle.

MARY-ANN DEVANTRO CALLED HER "THE LITTLE ONE."

When Devantro answered the knock at her apartment door, the round-faced child with a grinning, pink-eared kitten on her shirt was standing by herself. Fereshta was crying and clutching a scrap of lined paper.

Devantro had cried for hours when she heard the incomprehensible news that four of her downstairs neighbours were dead—those three sweet, beautiful sisters and their aunt. The rest of the family had just returned to Montreal that day, Thursday, July 2. Devantro didn't know any details, only that the four had been found dead in Kingston, in a sunken car, two days earlier.

The girls had been regular visitors to Devantro's apartment. She was more than a neighbour; she was a confidante and a friend. Devantro had told them they were welcome anytime to visit her and her sister Margaret. She remembered Zainab playfully pulling her sweater down to reveal her shoulder and giggling about how she'd never let her father see her *that* way. Fereshta had spent many hours colouring and making crafts with Devantro's granddaughter Alexandra. The girls hugged Devantro when they visited and treated Alexandra lovingly, like a sister.

Fereshta poked her arm toward Alexandra, who was standing beside her grandmother, and held the paper so Devantro could see it. The Disney stationery, a handspan tall and half as wide, was stamped in the top left corner with the likeness of Pluto, the energetic mutt with floppy ears. Devantro was startled by the scene beneath the dog, crudely drawn, but unmistakable.

It was a childish portrait of a car drawn with a thick, reddish-brown marker. Two spoked wheels protruded from the bottom of a simple rectangle, and another rectangle on top represented the passenger compartment. Three rows of undulating blue lines stretched across the bottom of the paper. The cartoon car's wheels were submerged in the lines.

Devantro's shock turned to horror. She reached forward to take the sheet, to keep it away from her granddaughter. Inside the car was a prone stick figure, drawn with a bright orange marker. The figure had long lines of hair cascading from its round head, and dots for eyes. Outside the car were three more orange stick figures with scribbles of hair. Only one had dotted eyes and a stroke for a grin. Two of the figures did not have faces, just long strands of hair. The figures were lying in the wavy lines.

There was a fifth figure, drawn with the same fat tip that had sketched the car's frame. This stick person was upright in the passenger compartment, where a steering wheel might be found. It did not have any hair. It did not look like the other four.

"Look, look!" Fereshta was saying, urgently, as Devantro held the paper, painfully aware of what the child had drawn. "The accident, the accident."

Devantro was momentarily paralyzed and could not speak. Half a dozen scenarios raced through her mind. What did this drawing mean? Who was the fifth figure, the apparent driver? Why was one horizontal figure inside the car and three outside?

Devantro had questions but asked nothing. She pulled Fereshta toward her and hugged her firmly.

"It's going to be okay," she told the child.

REPORTERS QUICKLY LOCATED THE SHAFIA HOME on Friday morning, after the release of the names of the victims late Thursday night. Journalists began knocking on the door, asking to speak to the parents about the tragedy. The typically reclusive family was accommodating, inviting television, radio and newspaper reporters inside.

Half a dozen journalists who had gathered asked to see pictures of the victims. Shafia and Tooba produced a photo album. They wept as they leafed through the pages, stopping occasionally to point at snapshots of three smiling, dark-haired girls.

"We went, my wife and I, to identify the bodies at the hospital," Shafia said, while crying. "They had no marks of violence or battle, or injuries."

"This is very hard," Tooba said, stopping frequently to bury her tear-stained face in cupped hands.

"It's bad, very bad," Shafia said after a bout of sobbing. "Three nights no sleeping, no eating."

They spoke in sometimes awkward English about the event.

"It's not Canada's mistake," Shafia said. "It's my family's mistake."

He explained that he had been a successful businessman in Afghanistan's capital, Kabul. The family moved to Canada in 2007.

"We came here for children because in Afghanistan, it became dangerous," Shafia said.

The reporters wanted to know how four people ended up dead inside a car submerged in three metres of water at an isolated and inaccessible location.

Tooba told the journalists the same story she had related to Dempster. Tooba and Shafia said Zainab was a rebellious girl who had taken the car without permission in the past, although she did not have a driver's licence. She was trying to teach herself to drive, they said.

"She did it for fun," Tooba said. "Maybe she wanted to go near the water."

None of their children could swim, the mother and father explained.

In fractured English, Shafia reinforced the suggestion that Zainab was to blame.

"Big mistake, take car, no driving lessons."

CONSTABLE ROB ETHERINGTON WAS BACK in the basement forensic lab at the police station before nine on Friday morning, even though he had put in an eighteen-hour day on Thursday. He had travelled to Ottawa for the autopsies, and then paid a late-night visit to the Kingston Motel East to photograph the rooms and collect evidence. He had seized an insulated bottle full of what appeared to be tea, a water bottle, a bag of Frosted Flakes cereal, a container of chocolate spread, a red purse-like shoulder bag that held women's jeans and other clothing, a pair of socks, a backpack and one toothbrush. Under one pillow, he found a pink hair tie.

Etherington's first priority was the ten pieces of fractured plastic that Steve Koopman had found inside the Lexus in Montreal. Three were transparent, and one large chunk was transparent and orange. He spread them out carefully on a workbench in the lab. He photographed them first and then began spinning them around to see if they would fit together. Etherington noticed that all the pieces had striations or lines that had been manufactured into the plastic. When he matched the striations, the pieces appeared to align perfectly, though there was a large gap on the right side of the plastic puzzle that he had assembled.

During the drive to Ottawa the previous day, Julia Moore had told Etherington that she had collected six transparent pieces of plastic at Kingston Mills. Four small chunks were on the stonework, less than a metre from the ledge where it appeared the Nissan Sentra had plunged into the canal. Two bigger pieces were in the grass, roughly thirty metres east. He looked at her photographs of those pieces and was startled by what he saw: the two larger pieces also bore the distinctive manufactured lines. Etherington got permission to retrieve the pieces that were recovered at Kingston Mills, which were being kept in secure storage, and conduct a more direct comparison.

He retrieved the pieces from Kingston Mills, set them out on the workbench and photographed them with a scale so that he could compare them on a computer screen to the photos of the pieces found in Montreal. He was careful to ensure that the pieces in the two sets never touched and were not laid out together on the table at the same time. If the pieces were related, it would be important to establish that material could not have transferred from one set to the other.

Using the scale photos, Etherington tried again to align the fractured pieces of plastic. He knew the account of events that Hamed had given to Dempster in two lengthy interviews. Based on that account, the pieces should not match, but there was no doubt in Etherington's mind what the images revealed.

HUSSAIN HYDERI WAS NERVOUS ABOUT TALKING TO POLICE, but he couldn't stay silent. He had heard the Shafia family's account of events in Kingston. They were saying Zainab had taken the car for a joyride. He had read news stories that portrayed Zainab as a rebellious girl who liked to sneak off with the car even though she didn't have a licence. It wasn't true, he thought. Hussain called Kingston Police and told them that he didn't believe the stories about Zainab. He explained that he knew her well; they were set to be engaged. Zainab had not shown any interest in driving, he told police.

THE TWO-CAR CARAVAN was about an hour out of Kingston Friday morning, on the highway, when Geoff Dempster's cellphone buzzed. He could see from the display that Chris Scott was calling. Dempster had been looking forward to this weekend with his wife, their two young children and their friends. The two families had hastily thrown together the cottage getaway when Dempster got the weekend off. He was tired from the nearly round-the-clock workdays since the car was found underwater at Kingston Mills on Tuesday. The pace had eased because of a lull in the investigation. The autopsy findings that all the victims had drowned left open the possibility it was a terrible accident, toxicology test results might not be available for weeks, and forensic analysis had just begun. The Shafias had returned to Montreal the day before. Several investigators who had put in long hours had the weekend off. Dempster knew that even Chris Scott was at the rink that morning for his teenaged son's hockey tournament.

There was a tone of excitement and urgency in the voice on the phone, Dempster thought. Scott said the pieces of plastic collected from Kingston Mills and from the back of the Lexus in Montreal appeared to fit together perfectly. They matched. All the investigators were assembling at the station for an emergency case meeting.

"I have to go back," Dempster said to his wife as soon as he ended the call. He was already looking for a place to turn off the highway and reverse direction to drive back to Kingston. The officer's mind was racing.

The Lexus was there, Dempster realized. He recalled his interviews with Hamed. *Everything he told me was bullshit, about not being there and not knowing what happened.*

Dempster felt a mix of anger and dismay. The family, particularly Hamed, had been stringing him along.

BY THE TIME DEMPSTER GOT TO THE STATION, Chris Scott was there. He convened the meeting as soon as the investigators arrived.

The officers heard about Etherington's visual match of the pieces of plastic. It placed the Lexus at Kingston Mills, though, by the family's account, the SUV was at the motel and then was driven directly back to Montreal. The officers wondered if Hamed's collision in Montreal was staged to conceal damage that happened at Kingston Mills. The officers were told about Hussain Hyderi's phone call and another call that had been relayed to investigators in Kingston by Montreal police. If this tip proved reliable, it established that Shafia was a liar. A relative of Rona who lived in Europe had called authorities in Montreal after reading online news stories. The caller said Rona was Shafia's first wife. They had married in Afghanistan more than thirty years ago, before he took Tooba as his second wife.

Scott told the team that, based on these new revelations, and the initial suspicions that stemmed from the inconsistent statements of the family members, the case was being reclassified as a homicide. Shafia, Tooba and Hamed were the prime suspects. A decision was made to use a rare tactic. The probe would be conducted covertly, without disclosing publicly that police believed the four people found in the car had been murdered and, most importantly, without tipping off the family.

The strategy called for investigators to play dumb. They would try to convince the Shafia family members that police believed their account—that the deaths were the result of a joyride that ended in tragedy. Detectives would give the impression that they were continuing to investigate for the sole purpose of understanding the mechanics and timing of the "accident." Kingston Police would channel the Keystone Cops, plodding, small-town flatfoots who were incapable of exposing a conspiracy. The investigation was dubbed Project Jigsaw.

THE FUNERAL SERVICE AND BURIAL of Zainab, Sahar, Geeti and Rona was still underway on Sunday, July 5, when a six-hundred-word email written six thousand kilometres away arrived in the inbox of Kingston Police Chief Stephen Tanner. In French, Diba Masoomi explained that she lived in Niort, France, and was a sister of Rona Amir Mohammad. Masoomi had read online news stories about the deaths, and wrote that she had "large doubts on the theory of the 'accident.'" She repeated what police had heard three days earlier in a phone call from another relative: Shafia had concealed Rona's true identity. She was the first of his two wives in a polygamous family. But Masoomi had more valuable information. She claimed that she knew why the victims were killed.

IT TOOK BENJAMIN GIRARD AND RAY HERNANDEZ TWO HOURS and thirty dollars to get to the Hamza Islamic funeral parlour and cemetery. The seventeen-year-olds felt that they had to be there, to honour the memory of their cherished school friend Sahar. The pair took a taxi to a subway station, transferred to a bus and then walked for about a kilometre to get to the remote property, located in Laval, a city north of Montreal.

Sahar's death had shocked many kids at St-Ex who knew her, including Sahar's closest schoolmate, Samia. The boys saw Samia at the funeral, sobbing uncontrollably. They had seen Sahar tell Samia, before the family left Montreal to go on vacation, not to worry, that she'd be back. They knew that Samia felt great guilt.

Many people were crying, including fifteen-year-old Zafar Shafia, whom they had hung out with at school from time to time, even though they called him a "wannabe gangster." There was that time he showed up at school with a shaved head and wouldn't tell anyone why. They didn't speak to him at the funeral, though Benjamin thought Zafar was looking at them strangely, across the room.

Near the end of the service, Benjamin and Ray saw Sahar's father collapse onto the floor, touching off a frenzy of activity. An ambulance was called and Shafia was loaded into the rig and taken away, accompanied by Zafar.

The boys did not notice the two plainclothes police officers in the crowd. Detective Steve Koopman had told Hamed that he and a partner would attend the service, out of respect for the family and the victims. It was, at least, a half-truth. Koopman and the other Kingston detectives were deeply saddened by the deaths, but they were determined to show their respect for the victims by catching their killers.

Koopman had been cast in a lead role in the investigative deception—helpful and slightly naive good cop—and this was the opening act. He had told the Shafias that he would be their primary contact with the police department as the sudden death investigation continued. He promised to do his best to help them get through this difficult time by assisting with arrangements that had to be made and with the return of their property that was still in the hands of police.

The lanky detective with an easy smile was perfect for the largely unscripted role. He was low-key and could talk convincingly about the importance of family. The father of two young girls still visited his boyhood home in Kingston almost every Sunday for a family dinner with his widowed mother and his siblings. With a thin face and dark hair, Koopman could have passed for Hamed's older brother. The family seemed to like him. They began referring to him as "Steve." The officer was polite when he ferried Shafia back and forth between the Holiday Inn in Kingston and the police station on July 1. Koopman was gentle when he interviewed Shafia to secure consent to search the Lexus. The detective was sincere when he expressed sympathy during a meeting with the entire family on July 2, before they left Kingston to return to Montreal.

Koopman's character was slow-moving and seemingly ignorant of the inner workings of the investigation. He wasn't in the loop. He wouldn't be able to swiftly answer all of the family's questions about the progress of the probe. "I'll have to check on that and get back to you" would be his regular refrain.

The real Steve Koopman was neither slow nor uninformed. A ten-year veteran of the Kingston force, a university grad with the equivalent of a criminology degree, he had been promoted to detective three years after joining the department, and four years later, he had been entrusted with the biggest cases as a member of the major crime unit. Koopman was an educated, articulate and technologically savvy cop.

Koopman and Detective Brian Pete had an important appointment after the funeral. They drove to a Montreal police precinct in Saint-Léonard and met with Sergeant Laurie Ann Lefebvre. She gave the Kingston officers a package of police reports including Zainab's missing person case from April that year. The package also included details of the Montreal police investigation that began April 17, the day Zainab ran away, the day that four Shafia children told investigators that they had been punched, slapped and threatened with death by their older brother and their father.

DIBA MASOOMI GAVE POLICE SOMETHING ELSE they had not had, a motive for murder.

"We are convinced that this is a crime of honour, organized under the guidance of Mr. Shafia, his wife Tooba and their oldest son Hamed," Masoomi wrote in her email to the chief. The message was a trove of information for investigators and seemed immediately credible. Masoomi referred to events that police already knew of and described circumstances that seemed verifiable.

> For some time, my sister, as well as the Shafia couple's old-est daughter, Zainab, had been receiving death threats for social, cultural and family reasons (a hidden marriage that should have been cancelled with a Pakistani man). My sister told me that she heard Shafia, her husband, say to second wife and his oldest son Hamed, that he was going to travel to Afghanistan and Dubai to sell some land and goods and then he would kill Zainab, and his second wife added: "And the other?" So my sister understood that they were talking about her.

The email claimed that Rona had no way to get out: "My sister was under the control of the second wife, who was holding her passport."

Masoomi explained that Zainab had "started proceedings with social services in Montreal."

"My sister tried to prevent Zainab from returning to the family home, using Sahar, who unfortunately also disappeared in the incident, as a go between," the email continued. Masoomi suggested that investigators might still find a copy of a letter that Zainab had written. She believed it was concealed in Rona's jewellery box or in her other belongings at the home in Saint-Léonard.

> Mrs. Tooba has a very large influence over the home and no longer wanted to see Rona with the children, and now that they were grown, she wanted my sister to disappear from her life. It must be known that, in Afghan tradition, only the husbands are allowed to divorce their wives, which Mr. Shafia had refused to do for my sister for twenty years, despite the demands of our brothers.

Masoomi also wrote that family and cultural rules did not allow women to be out alone at night.

> It is likely this was a crime of honour, designed to return honour to the father of the family who was tainted by the hidden marriage that we have already talked about. In fact, Afghan tradition allows the punishment of those at fault. In Afghanistan and Arabic culture, the crime would be "official" and approved by the extended family. However, when the family lives in the west, the crimes are often presented as domestic accidents in order to avoid trouble under the country's laws. We noticed that the deaths happened far away from their home, which can certainly hinder the investigation.

Chris Scott had never heard of an honour killing, and now he was confronted with the claim that the deaths at Kingston Mills were a *mass* honour killing. Only police in Calgary, Alberta, had experience with an honour killing in Canada that involved more than two victims.

Daljit Singh Dulay murdered his sister, her husband and a male friend in 1991. Dulay believed his sister Kulwinder had shamed their strict Sikh family by running away from their home in British Columbia and eloping with a man who had grown up with them in the same village in India. Under Sikh culture, Dulay's family considered the couple cousins who were forbidden from marrying. The third victim had helped arrange the couple's wedding. Dulay hired a private investigator, who tracked his sister to Calgary. He believed that killing her would restore his family's tarnished honour.

He armed himself with a semi-automatic assault rifle and hunted the victims to a parking lot, where Dulay sprayed them with bullets. He was sentenced to life in prison, with no chance of parole for twenty-five years.

He did not acknowledge what he had done until 2007, when he was eligible to seek early parole. He was denied.

14

The Match

ROB ETHERINGTON CONTACTED THE CENTRE OF FORENSIC SCIENCES, Ontario's government-operated central crime lab, the day after the victims were buried. The ident officer wanted to know if Kingston Police could submit automobile fragments for an urgent analysis. Detailed examination of the pieces of plastic found at Kingston Mills and inside the Lexus in Montreal was a priority. They appeared to fit together, and they appeared to have come from the Shafia family's Lexus LX 470, but investigators needed scientific certainty. Matching the pieces found in the two locations was the first step in the process. Next, police would have to seize the SUV so they could definitively prove that the plastic fragments came from the Shafia Lexus and not some other LX 470. Kingston Police didn't have the expertise for this job.

The CFS has a stable of scientists trained to analyze DNA, interpret bloodstain patterns, identify weapons based on spent bullets or cartridge cases, and conduct many other forensic examinations. Most Ontario police departments cannot afford to equip and maintain their own forensic labs so they rely on CFS scientists, who operate at two sites in the province, Toronto and Sault Ste. Marie.

If the CFS confirmed that the recovered pieces of plastic came from the Shafia family's Lexus, the evidence would place the SUV at the scene where the victims were found. This link was critical since it would also place one or more family members at the scene. Hamed and Shafia had told investigators that they were the only people who drove the Lexus on the evening of June 29 and during the early morning of June 30. If the Lexus was central to the crime, two people had already acknowledged having exclusive opportunity to use it.

Etherington was on the highway by eleven for the three-hour drive to the CFS lab in Toronto, carrying eighteen jagged pieces of plastic, a container of the tea that was found in one of the rooms at the Kingston Motel East, and other precious cargo. Zainab, Sahar, Geeti and Rona were with him, in twelve glass vials that held blood extracted from their hearts and femoral arteries. He also had vials of their urine. The fluids would be tested for evidence of drugs, poisons and incapacitating substances.

HAMED CALLED STEVE KOOPMAN'S CELLPHONE that afternoon, about the same time that Etherington arrived at the CFS building in downtown Toronto.

Hamed thanked Koopman and Brian Pete for attending the funeral on Sunday. They had not had a chance to speak at the event. Koopman again expressed sympathy for the family's loss and he told Hamed that he thought the event was poignant and very sad. He noted that Hamed's youngest sister had begun crying terribly at the sight of her sister in her coffin. Fereshta had cried out, "Geeti, Geeti, Geeti!"

"Yeah, she's just a kid," Hamed responded.

Koopman asked if everyone was okay. He had seen an ambulance arrive at the funeral parlour, but he didn't know the details of the medical emergency.

"My dad had a small heart attack," Hamed said. He explained that his father had developed trouble breathing during the service. He was taken to a hospital, examined and then released to return home.

Hamed moved on to the primary reason for his call. He asked Koopman about the return of items left at the motel in Kingston, particularly a digital camera. The officer fudged and said he'd arrange to have the items sorted and organized so they could be returned. Koopman was stalling. He didn't know whether any possessions found at the motel had been examined or deemed to be of significance as evidence.

THE CFS PHOTO ANALYSIS UNIT contacted Kingston Police on July 9 with preliminary results of the examination of the automobile parts that Etherington had delivered. John Stefaniak had studied the surface of some of the pieces in cross-section under a microscope, looking for tiny fractures and scratches that were imperceptible to the naked eye. Continuity of these fine marks across the pieces would be evidence that they were once joined as part of a larger structure. Stefaniak concluded that the clear plastic pieces found at Kingston Mills and in the back of the Lexus matched and had come from the same assembly. This information, combined with Koopman's photographs and observations of the car on July 1 in Montreal, cemented in the minds of investigators one key fact about the early morning of June 30: the Lexus was damaged because it was used to push the Nissan into the water at Kingston Mills.

By the time detectives got word of the definitive match of the fragments by the CFS, a plan was already in motion to seize the Lexus without alerting the Shafias that police had a court order empowering officers to take it. Detectives were concerned about losing critical evidence, the vehicle itself. The Lexus was no longer, in their minds, simply a vehicle; it was the murder weapon. Detectives wanted it under their control, so that the scientists could examine it as closely as they would a killer's knife.

Hamed had taken the Lexus to Montreal and locked it in the garage, out of reach of police. Though Koopman had seen it, photographed it and retrieved items from it, police needed to get their hands on it so that scientists could conclusively match the plastic fragments to *this* Lexus. There were likely to be other clues inside or on the vehicle. The luxury SUV had a built-in global positioning system that might have recorded its movements. Or the vehicle could have brushed up against other objects at Kingston Mills, leading to a transfer of substances or patterns that might still be detectable. But there was nothing to stop the Shafias from disposing of the vehicle or hiding it.

THE FAMILY WAS FULL OF QUESTIONS FOR STEVE KOOPMAN: How were the victims positioned inside the Nissan? How did they die?

They drowned, Koopman explained, in his July 10 meeting with Shafia, Tooba, Hamed and a woman he had never met before, Zarmina Fazel. The middle-aged woman introduced herself as a cousin of Tooba. She spoke fluent English.

"Is it true the car was found in neutral and the driver's door was open?" Fazel asked.

"I'm really sorry, that is information that can't be released yet," Koopman replied.

Fazel and the others nodded in apparent understanding.

Shafia asked the detective what time the accident happened.

"We believe that it occurred sometime between one o'clock in the morning and eight thirty in the morning," Koopman replied, providing a deliberately vague answer.

"That's really wide," Hamed remarked.

Koopman had come alone to the Bonnivet apartment to provide an update on the investigation. But he also wanted a favour. He asked if police could take the family's Lexus for a few days for examination by Kingston ident officers. The detective asked politely, but he knew that he didn't have to take no for an answer. He had a warrant, drafted under a section of the criminal law that permitted him to seize it without disclosing the existence of the court order. Shafia agreed to Koopman's request, however, and the SUV was loaded onto a flatbed truck and hauled to a Montreal police department impound lot, where the Shafias believed it remained. From there, it was whisked to Kingston and plans were made to have it moved in a sealed trailer to the Centre of Forensic Sciences in Toronto.

Two days after the Lexus was hauled away from the apartment, Hamed began calling Koopman to ask about its return. Koopman missed the first call, on July 12, but Hamed called again the next day. Koopman had a pre-fabricated lie ready. He told Hamed the vehicle wouldn't be available for another day or two because the Kingston ident officers had been called away on another matter and weren't available to go to Montreal to inspect the Lexus. To make up for the inconvenience, Koopman told him that the family could rent another vehicle and Kingston Police would cover the cost.

"That's not really necessary," Hamed said. "I was calling more because I have a friend who fixes cars and he's not busy the next two, three days. He offered to fix it."

Hamed said he'd call again the following day, to check on the Lexus. As promised, on the afternoon of July 14, Hamed left a voice mail on Koopman's phone, asking about the SUV.

The next day, just after noon, Hamed called the detective again. There were two reasons for this call. Hamed asked about the Lexus, but he also wanted to let Koopman know that the family was planning to visit Kingston Mills that day or the next. Koopman told him that he'd check on the status of the SUV and get back to Hamed. The next day, July 16, the detective called Hamed and apologetically explained that the Lexus still had not been examined at the Montreal impound lot so it could not be returned.

"Can I go there and get it?" Hamed asked.

Koopman said that only Kingston Police had authority to release it. He renewed the offer to pay the cost of a rental vehicle but Hamed declined again. Koopman said he thought they might be able to clear all this up in a few days. The officer asked if Hamed and his father could come to Kingston on July 18 to sort things out. Koopman said he believed police would be able to return the family's possessions at that time, including the Lexus. Hamed said he'd check with his father.

The following night, just before eleven on July 17, Koopman placed a call to Hamed. He said he could meet the two Shafia men at the police sta-tion at two the next afternoon. Hamed said he and his father would drive to Kingston for the meeting. Koopman called at that late hour because investigators had been waiting for an important judicial authorization that was the result of days of meticulous planning.

For roughly two weeks, teams of officers had been driving daily to Montreal from Kingston. They had completed dozens of interviews with extended family members, including Latif Hyderi and Fazil Jawid, with the boyfriends of Zainab and Sahar, Ammar Wahid and Ricardo Sanchez, and with school officials. They had amassed hundreds of pages of statements and documents that suggested a lethal plot had been hatched inside the Shafia home roughly ten weeks before the sunken car was found. The conspirators had closed ranks to protect their secret, and investigators had been unable to penetrate their familial solidarity. They decided to risk exposing their covert probe in a bid to hear what was being said behind closed doors. The payoff could be substantial.

Props were in place and the script had been rehearsed. The performance was scheduled for Saturday afternoon, July 18, at Kingston Mills.

PART FIVE

Closing In

"May the Devil shit on their graves."
—Mohammad Shafia

15

Intercepted

DETECTIVE CONSTABLE GUY FORBES HAD BEEN SUSPICIOUS from the very beginning, and what he had seen in the morgue, late on the evening of June 30, unnerved him. Shafia and Tooba had followed him to the basement of the hospital. The four bodies lay on their backs, side by side on waist-high gurneys. White sheets concealed them so that only their faces and hair were visible. The mother and father had been told that police needed definitive identifications. It would be painful to see the girls and Rona this way, they were cautioned, but it was necessary.

What was going through their minds? he wondered. Forbes's one-year-old daughter would have a sibling soon—a playmate and conspirator in household mischief. His family would grow to four members and he thought it was just the right number. Earlier that day, police had delivered to Shafia and Tooba the grim news that their family had lost four members, but until that moment they had not seen proof of it. They had not seen the dead. The Shafias still lived in the neverland of deniability. Maybe their daughters weren't dead. Maybe it was all a big mistake. Maybe it was a bad dream. Forbes had shepherded the bereaved to this crossroads before, where a mother, father or spouse peered into the face of death and gasped for air as denial was crushed from their chests.

Tooba seemed to feel the weight. Her legs quivered as she entered the room and she began to sob—big, choking, guttural sobs. She clasped her hands to her face and stopped walking. Shafia did not stop. He strode purposefully to the end of the first gurney and pointed one finger at the serene face.

"Zainab," Shafia said, in an unwavering voice. He did not linger. He did not cry. He walked to the next gurney and pointed at the face.

"Geeti," he said. He was still walking.

"Sahar," Shafia said, pointing, still moving.

Then, "Rona," as he pointed a final time.

His work identifying the bodies complete, he looked at his sobbing wife and spoke brusquely to her: "Tooba! Tooba! Tooba!"

The tone implored her to contain her emotion. He was not yelling, but he was reproaching her, Forbes thought.

Shafia led her out of the room. The couple's first opportunity to see their dead children had lasted a few minutes. The parents did not touch the faces of their daughters. They did not kiss them or caress them or clutch their hands longingly. They seemed devoid of any parental instinct to cherish them. Shafia completed his duty, to identify them, and then he left. Forbes concealed his reaction, but he was horrified.

Nearly three weeks later, on Saturday, July 18, as the detective rehearsed his lines, he wondered if Tooba had performed for him in the morgue that night. Investigators were certain that she, Shafia and Hamed had conspired together to murder the girls and Rona, but they weren't certain what role each had played. They hoped that the ruse they were about to employ would help answer this question.

Two vehicles, an unmarked police cruiser and the Pontiac Montana minivan carrying Shafia, Tooba and Hamed, pulled into the parking lot of the Kingston Motel East. Forbes, who was behind the wheel of the cruiser, and his partner had asked the trio to follow them from police headquarters to the motel where the family had stayed eighteen days earlier. Forbes walked up to the driver's-side window of the van.

"We want to take you through what we think happened. Like, just, we're not a hundred percent sure, obviously, 'cause we weren't there but just from, you know, trying to put the pieces together, this is what we think may have happened."

Forbes, a short, solid man with a bald head, had a golly-gosh tone.

"So, we think they started here," he continued, gesturing to indicate the motel parking lot. "Then the locks are north from here. So we think they pulled out of here and went north. Whether they were—"

Hamed interrupted. "Okay, is the place, like, about a couple of minutes?"

"Yes, it's maybe three minutes drive from here," Forbes answered. "It's close."

"'Cause the station, from the station to here was about ten minutes, right? So . . ."

"Yeah, it's about ten, but from here to where we're going, the site is about three minutes," Forbes said. "It's close."

"Okay."

"So we think that . . . plus it was dark so we think they may have pulled out here to just go for a drive and because it was so dark . . . You'll see, it's kind of confusing."

"Okay," Hamed said.

"So they may have gotten lost or something," Forbes suggested, improvising dialogue about the "accident" that police had told the Shafias they believed had claimed the lives of their family members. He told Hamed to follow him, then got back in the cruiser.

"Is this the motel that we were in?" Tooba asked, as soon as the officer was gone.

"Mmmm," Shafia mumbled, telling his wife that police had brought them to the spot to demonstrate that it was a three-minute drive from the motel to Kingston Mills.

The police car pulled out of the motel parking lot and headed north on Highway 15, and the minivan followed.

In a living-room-sized office crammed with desks and computers 130 kilometres north of Kingston Mills, buried inside a two-storey office building, an officer wearing headphones noted the time the conversation began inside the minivan, 3:40 p.m. The monitor officer in the Ottawa police department building on Greenbank Road checked to ensure that the digital recording system was capturing the conversation. He told Sergeant

Mike Boyles, the Kingston officer who was standing beside him, that the signal from the probe was good and the conversations were being recorded.

The minivan had been bugged at the Kingston Police station nearly two hours earlier. Conversations inside it were now being beamed to Ottawa and recorded at the surveillance monitoring site, the nerve centre of the bug and wiretap operation, known to investigators as the "wire room" or the "backroom." Police in the capital had made the facility, staffed by Ottawa officers and civilians, available to Kingston investigators.

When the Shafias had arrived in Kingston at two that afternoon, they were invited inside police headquarters to retrieve belongings they had left behind at the motel on June 30. They were told to park their minivan inside the police garage and leave it unlocked, with the keys inside, in case police needed to move it.

Forbes had taken the Shafias to a second-floor boardroom where an ident officer with a camera was waiting. Socks, shirts, dresses, sweaters, tote bags, toiletries and dozens of other personal items were spread out on the big wooden table. Forbes explained that police needed to document the items handed over. He held up each item and asked the Shafias if they recognized it, knowing that they would. Each item was then photographed and returned to the family.

The laborious process took more than an hour, plenty of time for officers on the ground floor to attach the listening and tracking device to the minivan.

Forbes also told the Shafias that the Lexus would be returned to them later. Before he could outline the final component of the ploy, Tooba asked if the family could see the spot, the place where her daughters and Rona died. Forbes agreed to the request, though the trip had always been part of the plan. Props were in place at Kingston Mills.

THE VEHICLES APPROACHED THE MILLS FROM THE EAST, following the same route that the Nissan Sentra might have taken. They parked in a lot on the west side of the locks and walked across the bridge to the east side of the canal. Forbes and his partner, Detective Brian Pete, led the trio to the stone ledge where it appeared the Nissan Sentra had fallen into the canal. Forbes pointed to the water and explained that this was where the car was found.

Tooba wobbled, as she had in the morgue eighteen days earlier, and began to weep. Hamed steadied his mother as she clutched her face. Forbes wondered whether the theatrics were the product of guile or guilt. He thought Tooba seemed genuinely distraught, and he feared she might fall off the ledge. Shafia seemed unmoved, just as he had appeared in the morgue. Forbes detected no flicker of emotion. The officer gave the family members a few moments to digest the scene before he began his monologue.

"Now, I wanted to tell you that, we haven't made this public knowledge yet, for investigative purposes, you know, but there's a camera here," Forbes said, gesturing toward a squat, two-storey building thirty metres east of where the group was standing. Even at that distance, the unmistakable half-dome of a plastic surveillance camera housing was visible on the blockhouse that overlooked the property on the east side of the canal. Police had just installed the dummy camera housing.

"Just so you understand, we haven't released this information because we're analyzing the data," Forbes continued. "We're still going through it."

Hamed began to speak in Dari, translating for his parents what the officer had said.

Forbes thought the trio looked concerned. They were staring at him blankly but did not ask him to explain the import of his information. As the group stood in silence for a moment, Forbes spotted the characteristic, stiff-legged stride of his boss. Staff Sergeant Chris Scott was right on cue, storming across the swing bridge toward the group standing at the canal ledge. The stern look on Scott's face was obvious as soon as he turned toward them. He was still a few strides away when he asked Forbes what he was doing.

"We're just, you know, showing them the spot, and we told them about the camera and then we'll take them back to the station and give them the Lexus," Forbes said.

"Whoa, whoa," Scott said, frowning. "What are you talking about?"

Forbes recoiled but didn't reply. Scott seemed angry and his voice grew louder.

"What's wrong with you guys? How stupid can you be? They're not getting the Lexus back. I didn't authorize that. You shouldn't be talking about the camera."

Scott turned to the Shafias. His face softened and he lowered his voice, making it clear his anger was directed at his investigators, not the family. "We didn't want to say anything yet," Scott said, gesturing toward the camera that Forbes had pointed at minutes earlier. "The camera is right there but we haven't got anything from it yet."

Scott didn't offer the Shafias the opportunity to quiz him. He shot his officers a disapproving look as he turned and walked away. Forbes waited until Scott was out of earshot before he spoke again.

"Oh, jeez, I'm sorry, I guess we're not giving you the Lexus back today," Forbes said sheepishly. "I'm sorry about that. I guess there was a miscommunication at our end." The Shafias seemed unfazed and accepted that they would have to return to Montreal without the Lexus.

Within minutes of getting back in the van and heading toward home, the Shafias seized on the suggestion that there might be video footage of events at Kingston Mills.

"They said that big white place, that room there, it has a camera," Hamed told his parents, speaking in Dari. "They say they want to see if the camera has recorded anything or not. They said there's a camera near the water."

"They're lying," Shafia said dismissively. "If there was a camera, they'd access it in a minute. A camera is supposed to be placed outside, not inside. It can't take a picture from behind a wall."

Shafia did not seem to understand that the camera was attached to the exterior of the building. He asked Hamed to explain more clearly what the police officers had said.

"The guy that came later, he said that?" But he didn't wait for Hamed to answer. "If there's a camera, it's outside, not on the inside."

Tooba parroted her husband's dismissiveness. "If there had been a camera, they would have taken it out a long time ago and checked it," she said.

"Yeah," Shafia agreed.

"They wouldn't have left it like that," Tooba continued. "They're just lying. They're trying to sound us out."

"No, there's no camera there," Shafia repeated. "The other one told me there's no camera there. Had there been a camera there, the other two would have mentioned it. He said, 'We don't know where the car came from.' Did he say that to you too?"

"Yeah," Hamed replied.

Shafia asked about other things that the police officers had mentioned, the gate at Kingston Mills and the Nissan.

"He said the gate might have been open, then he said the government opens it," Shafia said. "Isn't that what he said?"

"I don't know," Hamed answered. "God knows."

Shafia repeated his belief that police were lying. "Now they are looking at the impacted part of the Lexus. It does not match that other."

"There was no camera," Tooba interjected again. "They're lying."

"Huh?" Shafia said.

"There was no camera," Tooba repeated. "If there had been a camera, they would have taken that out first thing on the very first day."

"Yeah," Shafia agreed.

Tooba hesitated. "It's been twenty days now," she said, apparently forgetting how long her daughters had been dead.

"Yeah," Shafia agreed.

Tooba suggested that they should not tell the three children at home in Montreal, Mina, Zafar and Fereshta, where they had been and what they had seen. They should say only that they retrieved clothing at the police station.

Shafia wondered aloud where the police had taken the family's Lexus, and remarked that the officers had made a big fuss about returning the clothing, but Tooba seemed preoccupied. She said nothing about the Lexus or the clothing.

"There was no camera over there," she said for the fourth time. "I looked around, there wasn't any. If, God forbid, God forbid, there was one in that little house, all three of us have come, no?"

Police had been eavesdropping for just fifty minutes when Tooba implicated the trio in a secretive visit—"all three of us have come"—to a building at Kingston Mills—"that little house"—together. In that little house, something had happened that would somehow imperil them if—"God forbid"—a camera had witnessed it. Shafia agreed that police would have taken Tooba into custody on June 30 if there had been a camera.

"No, had there been one there, they would have checked it and I swear they wouldn't let you that night," Shafia said. "It earlier [unintelligible (u)]"

The remainder of his sentence wasn't intelligible, one of many frustrating blank spots for investigators. Bugging a vehicle is a tricky enterprise. Wind, road noise and background sounds muddied the recordings, but already, Kingston investigators had collected a critical piece of information: the Shafias had been to Kingston Mills, an admission they had not made in the eighteen days since the deaths.

"God so took away their common sense, they didn't think," Tooba said. "They had no business there."

"God knows and his works," Shafia said. "That night, there was no electricity there, everywhere was pitch darkness. You remember, Tooba?"

"Yes," his wife answered.

"There wasn't the slightest glimmer of light or electricity," Shafia continued. "Even that room's light was off." Shafia didn't explain which room's light was off.

He reminded his son that the pair had been to Kingston Mills previously: "If they take picture, you and I have been once before, neh?" Shafia said. "Once, we came before that, you and us and once after. We came to Niagara, then once more, it was three, four times."

"Unless they have a camera, it's going to be hard for them to find," Hamed said. "He said, 'We're going to search the cameras.'"

"Did he tell you that?" Shafia asked. "Where are they going to look?"

"They will be looking. Heard in news."

"It was mentioned in the news? Did you check the news?"

"On the Internet several days ago," Hamed said. "They said they're going to check the video."

"Cameras on the road and other places, eh?" Shafia remarked.

"Those places," Hamed said.

The discussion of roadside cameras rekindled Tooba's concern about a camera at Kingston Mills. "Hamed, do you think that little house had a camera?" she asked, but she did not wait for a reply. She seemed content to repeat what they all had agreed upon earlier: "If it did, they would have taken it out a long time ago."

"No, Tooba," Shafia offered reassuringly.

"No, no, not known," Hamed said. "If they look, for example, they want to find proof that this person was sitting in the car at that time. Something like that."

"A camera is supposed to be visible," Shafia suggested. "It won't take pictures if it's in a hidden spot. If you put your finger in front of the lens, nothing will be there. Doesn't make sense."

"No, if it's behind a glass, it can still capture an image," Tooba said.

"Yeah, it can," Hamed agreed. "No, that camera, it can record anywhere."

"That little house had a glass," Tooba noted. "I saw it."

Shafia did not agree with his family members about the possibility of a camera on the building. "It did have a glass but wouldn't be placed behind the glass. They need to place the camera above the thing. If they put it behind the glass, you can't tell from there."

After nearly two hours of bugged conversation in the van, Hamed thought to warn his parents: "Right now the car was at the police place, it was with open," he announced. "They can fasten something to record your voice."

"Why did you leave it open?" Shafia asked.

"They themselves said to leave it open, in case a person wants to get out."

The caution had no effect on Shafia, who seemed unable to stop talking.

"Whatever type of camera it may have been, they would have checked it during the twenty days. If they had had any proof, they would have come a long time ago. They wouldn't have left you, me, or your mother, alone.

Or they would have [u] had they suspected . . . they're only thinking about the accident of it. If there had been cameras, and there hadn't been any accident [u] this and that didn't have any role on this . . . They're keeping the car because they want to render a person's morale weak, do you understand, Tooba?"

"Mmmm," she responded.

The more he talked about cameras, the more Shafia convinced himself there were none, or if they existed, they did not yield "any proof" that incriminated the trio because, if police had perused the footage, they would surely have arrested the father, mother and son by now.

When the trio arrived home in Montreal, Tooba awoke from a light sleep and spoke about her dead daughters.

"Their boyfriends and all are wandering about fit and happy," she said. "They've gone under the ground."

Shafia refused to join her commiseration: "Damn on their boyfriends. To hell with them and their boyfriends [u] filthy and rotten children. They exceeded all [u] they run away or do this or do that."

Shafia's curse was the last recording captured by police from inside the minivan on July 18, but the three were inside the vehicle again the next evening. The conversation focused first on Mina, who was resisting the family's plan to move to the new house under construction in Brossard, on Montreal's south shore. Mina would have to switch schools.

"You would say we've taken them and thrown them into hell," Shafia said. "They take on such airs! You can see yourself that we are going to a better house, not a worse one. For example, if we move from here to our own house, it is bigger and newer. If we don't like it here, if it messes up our program, we'll go to Toronto. Then where we would go?"

Shafia had not forgotten that some of his children had appealed to youth protection authorities for help. "Do they want to go to what is called DPJ or MPJ? Like others? We do this way. [u] this so God's curse wouldn't be coming upon them like it did on the others. [u]"

"Let this current problem resolve, then we think of this," Hamed said.

Tooba defended Mina. "She says, 'I went to this school for two years [u]

I never, for even one day, had either a boyfriend nor have I even once called the number of neither boy nor girl from home.'"

"Tooba, they said the same thing," Shafia remarked dismissively, apparently meaning he had heard the same protestation from Zainab and Sahar.

"She says, 'They found one from the very beginning,'" Tooba continued, still in defence of Mina. "Immediately upon going, on the following day, they found one but, 'I went there for two years, I kept myself' [indistinct] and also, she says she would be with Zafar at the same school so she would go with Zafar and come back with Zafar."

"Zafar is not that mature. He was with the Pakistani boy, used to take Sadaf there," Shafia complained, using Zainab's first name. "Used to sit with him. Would a son be like that? God's curse on such a son."

Shafia made it clear he did not trust his younger son, who had befriended Ammar Wahid. Shafia referred to Ammar as *lunda,* a Dari slur for "lover." "Used to chat on the phone with his sister's *lunda.* Used to, you know, with his sister's *lunda.* I don't count on Zafar until he grow up. I'm even fearful that he might find her a boy like the other God-cursed girl who took Zafar's friend as her boyfriend."

"She did it herself," Tooba insisted. "Zafar didn't find for her."

"No, Tooba, he spoke with the Pakistani just now," Shafia said.

Tooba insisted that Zafar only spoke to Ammar, "the Pakistani," "because of photos."

"Whatever she threw in our way, she did," Shafia said. "We lost our honour. For me, the issue was no taunt because even if they were to wear clothes made from Koran, the four of them, even if they were to scatter the pages of the Koran in front of me, I wouldn't tell to their face. This because even my father couldn't have accepted such [u] I don't say they are doing such behaviours, but I think it will create more headaches."

Tooba and Shafia continued to bicker about whether Mina should be permitted to choose a new school. The conversation seemed spurred by concern that she too might begin consorting with boys and acting shamelessly.

"The important thing is that they are away from these friends and stay away from such friends," Hamed told his parents.

Shafia had either forgotten Hamed's warning the day before that the van could be bugged, or he did not care if it was. Eighteen minutes after the police recording began, he unleashed a venomous rant about Zainab and Sahar.

"Even if they come back to life a hundred times, if I have a cleaver in my hand, I will cut him/her in pieces. Not once but a hundred times, as they acted that cruel towards you and me. For the love of God, what had we done? What harm did we done to them? What excess had we committed that they found so rear up and, as Iranians say, undressed themselves in front of boys? [u] I swear by God, every night when I see shed tears of blood in your eyes. Every night I used to think of myself as a cuckold [u] Everyday I used to go and gather her from the arms of boys. If we remain alive one night or one year, we have no tension in our hearts, our daughter is in the arms of this or that boy, in the arms of this or that man. God curse on their graduation! Curse of God on both of them, on their kind. God's curse on them for generation! [u] May the Devil shit on their graves! Is that what a daughter should be? Would be such a whore? [unintelligible exchange]Honourless girl! I doubt they even were doing this there. They might have removed their scarf once going out of the house."

Tooba reassured Shafia that his daughters had been good girls in Dubai—"there"—before they moved to Canada. "No, I am sure they were not like this there," she said. "I didn't see them doing that."

Her reassurance did not cool his anger.

"No, no, what you saw or didn't see doesn't matter much, you know [u] Shameless girl, with a bra and underwear. I swear to God that even those who do ads of such clothes are not like that."

Shafia believed Zafar and Mina had concealed the shameful conduct of their siblings.

"And these two others are hiding her photos," he continued. "That is why am afraid. If they were good children, they should have told us on time that, 'dad or mom, they are doing this or that."

"I'm not defending Mina," Tooba said. "In the two years that s/he has come [u]."

Shafia interrupted her. "I heard later about their *rafiqbazi?*" he asked, using a Dari word with no English equivalent that describes promiscuous behaviour with friends.

"She began the *rafiqbazi* after Sadaf ran away," Tooba offered, blaming Zainab's flight from the house as Mina's motivation for misbehaviour. "There was no *rafiqbazi* before that. I told you, once Mina came to me and said that Ukrainian boy came and said, 'What kind of religion is this? You guys don't have fun. Why are you so down?' Mina told me everything."

"I am not saying that Mina is lying to us," Shafia said. "I am saying that if they could trick us in this age, they could possibly trick them as well."

"Both Zafar and Mina said that we should be careful of their behaviour," Tooba added.

"We shouldn't be discussing what has happened, but once we come up the current problem, we would move to Brossard and have them continue their school there," Hamed interjected. "We will pick them up from school and drop them back to school."

Shafia made it clear that he would have the final say on the family's course and would consider drastic action if the children could not be kept in line: "Or if we feel that it is not working that way, we will move back to Dubai."

16

"Sadaf Was Already Done"

CHRIS SCOTT COULDN'T BELIEVE WHAT HE WAS BEING TOLD.

"Are you sure that's what you heard?" he asked the officer who relayed translations of some of the intercepts: "May the Devil shit on their graves." "Filthy and rotten children." "Whore." "Honourless girl."

Scott didn't doubt the wire room monitors or the interpreters, but with two teenagers at home, he had a hard time believing that any father would speak this way of his children, of his dead daughters. It was a new element to consider in the arrest planning. *Did Shafia pose a danger to his other children?* Scott wondered. The decision to arrest Shafia, Tooba and Hamed had not yet been made, and, as case manager, Scott was ultimately responsible for making the call. The wiretaps had been in place for only two days and already investigators had accumulated lengthy passages of incriminating conversation. Two key questions remained unanswered in their minds: How were the victims killed, and what role did each conspirator play?

It was too soon to make the arrests, but an important date was approaching. Scott knew that Hamed was scheduled to fly to Dubai at 7:55 p.m. on July 22. Hamed had booked the flight on the same day that the bug was installed in the minivan. That day, police also began eavesdropping on the Shafias' phone calls.

On Monday, July 20, Hamed had a conversation with an agent from Qatar Airways that piqued Scott's interest. The agent called Hamed to confirm the details of his booking and credit card payment. Hamed confirmed that his departure was set for Wednesday, July 22, but then made an unusual request for a last-minute change.

"Is it, ah, possible to make it tomorrow, or uhm . . . or, or, is that a problem?" Hamed asked.

"Actually no, we . . . it's just, you know . . . you already received a confirmation e-mail, Mr. Shafia," the agent responded.

"Ah, yeah, okay."

Hamed did not tell the agent why he had hoped for an earlier departure date. Scott wondered if the Shafias sensed that investigators were closing in. He knew that he would have to make the arrest decision soon.

LATER THAT MONDAY EVENING, at seven thirty, Shafia and Tooba were together inside the minivan, talking again about their dead daughters. Tooba said the girls had complained that he meddled in their lives, and she noted that he had called his daughters filthy and *padar la'nat,* a caustic slur literally translated to "child of hellhound father."

"Tooba, except for their sinning and fornication, whenever did I call her 'filthy' and '*padar la'nat'*? Whenever did I call her filthy except when they ran away? Which one did I call filthy? You tell me."

"No, before you tell, she wrote that," Tooba answered, apparently referring to Zainab.

Shafia protested that if he used the slur, he had insulted himself. He insisted that he had hit the children only once, when they were out late.

"They're gone now, shit on their graves," he said.

Tooba's response was unintelligible against the background sound in the car. But half an hour later, the bug in the minivan captured another diatribe by Shafia that began with a cryptic remark from his wife.

"I know Sadaf was already done, but I wish two others weren't," Tooba said.

Investigators wondered: Had a guilt-ridden mother voiced regret that Sahar and Geeti—"two others"—were killed, while acknowledging that

Zainab had sealed her fate with her extreme misconduct—she was "already done"? Had she so tarnished the family's honour that she must be killed?

"No, Tooba, they messed up," Shafia responded. "There was no other way. Look, Tooba, consider all the options. However you look at it in any way, she messed up big time."

Shafia puffed himself up with conspicuous indignation. "These others, was there a *talabgar* who had come for them, was it time for them to take husbands, had we refused the request? Tooba, for the love of God, look at what they did! For Sahar, it was neither the time for her, nor did she have a *talabgar,* so she had no excuse to say, 'You have refused the *talabgar*.' Right?"

"Mmmm," Tooba murmured, conceding to him a pulpit from which to excoriate their dead children. Shafia declared himself blameless because Sahar had ignored tradition. No suitor had come to ask her family for her hand. They had not refused any request for marriage. Yet the girl had sneaked off to engage in indecent acts.

"No, Tooba, they were treacherous," Shafia continued. "They were treacherous. They betrayed both themselves and us. Like this woman standing on the side of the road and if you stop the car, she would go with you anywhere. For the love of God, Tooba, damnation on this life of ours, on these years of life that we lead! When I tell you to be patient, you tell me that it is hard. It isn't harder than watching them every hour with *lunda*. For this reason, whenever I see those pictures, I am consoled. I say to myself, 'You did well. Would they come back to life a hundred times, for you to do the same again.' That is how hurt I am. Tooba, they betrayed us immensely. They violated us immensely. There can be no betrayal, no treachery, no violation more than this. By God! There isn't any!"

Shafia was fixated on snapshots that he had seen of Zainab and Sahar dressed in miniskirts and in bikinis, and embracing boys. He had congratulated himself—"you did well"—though he did not enumerate the creditable acts he vowed to repeat "a hundred times." Eavesdropping investigators believed that a patriarch obsessed with honour had just confessed that even if his "treacherous" daughters came back to life a hundred times, he would kill them again and again.

"Look, you and I, we carried these children on our backs," Shafia boasted. "We take them to Afghanistan, Dubai, here and there with the use money, we subjected ourselves to hardships, we took on drudgery for them. We wash their shit and pee, we wash their clothes, we take them to school and bring them back, however being in hard work, take them on picnic on Fridays, after all, should this have happened? No one does this. As far as home and cars and money go, everything was there, we used to give them money, we used to spend on them and for them, the only thing that we inhabited them from was *lundabazi*. That was the only 'wrong' we did them."

It was clear that for Shafia, the fact that he was willing to bear the cost of raising children elevated him to good-father status. He had been a provider of worldly comforts and he was willing to admit only that he denied his children freedom to be promiscuous—*lundabazi*.

Shafia returned to the theme that dominated his thoughts: loyalty to family and devotion to values passed down for generations. He believed his children were guilty of apostasy. It was a rationalization to explain their deaths, and, police believed, an excuse to justify his deeds.

"It was all treason," Shafia continued. "They committed treason from beginning to end. They betrayed kindness, they betrayed Islam, they betrayed our religion and creed, they betrayed our tradition, they betrayed everything."

THREE DAYS OF SHAFIA'S INVECTIVE WAS ENOUGH FOR CHRIS SCOTT. He believed that the other children could be at risk. Police shared their concerns with child protection authorities in Montreal and a plan was made to remove Mina, Zafar and Fereshta the next day. As soon as the children were out of the home, police would make a dramatic move that would mark the end of the cat-and-mouse game in which they had feigned incompetence. Investigators believed vital evidence was still beyond their grasp and the only way to get it was through a search warrant. In order to get a warrant, police would have to describe, in writing, the crime they believed had been committed. The warrant would reveal to the Shafias, if they didn't already know, that police suspected them of murder and that their arrests were imminent.

Rona's sister told investigators in an email that Zainab had written a letter before she fled the home in April, cataloguing abuses she had suffered. Police wanted to get their hands on the letter or any notes she made while writing it. Investigators also hoped that they might find evidence on computers in the Shafia home. They didn't know that one laptop would yield a trove.

Roughly a dozen Kingston Police officers, split between two teams, travelled to Montreal on Tuesday, July 21. The three children were removed from the apartment around suppertime that day by youth protection workers and police officers, and minutes later the search team, led by Chris Scott, moved in. The other team, led by Sergeant Carolyn Rice, interviewed the children at a Montreal police station.

At the apartment, Detective Constable Geoff Dempster showed the search warrant to Hamed. "Hamed Mohammad Shafia, Yahya Tooba Mohammd and Mohammad Shafia did unlawfully murder Rona Amir Mohammad, Zainab Mohammad Shafia, Sahari Mohammad Shafia and Geeti Mohammad Shafia, contrary to the Criminal Code section 235," was written in bold on the first page of the document. Hamed translated the accusation to his parents, and Shafia asked him to translate a question back to the officer.

"My dad wants to know why you think it's a murder and why you think we murdered them," Hamed asked.

"I'm not going to discuss the grounds, but I'm willing to explain anything that's on the face of this document," Dempster said.

The warrant empowered officers to search the residence on July 21 between 6 a.m. and 9 p.m., for "Notes of a letter made by Zainab, laptop computer, Pieces of Debris of the Lexus motor vehicle, Bank receipts, credit card receipts, financial statements." The Shafias were told they had to leave the apartment until the search was completed, although they were not being taken into custody. They weren't told that investigators were concealing listening devices inside the home. While one group of officers scoured the apartment, snapping photos and collecting items, others planted bugs. Dempster had fulfilled one of his key tasks. He had ensured that the Shafias knew police suspected them of murder. The newly installed bugs were expected to capture the family's reaction to this revelation.

Detective Nancy McDonald, who was part of the team cataloguing and collecting evidence, was struck by the spartan state of the home where ten people had lived for the past two years. Several rooms had area rugs, perhaps Iranian, with intricate patterns, but there were no pictures, posters or decorations on any of the walls in the eight rooms. Only two of the four bedrooms had furniture, small computer desks with folding, camp-style chairs. Slabs of foam, covered in fabric, served as beds. One of the foam mattresses was shoved up against the wall in a hallway leading to a common area that served as a family room, in the centre of the apartment. Six dining-room chairs lined the walls of this room, which had a small tube television on a stand.

Only the living room was fully furnished. It was stuffed with a matching tan-coloured couch, love seat and two plush chairs, plus two dining-room chairs, two end tables and a coffee table. On top of one end table was a pink photo album with "Princess" printed on the cover, above drawings of three cartoon princesses. It appeared to be the same album that Mohammad Shafia had tearfully shown reporters in early July. McDonald took the album.

One bedroom appeared to be a storage area. Two large plastic tote boxes and three full-size suitcases were strewn about the room, along with plastic bags, shoes and jewellery. The kitchen was littered with nearly a dozen steel cooking pots, scattered on the floor, on boxes and on the counters. There was no table in the attached dining area, nor did there appear to be any place for the family to sit and eat meals together.

McDonald looked through a small black suitcase that she found on the floor in one of the bedrooms. It was full, as if packed for a trip. In an outer pocket were Hamed's passport and the boarding passes from his visit to

Dubai in early June, just seven weeks earlier, when he had joined his father there. McDonald also found an odd assortment of forty snapshots inside the suitcase. There were ten photos of Sahar, including one image of her embracing Ricardo Sanchez on an outdoor veranda. Sahar wore sunglasses to shield her from the bright sun, a banana-yellow sweater and a denim miniskirt. Ricardo, dressed in a grey tank top and shorts, had his right arm wrapped around her waist and was pulling her tightly against his body.

Other photos showed Sahar with schoolmates, including several shots in which she hugged boys or was embraced by guy pals from the reception classes at St-Ex high school. They were not boys that Sahar dated. But for a father fixated on virginal modesty, the playful snaps of a pretty girl and her school friends would have appeared to be overwhelming evidence of promiscuity.

Investigators would soon conclude that these were the photos that reminded Shafia that he "did well." They believed the snapshots were taken to Dubai by Hamed when he travelled there May 31 to meet his father. Shafia had seen the photos only because his dutiful elder son—who spied on Zainab at school and who had tattled to his father that she had brought a boy to their home—hand-delivered the evidence of immodesty. When Shafia saw the images, his anger boiled over, police believed, and he decided to include his "treacherous" daughter Sahar in the plot already underway to murder Zainab. The discovery that some of the photos were printed from pictures on Sahar's cellphone was evidence of an unfolding conspiracy. Prosecutors considered it valuable proof that the killings were carefully planned.

Two dozen photos of Rona also tumbled out of the black suitcase. In most of the images, she was alone, smiling or grinning at the camera, and often dressed in a sleeveless gown or stylish top. In most of the photos, she wore makeup and jewellery. In some of the images, she mugged like a teenager, holding her arms above her head, crossing them on her chest, or pouting. Many of these photos of Rona had been taken in 2007, before she came to Canada. Investigators concluded Hamed had also couriered this evidence of immodest behaviour to Shafia too.

Officers scouring the apartment were frustrated in their search for the letter Zainab had reportedly left behind when she fled in April. They could not find any trace of it or any notes that she might have made as she drafted it, but as the search team pored over books and papers, they found an unexpected piece of documentary evidence. On a closet shelf, just above the hook where Shafia's favourite brown houndstooth sports jacket hung, was a steno-sized, spiral-bound notebook. Many of its 120 pages were filled with writing in Dari. The first inside page had three upper-case English words, including one that was misspelled: "RONA'S DAIRY BOOK."

The investigators had stumbled upon a seven-thousand-word account of life inside the dysfunctional Shafia home, in which a mostly absent patriarch abandoned all domestic responsibility to two feuding wives. By Rona's account, Tooba was the aggressor who sought to isolate Rona and push her out of the family. The diary, written between April and August 2008, in Canada, documented violence by Shafia and psychological abuse by Tooba, including taunting that had begun immediately after Rona's arrival. Police read that Rona was "miserable and upset." She had written that Tooba once told her, "Your life is in my hands."

Investigators marvelled at their good fortune. Shafia and Tooba had not made any effort to hide or destroy the damning record that portrayed them as a tyrannical pair who abused and alienated Rona.

Officers also seized a handwritten school assignment found in Hamed's room. Printed, block-letter words filled one and a half lined pages. It was written in English and titled, "Importance of Traditions and Customs." Littered with grammatical mistakes, misspellings and run-on sentences, the essay began:

> Traditions and customs are to be followed till the end of ones life, actually it doesnt matter at all weather your close to the community following the specific traditions or living millions of miles away. Tradition and customs of a person is like his identity and what makes him special even though living in another country.

Hamed, who was old enough to be attending a post-secondary institution, had earned a grade of 70 percent on the error-filled essay of juvenile ideas. It exposed him as a dullard who had been trained to follow family tradition.

Police left the apartment shortly after nine with an assortment of documents, two laptop computers and several pieces of jagged plastic that appeared to have come from the shattered headlight assembly of the Lexus, found in the attached garage. The Shafias were allowed back inside and told a lie—that police would contact them in a few days. Investigators wanted to surprise them when they appeared to arrest them, which they knew would be soon. The newly installed listening devices picked up their activity. The trio seemed to be moving around the apartment, trying to determine what police had taken. If there was panic or fear after the surprise police raid, the bugs did not capture it. All three family members noted that photos had been taken, passports and some financial papers.

Ten minutes after police left, Hamed called a youth protection worker who had been present when his three siblings were taken earlier that evening. Hamed left a voice mail asking if the family could schedule an appointment to see the children the next day. Shafia seemed more concerned about his business interests, now that it was clear police were closing in. He would need a capable proxy if the police put him in jail. Shafia wanted to talk to someone he trusted, a fellow Afghan.

"Make a call to Nabi," Shafia ordered Hamed. "I want to see him."

SHAFIA, TOOBA AND HAMED DROVE TO NEDA'S HOME on the south shore of Montreal and explained that the children had been taken. Shafia ranted about the Canadian government and Neda advised him to get a lawyer.

"If some things happen to me, you take care of my business," Shafia said. "I don't know tomorrow what will happen." Shafia did not tell Neda that police suspected the family of murder.

The Shafias also visited Zarmina Fazel, Tooba's aunt, who had helped the family navigate government regulations when they immigrated to Canada. She provided the name of an Afghan lawyer in Montreal and arrangements were made to see him the next morning. On the ride home to the apartment on Bonnivet, Shafia mused that some extended family members, including Latif Hyderi and Fazil Jawid, had talked to police.

"Good people said good things and bad people said bad things," Shafia said. "I know who said what."

As always, Shafia dominated the conversation. While his previous diatribes had been addressed to Tooba, this was for Hamed's benefit, exhorting his son to stoic resolve.

"I am happy and my conscience is clear," Shafia said. "They haven't done good and God punished them. No need to talk about it at home [u] my conscience, my God, my religion, my creed, aren't shameful [u] your mother's family. I could not tolerate this. I don't know about you. [u] Even if they hoist me up onto the gallows [u] nothing is more dear to me that my honour. Let's leave our destiny to God and may God never make me, you or your mother honourless. I don't accept this dishonour. So don't think about it anymore. World, these things happen. Either you accept that or this. Either you see them doing those bad things or hear that they did, but they did wrong. Who knows what we went through [u] we know and our life. We know and our work. We know what we have been through. We eat and do our routine work. We are not ashamed of our conscience, neither you, nor I, nor your mother. Be like a man. Your mother is also like a man. You should have tolerance you should have patience [u] I had told your mother in the past and I am telling her again now, 'Don't be a woman, be a man.' I know that your heart, your body, is different, that is, I know, but I am telling you, this is my word to you, be I dead or alive, nothing in the world is above than your honour like, if your sister or my daughter, or your mother's daughter to be with a *na mahram* and do nasty or dishonour work, even if, God forbid, they hoist us onto the gallows [u] isn't that right, my son?"

Hamed had no opportunity to answer. This was a rhetorical lesson on the honour code to which Shafia subscribed and on Islamic law, which forbade a female from associating with a *na mahram*—someone who was not a close relative and who therefore was a potential spouse—outside of marriage. Zainab and Sahar had both committed this sin—"nasty or dishonour work"—which Shafia refused to tolerate. It was sanctimonious vilification of the victims.

But Shafia was devoid of piety.

He did not attend mosque and he did not read the Qur'an daily, as had Rona. He knew only what he had seen growing up in Afghanistan, that women were the property of men and should be obedient, passive and chaste. In his household, the girls had been ordered not to associate with boys until they had completed their studies. Shafia saw no offence in calling his daughters "prostitutes" and "whores" when it was clear that they had ignored that rule. He was prepared to accept the consequences of his deeds, and he exhorted his son and wife to follow him.

"Don't think about it," Shafia continued. "Don't worry about it, whatever the eventuality, it is from God. We accept it wholeheartedly. Have your meals [u] we are not ashamed of our conscience. We have not done anything bad [u] just be a man, matured, and think of yourself like me [u] I know my enemies as of your mother's brothers. [u] I have worked all my life and collected whatever I have for you and all kids. God is great. We don't have any solution. There is nothing more valuable than our honour. I am telling your mother that be like a man as you have always been. I know it hurts. I have passed more experience in life than you. Don't worry at all. Don't regret or wish that this would have happened or that would have happened [u] I am telling you now and I was telling you before that whoever play with my honour, my words are the same [u] there is no value of life without honour."

Chris Scott had made the decision by the time Shafia's soliloquy in the van was complete. The trio would be arrested the following day in a surprise raid on their home, even though the wiretaps had not provided the *how* that police were seeking. Investigators had developed a theory that the victims were rendered unconscious with drugs or poison, or perhaps were drowned first, then stuffed into the Nissan Sentra before it was pushed into the canal. It seemed the only reasonable explanation for the failure of any of the four to attempt to escape the sinking car: they must have been dead or unconscious when the Nissan sank.

There were tantalizing bits of evidence to bolster this theory. Sahar had talked and texted non-stop during the Niagara Falls vacation, but her communications ended abruptly a half-hour after the family's late-night pit stop. Investigators wondered if the four victims had consumed spiked drinks during that stop.

Autopsies had found bruises on the tops of the heads of three of the victims, suggesting that each had banged into something hard or was struck by something in a similar place or position. Perhaps the victims were struck on the head to render them unconscious.

Investigators had also found unexplained references to antifreeze and to drugs in a text file concealed on Hamed's computer.

But investigators had not collected any definitive evidence that the victims were incapacitated, and there was nothing on the wiretaps to confirm the theory, save for Tooba's cryptic comment that "God forbid" a video camera captured the group, that night they were at a small building at Kingston Mills. Detectives wondered if it was a vague reference to the public washrooms at the site, a place where someone's face could be held underwater in a sink or a toilet. There was also a shallow pond, the turning basin, where someone could be held underwater.

17

"One Hundred Percent Caught"

SHAFIA'S PITILESS RANT IN THE MINIVAN about the treachery of his daughters and honour above all didn't end until almost midnight on July 21, his last full day of freedom. At about the same time, Kingston Police officers were completing their interviews with the three children who had been taken into protective custody earlier that day. They were the only other people who might have witnessed what happened the night the family stopped in Kingston and the Nissan plunged into the canal. If the victims were somehow incapacitated or killed before the car went into the water, surely the other children knew something of it?

But Mina and Fereshta each told police they did not know what had happened to their sisters and Rona. They were dropped off at the motel around 2:00 a.m. and awoke the next morning to the news that the four family members were missing, they said.

Zafar was interviewed last. He parroted the story that Shafia, Tooba and Hamed had told investigators when they were first interviewed on June 30. Zafar told the detective who interviewed him, Sean Bambrick, that the family decided to stop in Kingston on the way home from Niagara Falls because they were tired. He was asleep in the Lexus when his father woke him and told him to go into the motel, along with Mina and Fereshta. He recalled that it was exactly 1:53 a.m., because he looked at a clock. He went straight into the motel room, flopped onto a bed and went to sleep.

"And once I remember sa—, I think it was my sister coming to ask me for my cellphone and I had told her that, 'No, I don't know where it is. I'll give it to you later.' I mean, 'I'll gi—, I don't know where it is, like, I'm sleepy. I'll, I can't search it for you,' ya know," Zafar said.

"Which sister?" Bambrick asked.

Zafar said he believed it was Zainab.

"Why do you say that?"

"Because, like, I don't know, like, it was either my mom or my sister, one of these two."

"How could you get them confused?" the detective asked.

"Because, like, it was really late night and I was sleepy and they had just, like, came and asked me where was the cellphone so I had no, like, ya know, 'Leave me alone,' like, I was kind of like that, so I turned my back and slept."

This was the second time that Zafar had told police that someone came to his motel room and asked for his cellphone soon after they arrived in Kingston. He had given the same account during his interview on June 30, but with one significant variation. In his first account, Zafar said he was certain that it was Zainab who asked for the phone. Now, he was unsure whether it was his sister or his mother. The boy had never told investigators that he heard Zainab ask for the keys to the Nissan.

When the detective asked Zafar what he thought had happened to his sisters and Rona, he referred to his previous statements that when they were in Niagara Falls Zainab used to secretly take the keys to the Nissan and drive the car around the parking lot.

"They could have gone for a ride, either they could have went to get some food," he said, affirming the joyride theory his parents had promoted publicly and to police. When Bambrick suggested his fifty-year-old aunt was unlikely to agree to a joyride at 2:00 a.m., Zafar said his sister wouldn't respect what Rona said, if Rona tried to stop her.

Zafar corroborated the bulk of what police had already heard about a violent confrontation at the Shafia home one evening in early April, when the boy and two of his sisters, Geeti and Mina, returned home late from a trip to a shopping mall. Zafar left out Sahar, who, police had been told previously, was also with them. Zafar said that his father began shouting at them when they arrived at the house.

"Okay, and we had came, so he was like, 'Where were you guys?' and he started shouting so I kind of, like, told them that, like, you know, piss off," Zafar said. "Like, we didn't, we, it's only nine o'clock, like, we're not home like twelve at, at night, you know. So he had gotten physical with me and then physical with my sister so I stepped in. I was like, 'No, you can't touch her like that,' and then, ya know, he, he gave us some slaps and all that. But then next morning and a few weeks, like, a week after, we weren't really good with him, like we were, we weren't talk to him, like, we were mad at him but then, like, stuff got better."

The boy said the incident happened in the common area of the apartment on Bonnivet, about a week before Zainab ran away.

"Uh he, he kept on telling me, like, um, like, shut up and, and, uh, I kept on talking," Zafar explained.

"Right."

"So every time I spoke, he would slap me."

"And where would he slap you?" Bambrick asked.

"On my face." They were open-handed slaps, Zafar said, gently patting his cheek.

The detective asked which sister was hit.

"With both of them, I guess, so, he had given Mina a slap too."

"Yeah?"

"And Geeti too, a slap, but I, I, like, I got, like, most hits."

"Yeah? 'Cause you're older?"

"Yeah," Zafar answered but then quickly reversed himself. "No, I'm not older but, you know."

"Well, no, you're a guy," Bambrick noted.

"Yeah."

"Older than Geeti, sorry," the officer said.

"Yeah."

"Okay. Um, so how many slaps did you get compared to them?"

"Like, four, five, something like that."

"Okay, and those guys?"

"Uh, like, one, probably two, something. I don't know. Like, the thing was, I was in, like, ya know, I was going crazy 'cause I was getting hit for no reason."

When the hitting was over, Zafar said, Mina had "a mark" near her eye. He wasn't sure who had delivered the blow. "Uh, I don't know," he said. "I guess it was either my dad or my brother."

"Okay, 'cause I understand Hamed sometimes helps your dad?"

"Mmm-hmm," Zafar mumbled.

"With that kind of thing?"

"Mmm-hmm."

"Um, has he helped your dad with that kind of thing with you?" Bambrick asked.

"Yeah, once."

"Tell me about that one."

"Well, he didn't do much, like, after, like, he hit me, he just got me by my neck and he pulled me. That's, uh, what, the only thing I remember him doing to me."

Zafar told Bambrick that his mother usually tried to stop these assaults, by screaming and grabbing Shafia and Hamed.

In the final few minutes of the interview, Bambrick asked if he had been instructed by anyone to say certain things or to withhold information. Zafar insisted that he was being "completely honest."

Bambrick said police were certain that his father, mother and older brother had killed Zainab, Sahar, Geeti and Rona. Zafar did not flinch. The gangly boy, in a baggy grey T-shirt, blue nylon shorts and runners, seemed a guileless witness. He had been relaxed and attentive throughout most of the interview. He did not cry or tremble as the detective quizzed him about the deaths. But he had grown more fidgety as the conversation wore on, as Bambrick probed his memories in greater detail. By the end, he was pawing at the back of his neck with one hand, bouncing his left leg up and down, and twisting the collar of his T-shirt into a knot.

"One more thing," Zafar said. "That if I would know that they had done it, if I was a hundred percent sure, I would never have keepen quiet, like, ya know. You know, like, I would do the most arguing. The first time, I was the one who called the cops, ya know."

The boy seemed desperate to draft one final, grand argument that absolved his parents and brother. He suggested that they could not be murderers, because if they were, they would have killed him, because he was more troublesome than his dead sisters.

"I was the first one, ya know, to push them off me, you know, like, I would do the most stuff around here, you know, like, I've disobeyed their rules and everything, so the thing which makes me think, 'Why am I, I alive?' ya know, if, if it was me. I used to do, like, more stuff than any one of them then."

"So why not you, right?" Bambrick asked encouragingly.

"Yeah, so why not me? That's what I'm thinking. That's the second thing which gets it off my mind that it's that, ya know."

Zafar hadn't given a first reason, but his logic was absurdly simplistic and profoundly insightful. If his parents were capable of murder, why had they not killed him, since he was more mischievous than his siblings? His privileged status in the tribal patrilineage blinded him to an obvious answer: he was not female.

ONE HOUR AFTER ZAFAR TOLD DETECTIVE BAMBRICK that the possibility that his parents and Hamed were murderers was off his mind, he made a phone call to his big brother from the emergency foster home where he and his sisters had been taken. He no longer sounded like the ignorant child who knew nothing about the deaths and who had no doubts about the innocence of his family members. He sounded as if he had a secret, something that fostered dark thoughts.

"Hamed, like, this thing, um, like, Hamed, ah, should I kill myself, Hamed?" Zafar asked in a near whisper.

"No, man, don't do anything like that," Hamed replied in English.

"Hmm?"

"Don't do anything like that," Hamed repeated. His tone was flat. He didn't seem surprised to hear his little brother talking about suicide.

"Look, Hamed, you are one hundred percent caught, see," Zafar said breathlessly.

"[u] They are making up stuff," Hamed replied, in English. "Don't say these stuff on the phone, they'll say, they'll, you know [u] sort of thing for them."

"They won't know that we have called."

"Yeah, but still. But still, it's like, easily recorded."

This warning was too late, because it *was* recorded. Police continued to eavesdrop.

"Okay, you mean, okay, it's not safe to talk?" Zafar said. "All I'm saying, Hamed, keep a sharp ear, okay?"

Hamed told his little brother to call him back later that morning and urged him to take care of his sisters. When he hung up, it was 3:04 a.m. His father immediately quizzed Hamed about the eight-minute phone conversation.

"What did Zafar say?" Shafia asked.

Tooba wanted to know if Fereshta was there and if she had cried.

"Uh, he said no, when she cry here, after that, she hasn't cried," Hamed said. "What is it? You can tell by the way he's talking that he's saying that they took a video of them."

"When?" Shafia asked. "Who was talking?"

"Zafar," Hamed answered.

"Now they're going to see that from the beginning," Shafia said. "That, what was it [u] possible that [u] what did he say, meaning what did they ask him?"

"Lots, they asked him lots," Hamed said. "Said, they said, police from Kingston came and said, 'We are one hundred percent proof that the Lexus vehicle hit it from the back.'"

Shafia asked Hamed if the children had told police "that they saw in the hotel," an apparent reference to seeing Zainab at the motel in Kingston. The detail was a critical building block in the family's joyride story.

Hamed reassured Shafia that Zafar had told police he had seen Zainab at the motel. He told his father that investigators had told Zafar that they had proof the trio used the Lexus to push the Nissan into the water.

"They're taking it from the beginning," Shafia said. "They're lying. They're making things up."

Shafia peppered Hamed with questions about what police had asked his children, but not once did he ask *about* the children. He did not inquire about their emotional state, their fears or anxiety since they had been forcibly taken from home nearly ten hours earlier.

At 3:23 a.m., Hamed's cellphone rang again.

"Hello, Hamed?" asked eight-year-old Fereshta, her voice a barely audible squeak.

"Yeah."

"Hamed, are you able to pass it to my mom?" the child asked.

"Yes, just wait a minute."

"Okay, thanks."

She sniffled as Hamed passed the phone to Tooba.

"Hello?"

"Hello," Fereshta answered, her voice tiny and quivering.

"Yeah, Fereshta?"

"Yes, mother?" the girl said, the words barely escaping her throat.

"Yes?"

"How are you?" the child asked.

"I'm good," Tooba replied. "How are you?"

Shafia seemed to admonish Tooba in the background: "Don't cry."

"Good, mother," Fereshta answered. "Are you coming tomorrow?"

"What?" Tooba asked.

"Are you coming tomorrow?" Fereshta repeated. "I want to see you."

"Yes, I am going to come to you tomorrow. Okay?"

"Okay."

"Yeah, did you eat food?"

"Yeah." Fereshta was still sniffling through the remnants of sobs.

"Don't cry, okay?" Tooba said. "You are with Mina and Zafar."

"Okay."

"Nothing is going to happen."

"Okay."

"Don't cry, okay?" Tooba repeated.

"Okay."

"Is Mina with you?"

"Yeah."

"Always stay with Mina and Zafar. Okay?"

"Do you want to talk to Mina?" Fereshta asked.

"Yeah, eat your food properly. Okay?"

"Okay."

"Don't cry anymore. Okay?"

"Okay."

"Give it to Mina," Tooba said.

"You want me to give it to Mina?"

"Yes, give it to Mina."

Fereshta could be heard telling her sister, "Here, take it. It's Mother."

Tooba's conversation with her youngest child, their first chance to speak since the little girl was wrenched from home, lasted fifty seconds. The mother did not tell her terrified, tearful child that she loved her, that she missed her dearly, or that she was anguished to be apart from her.

Tooba then spoke to Mina for three and a half minutes. As soon as Mina came on the line, Shafia wanted to know about his daughter's conversation with police.

"What did they tell this one? Ask," he instructed Tooba.

Tooba asked Mina if she had been given something to eat and if she was with her siblings, and she said that "hopefully" she would visit the next day. But after those perfunctory questions, she began to quiz the girl.

"What did they ask you? Did you all tell them the same stories?"

"Yes, yes," Mina replied.

"Okay, okay. Did they tell you anything else?"

"They said, what was it, I said, 'Why are you asking questions like this?' They said, 'We have suspicion over your mother, father and Hamed.'"

"They said they have suspicion?"

"Yes."

"Okay."

Mina explained that police had told her they wouldn't have taken this action unless they were certain about what happened.

"Say they're lying," Shafia told Tooba.

"They said, 'Unless we are one hundred percent sure of something, we don't have the authority to talk about it or take the children like this,'" Mina said.

"Okay, just let them say what they want," Tooba responded. "At no time did I do something like this and at no time did this happen. Let them take us wherever they want. If they want to take us somewhere, they can take us."

"They told us, 'We are not allowed to just take them to jail, we have to prove it.' Do you understand?"

"Yeah."

"For example, you should get a lawyer and keep saying, 'No, we didn't do it.'"

"Yeah, besides we didn't do it," Tooba said. "They said, 'We're not allowed until to take them to jail until it proven?'"

"Yeah."

Tooba asked about the sleeping quarters and other children in the foster home, and then asked Mina to pass the phone to Zafar. The boy asked his mother what police had said.

"They didn't say anything to us," she answered. "They took us out and they said, 'We are going to search the house.' They didn't say anything else. They made us sit outside."

"Hmm."

"They searched the house. They took the laptops. They searched the house. They didn't say anything else."

"They took the laptops?"

"Yes. They took the laptops."

"Both of them?"

"Yeah."

"That's it?" Zafar asked. "They only took the laptops, or anything else too?"

"They took the laptops and apparently some papers here and there and some bank documents," Tooba answered. "They took these. They put those things in a bag and they didn't show us but they took it. And what else, they didn't tell us anything else. No. No, they said we're going to do, what was it, we're going to take the laptops and we have permission to search them and take these things and search your house. Finish."

"It's just that, why would they take the laptops?" asked Zafar, who seemed preoccupied with the revelation.

His mother was worried about what her son had told police.

"The things you said before, did you tell them the same thing again?" Tooba asked.

"Yeah."

"Okay, well done," Tooba said, relieved that her son had offered consistent stories. "Let them be, say, they have suspicion. Wherever it be, we'll go with them. Let them have suspicion. One thing [u] tells them to separate my children from me. We have suspicion."

Shafia interjected again, while Tooba continued to talk to Zafar, telling her: "They should say, 'We want to go home.'"

"What was it, so they said they're going to take the laptops for the reason that . . . are the police [u] the door so they don't let you go anywhere?" Zafar asked.

"No, they left."

"Oh, they left?"

"Yeah. They left at the same time. It was around nine thirty or ten when they left. They finished their search and they left."

"Okay."

"Yeah."

"Besides, what does Hamed have to say about all this?" Zafar asked.

"Hamed says that, he says that people told many times. Perhaps people called a lot from all four sides from our family and community that, 'They did it.' The woman said that because of that, we took all the bank papers to check the account to see what types of thing you took money out for."

"Okay."

Tooba wondered what police had told her youngest son: "Are they saying that they have one hundred percent proof or just suspicion?"

"The man told me that, 'I believe that those three did it.'"

"Yeah, let them," Tooba scoffed. "Let them say that. Let them say. People have called and told them. Sadaf would always go to Hussain every minute and tell him. Go here and there and he told Anwar and that cursed woman told everything."

It was everyone else's fault that police were after them, Tooba was complaining, even her dead daughter Zainab, who had spent "every minute" sharing family secrets with her boyfriends. Investigators believed "that cursed woman," who also had broken the code of family secrecy, was Rona and "Anwar" was actually Ammar.

"I say, let them say what they want to say, my child," Tooba continued. "As long as you are happy and you don't worry about anything, I will, hopefully, I told you, come to see you. If you guys act stubborn and say, 'Let us go home,' they won't let you?"

"No. We asked so much. They said, 'It's not safe for you there.'"

"Okay."

"So now, my father, are all three of you awake?"

"Yeah. Yeah, we're awake," Tooba answered.

In the background, Shafia told Tooba to tell the children they should run away from the foster home. Tooba didn't repeat Shafia's suggestion, but passed the phone to Hamed after Zafar asked to speak to his brother. Hamed left the room where he had been with his parents.

"So everything's going okay there?" Zafar asked.

"Like, we don't know for sure yet cause I don't want to lie too," Hamed answered. He asked if police had interviewed his siblings for a long time.

"Yeah, for, like, each one of us a long time, like, one hour each, I guess, so."

"And they just told you, like, 'Say the story now'?"

"Yeah. They're like, 'Say the story. Where did you guys stop and everything.' The guy was like, 'Me, I think that, what do you think?' I was, like, I told [u] nothing like that can happen, you know, like, these are our parents and everything. They liked us. They said there was a complaint before that they used to hit Zainab and everything. I was, like, 'Yeah, but you know,' what did I tell them, I was, like, 'Yeah, but, you know, I use to do the most bad stuff and all that but they didn't kill me and everything.' I said them, all those kind of stuff. But the guy was, like, 'Me, you know, I think they did it.'"

"Which one?" Hamed asked.

Zafar explained that it was a policeman that he had not met before, a reference to Detective Sean Bambrick.

"What do you think will happen?" Zafar asked.

"I don't know. They are saying that they have, they think we ki—, we did it. But, um, if, uh, I don't know if they [u] a lot, you know, maybe they are going to put us in jail. I don't know, but don't tell this to Mina and Fereshta 'cause they'll be crying."

Zafar said police could not do anything if they didn't have proof. He seemed to be trying to reassure his brother.

"We're gonna tell the truth," Hamed said. "We're gonna say, 'Yeah, we didn't do it.'"

Zafar said he and the girls would "keep saying the truth," that their parents and Hamed were innocent. But he didn't seem to believe that this protestation would be enough to save his family.

"What are we going to do till the end?" Zafar asked. "If nothing happens, the best thing is everyone suicide. Or we can fight till the end."

"No, we'll see, man," Hamed replied blandly, as if he had not heard his little brother suggest that *everyone* in the family should commit suicide. "We'll see what life shows us. But you guys just take care of yourselves again. Like, let it be. Don't worry a lot. Just uh, just take care of your sisters and, you know, stay home a lot and—"

Zafar, worried by Hamed's entreaty to stay calm and care for his sisters, interrupted his brother. "Hamed! Don't say me that, like, uh, like if you say me that, I think like, 'Oh, you're saying me that because you're going.'"

Though Zafar had first raised the idea of suicide, he believed that Hamed was bidding him farewell; he was going to die.

"No, man, I can't help it, you know?" Hamed said. "The things the cops told us, you know, like, we can't help it. So, you know, I don't know what's gonna happen."

Zafar interrupted him again. "Why did they say that we can't help it?"

"You know, 'cause in the papers it was written there, it was a search warrant, right. It was a search warrant. It was written there that these people, they murdered those people. It was written like that on the search warrant. So, if it was given like that, they're saying we did it. We're telling them, like, 'No, we didn't do it.' They're not believing us. Like, what else can we do. Just, I will tell you this in advance, don't like be shocked when you hear anything but, like, um, like, take care of your sisters and everything. That's all, you know, that's all I have to tell you."

Zafar was growing more agitated by Hamed's fatalism. "Hamed! But I'm just saying, don't do nothing stupid, okay?"

"No, no, nothing like that," Hamed insisted.

"Don't do anything stupid, 'cause, Hamed, you guys think of suicide and all that. Don't do it! Okay?"

"Yeah, yeah," Hamed said, unconvincingly.

"You're not lying to me, right?"

"No, no. As long as you people don't do anything stupid too, you know?"

"Yeah, like, but, uh, I'm telling you, as soon as we hear something on you guys, like that's it for us, you know?"

Hamed did not respond immediately to Zafar's threat of tit-for-tat suicide.

"Hello?" Zafar asked.

"Yeah."

"Like I said, as long as we don't hear anything stupid from you guys. Okay? Don't do nothing Hamed."

The brothers then discussed which relative the children should stay with, but Zafar's anxiety had not dissipated.

"I have a feeling you're going to do something stupid," he said accusingly.

"Why?"

"Hamed! Make sure you don't, okay?"

Zafar appealed to whatever sense of familial duty his big brother felt for their youngest sister, showing concern for the little girl that neither Tooba nor Shafia had exhibited. "Think of Fereshta before you guys do anything," Zafar pleaded.

Hamed tried to reassure his brother, but his words betrayed him.

"Our life is over for us," Hamed said. "That's all I'm telling you."

"Hamed, but just think before doing something. Just think of Fereshta, okay?"

"Is she crying a lot?" Hamed asked.

"Yeah, like right now she's crying."

Hamed told Zafar to take care of the family's business affairs "if anything goes wrong."

"If God helps us, knows the truth, we'll be out," Hamed said.

Zafar reminded Hamed that he was still under eighteen. "Hamed, because look, you understand that this thing, everything will be gone if you guys do something. Everything. Everything you're talking about, the money, the case of money isn't up now but still I'm saying you, the building is gone, everything is gone from my hand. That all goes to charity, to the government. That's what will happen if something like that happens."

"Yeah, we'll see, you know?" Hamed said. "Just try to get some sleep, you know. If you don't get some sleep, then call me back whenever."

"But, Hamed, don't do nothing, okay?"

"Yeah, yeah."

"I swear to God and the Koran, please don't do anything," Zafar said, in Dari.

"Yeah, yeah."

"Give the phone to Mom," Zafar said. "Fereshta wants to talk to her."

"Zafar, she's sleeping right now. When she talks to Fereshta, she starts crying, you know?"

"Oh, okay. What about Dad? What is he doing?"

"He was lying down there. He heard the call so he got up, you know, but I don't know what he's doing right now."

"Okay, tell him some stuff about me, like I told him, 'How are you? Don't worry. You'll get out.' All that, okay?"

"Okay."

"Just make up some stuff and tell him. Okay?"

"Okay, bye."

"Bye."

18

Takedown

THE ARREST TEAM OF TEN OFFICERS in five vehicles was just arriving at the staging area, a gas station about a kilometre from the Bonnivet apartment, when Chris Scott's cellphone rang. Geoff Dempster, who was driving, pulled the unmarked sedan into the Petro-Canada lot where three marked Montreal cruisers were waiting while Scott talked to Corporal Nathalie Bernard, who was in charge of the RCMP surveillance unit. She told Scott that the Shafias and a fourth man, Tooba's brother Zia, were leaving the apartment in the bugged minivan. Zia, who had arrived earlier in his own vehicle, was driving. The Mountie, who knew of the morning arrest plan, asked Scott if he wanted the "spin team" to intercept them immediately.

Scott was surprised. The Shafias had been awake until four in the morning after the dramatic developments of the previous evening. He had not expected them to be up and out of the house so early. It was just 8:40 when the surveillance team spied them leaving. The arrest plan that had been fine-tuned an hour earlier, during a meeting at the Montreal police homicide squad offices, would have to be abandoned. Police would have to improvise, but they should still have the element of surprise.

Scott told the surveillance supervisor that her team should follow the Shafias and wait for his instruction. He kept the RCMP officer on the line while he grabbed Dempster's phone and dialled the detective in the wire room in Ottawa, to see if the bugs had picked up any conversation that would explain where the family was headed. The people in the minivan had been overheard talking about "an uncle." Scott switched phones and asked the surveillance supervisor about the minivan's direction of travel. The van was heading southwest, in the direction of Trudeau International Airport.

Scott felt a twinge of anxiety. He recalled the discussions Kingston Police had had with senior RCMP INSET officers about the hurdles they would face if the Shafias fled to another country like Dubai or Afghanistan. The Integrated National Security Enforcement Team knew better than anyone the difficulties of tracking highly mobile fugitives who had the means to hop from country to country to duck Canadian justice. Scott did not want to pursue his quarry across international borders.

"Take them down at the first opportunity," Scott told the surveillance supervisor. He relayed the developments to the Montreal officers at the staging area, and all the vehicles roared out of the lot, heading southwest toward the minivan and the dragnet of ghost vehicles trailing it. The marked cruisers led the procession. Moments later, Scott heard from the surveillance supervisor. The Shafias were being taken down at Saint-Laurent and Crémazie, a busy intersection nearly ten kilometres southwest of their apartment in Saint-Léonard. The minivan was stopping at a red light, where the surveillance vehicles would box it in.

The arrest team convoy, a blaze of screaming sirens and flashing lights, was only a few minutes away, threading through traffic. Scott's mind raced. Weeks of digging by a dozen exhausted investigators who had clocked eighteen-hour days since July 4 would crescendo in the next forty-eight hours. The takedown. Cautions. Booking. Transport in bugged vehicles. Interrogations. Media frenzy. Scott was alive with adrenalin, but he would not unholster his weapon or relish the shackling of the quarry. He had to manage the chaos and ensure that the prisoners were properly separated, given legal cautions and advised of their rights to counsel. He was anxious for the arrest team to get to the scene with Azi Sadeghi, a Farsi-speaking female constable on loan to Kingston from Toronto. Scott didn't want a lawyer to complain later that the Shafias didn't understand the cautions and their rights to counsel because police didn't explain them in their native language.

When the convoy roared up to the intersection, it was clear that the takedown had begun only a moment earlier. The streets were clogged with morning commuters blocked and befuddled by the strangely positioned RCMP vehicles. The surveillance officers, with their guns drawn and pointed at the minivan, were moving slowly toward it, but none of its occupants had emerged. Drivers stuck at the chaotic scene gawked at the unfolding drama. Scott's team members jumped out of their vehicles and bolted toward the Shafia minivan. There were now twenty police officers, many with their weapons out, scattered about the intersection.

Sadeghi pulled Tooba from the minivan. The three men were brought out. All four were handcuffed and Sadeghi advised them, in Farsi, that they were being arrested, that they had the right to retain and instruct counsel, and that they were not required to say anything to police. It was 9:08 a.m.

Tooba's brother was placed in the back of a police car while she was escorted to a Kingston Police minivan. Her brother was later released without charge. Shafia and Hamed were hustled into the back of an unmarked car. For days, Shafia had railed about police trickery and lies, and Hamed had warned his parents about the possibility of eavesdropping investigators, but the pair immediately began to discuss their predicament.

"Don't worry, my son," Shafia said.

"I'm not worrying, only about my mother," Hamed responded.

"It's okay, my son."

"It's not difficult for me these [u] she can't, she might lose her mind."

"Whatever is God's will. It's a false accusation." The bug hidden inside the police car captured Shafia's continued indignation. "Your poor mother," he muttered. "May God's fury descend on those girls."

Hours later, the pair talked again about Tooba, who was inside the police minivan with three female officers, including Constable Sadeghi. Shafia and Hamed knew that Sadeghi spoke their language. She had been at the Bonnivet apartment when their home was searched the day before, and they thought she had been trying to eavesdrop on their conversations.

"What do you think, what is the truth now?" Hamed asked his father.

"I [u] don't know."

"Is it possible?"

"Perhaps your mother has made a mistake, said something in the car," Shafia said.

Several times he announced his innocence. "We haven't done anything wrong," Shafia told Hamed. "They did it themselves." He called the family members "innocents."

The conversation between the pair also turned to surveillance cameras, the subject that had possessed Shafia since July 18. "It may be that in the car that you departed in there was a camera or something," Shafia said.

Several times during the hours that the father and son sat together in the bugged car in Montreal, waiting to be processed, Shafia voiced concern about his businesses. He wondered whether he'd be able to talk to his partner and whether the law would allow him to make arrangements related to the shopping plaza that he owned, where he collected rent from half a dozen tenants. He did not express concern for the welfare of his three other children, and it was not until Hamed articulated the gravity of the situation that Shafia seemed concerned about the handcuffed son beside him.

"It may be that we won't be able to see each other again after this," Hamed told his father.

"I commend you to God, my son."

Shafia needn't have worried about Tooba, who spent four hours alone in a bugged police van with Sadeghi and two Kingston detectives, Nancy McDonald and Kelly Haird. Tooba grudgingly spoke to Sadeghi but she did not make a "mistake," if a mistake was an admission of wrongdoing. She sparred with Sadeghi, who struggled to draw Tooba into conversation.

"I don't know what to say. I don't want to talk," Tooba said.

Moments later: "I am cold too but I don't want to talk. I don't have the patience."

Sadeghi asked about Tooba's children, where she grew up, when she came to Canada, her relationship with Rona.

Tooba's answers were curt and sometimes sarcastic. Her tone and demeanour conveyed her disdain for the police officer. "I have no patience for you," she said.

Early in the four-hour ride from Montreal to Kingston, Tooba presented an argument she believed a woman would understand, a simple piece of intuitive truth: "A person cannot kill their child." Tooba asked Sadeghi if she had children.

"How sweet are children. You can be away from your kids?" Tooba asked. "You are a mother. My children were all the same to me. They were all the same to their father and brothers. Every house has problems. That doesn't mean you kill your children unless there is an ongoing problem or they're crazy."

Later, Tooba was more direct: "I haven't committed any crime."

Sadeghi rejected the denial and asked why the children were killed.

"They did it themselves," Tooba answered. "They did it themselves. No one else did it."

"They themselves?" Sadeghi responded. "Who?"

"The children themselves. The daughter herself took the keys from me. After that, I don't know."

When Sadeghi suggested the girls had been causing problems, Tooba insisted that she had no reason to kill her children.

"No, I was satisfied with my daughters. I am still telling you this. I was happy with my daughters."

Sadeghi prodded Tooba with suggestions that the accused woman found transparent. The officer said everything would work out for the men, but Shafia would sell Tooba out and she would go to prison, penniless.

"No, he's left money for me," Tooba shot back. "The building that he has bought in Laval, it is joint. It is fifty-fifty. The money that he has in the bank, the authority is with me."

On this subject, Tooba was telling the truth. Her name and Shafia's appeared on the legal documents related to the family's purchase in 2008 of a suburban Montreal strip mall valued at $2 million. She was not similarly truthful when Sadeghi asked about Rona.

"I thought you were the second wife?" Sadeghi asked. "I think he has two wives."

"No, when I got married to him, he was not married or previously married!" Tooba snapped.

Perhaps Tooba did not consider that a lie, because she did not consider Rona a *real* wife. Rona did not bear any of the babies; she cooked and cleaned and chased after the children, like a servant. When Shafia moved to Canada, he could name only one wife in the immigration documents. He chose Tooba. He had stopped sharing a bed with Rona.

Tooba professed affection for her husband, although she acknowledged it was an arranged marriage.

"Do you love him, Shafia?" Sadeghi asked.

"Yeah, my husband was always very good to me," Tooba answered. "The children and me, I love him very much. I love him so much."

"Did you love him before marriage? How old were you when you got married?"

"I was eighteen."

Sadeghi asked if Tooba was Shafia's girlfriend when they married.

"No, I loved him but the family asked for my hand and they took me. It wasn't dating though."

"Oh, okay. Are you in love?"

"I wasn't. I was not in love but I fall in love after we got married! I wasn't."

Tooba's defiant tone ebbed when Sadeghi pressed her about her dead "innocent children." The officer became more aggressive, hoping that a surge of emotion would loosen the truth. "How many times do you hear their voices?" Sadeghi asked.

"A hundred times in every moment," said Tooba, who seemed to be sobbing softly.

"Aren't they telling you [u] Aren't they telling you, 'Mommy, we were innocent.' Don't they ever say, 'Mommy, what was my culpability?' Don't they ever say that? Don't they ever say, 'Mommy, what was my culpability?'"

"They come into my dreams but the following morning I forget. I don't know what they said."

Sadeghi saw an opening and clutched at the emotions. "The sound of their cries will forever remain in your heart," she told Tooba. She warned again that Shafia would save himself and abandon her.

"Why did you allow him to do such a thing?" the officer asked.

"I didn't allow him."

"Did you speak with him?"

"He didn't speak a word of this to me, that he was going to do such a thing. He didn't say a word of this to me."

It seemed that Tooba was on the cusp of telling Sadeghi that her husband had done "such a thing," though she did not know he had planned to do it. But a moment later, Tooba seemed to correct herself, to suggest that Shafia had not spoken to her about "such a thing" because he had not done anything.

"He told me it was an accident," Tooba said.

Sadeghi's success was suddenly nullified. She said she knew Tooba was protecting her husband—perhaps she was afraid of him—but he would let her go and protect himself. Tooba remained silent so Sadeghi scratched for more emotion.

"Have you buried them? Have you buried the children? You saw all of them? How were they?"

Tooba sobbed but made no admission. The victims died in an accident, and she did not know anything about a plot by her husband.

"If he had told me he was going to kill them, I would have taken all my children and gone to the police," Tooba said.

IT WAS AFTER FOUR THIRTY when the convoy ferrying the arrested trio arrived at the Kingston Police station, where investigators had a surprise for them. Tooba would be first to meet Shahin Mehdizadeh, a middle-aged policeman with a balding head of salt and pepper hair, dark brows, a hawk nose and a perpetual grin. The officer had travelled from British Columbia, on loan from the RCMP, to act as the kind and compassionate officer in whom Tooba could confide. When he spoke English, in his characteristically soft voice, an accent or lisp was noticeable in words like "with." Born in Iran, Mehdizadeh had lived in Canada since 1984. Soon after arriving, he had joined the RCMP, where he rose to the rank of inspector with a reputation as a clever undercover operator.

He had been studying the Shafias. He had watched the video recordings of their interviews by Kingston Police officers on June 30. He had reviewed newspaper stories and television reports based on interviews given by the grieving family. In the past forty-eight hours, Mehdizadeh had driven the two hundred kilometres between Kingston and the wire room in Ottawa three times to listen to some of the secret wiretap recordings. He had studied the forensic evidence that suggested the family's Lexus pushed the Nissan Sentra into the canal. He had pored over cellphone records showing that Hamed and Shafia had travelled to the Kingston area on June 27, while the rest of the family remained in Niagara Falls. Mehdizadeh knew their story intimately, and he knew the key pieces of evidence that police had amassed that pointed to their guilt. More importantly, he knew their language and culture, and he understood displacement and cultural assimilation. His family had fled the revolution in Iran in 1979 before immigrating to Canada. He had a strategy that he hoped would wrest a confession from the accused mother.

After more than twenty years with the RCMP, Mehdizadeh had outgrown the job of chasing crooks down alleys. Now, he buddied up to gangsters and killers, though he didn't look like the criminal that he sometimes portrayed. He sometimes played a key role in Mr. Big stings, an ingenious but controversial ploy invented by the Mounties in which a "target," often a suspected murderer, was initiated into a fictitious criminal organization. In a meeting with the crime boss or associates—undercover police officers— the target was asked to confess past misdeeds as evidence of his criminal success. The meeting was secretly recorded and the video often used later as evidence to prosecute the target. The Mounties had successfully used the ploy to catch killers in long-unsolved murder cases.

Mehdizadeh's undercover encounters with accomplished criminals had taught him to think on his feet, to adapt to the personality of his target and to gently coax admissions from crooks accustomed to concealing their crimes. This time, however, his target was a middle-aged mother with no criminal record. Knowing that solidarity was valued and rigidly enforced in Afghan families, he wasn't certain that he would be able to get anything from Tooba, but he believed he had two sharp tools with which to attempt to pry loose the family seal: appeals to her as a mother and as a Muslim.

19

"This Car Has Fallen into the Water"

WHEN AZI SADEGHI BEGAN INTERVIEWING TOOBA, fifty minutes after she was placed in an interview room in Kingston, Shahin Mehdizadeh was watching on a screen in a nearby monitor room.

Sadeghi had spent most of the day with Tooba, including the four-hour van ride from Montreal. Mehdizadeh wanted to see if Sadeghi had built any bond with Tooba before he stepped in. Tooba leaned back in the chair, her arms folded across her abdomen, when Sadeghi entered the room. Sadeghi sat in the comfortable office chair and leaned forward onto the table, looking at Tooba.

"Do you know that you are in Kingston right now?" the officer asked.

"Yes."

"Do you know why you are here?"

"Yes."

"Why are you here?"

"Because of the accident that has happened, they have brought me here. I can't talk to you more than that. If anything else you want, you can talk to my lawyer tomorrow. I can't talk to more than that. Excuse me."

Sadeghi corrected her: "You are here because four people have been killed."

"Umm," Tooba mumbled.

"I am also here because four people have been killed. Have you killed any of them? Haven't you conspired or planned in killing them?"

"I don't know," Tooba answered. "I don't want to speak about it." The accused mother seemed indifferent. She glanced at the floor and at the table, but she did not meet Sadeghi's gaze.

"You don't want to speak with me?"

"I don't want to talk about it."

The officer asked if she wanted to see pictures of her children. Tooba nodded her head and her lower lip quivered as Sadeghi flipped open the "Princess" photo album. Two pages in, Tooba reached for the book and began to sob. She clutched the album tightly to her face as tears rolled down her cheeks. After a few seconds she held the album away from her face, flipped a page and continued sobbing, pulling the open book against the left side of her face. Sadeghi persuaded her to put the album down and identify the children in the photographs. Tooba pointed, identified a child and sobbed. The page was flipped. More pointing, more sobbing. After five minutes, Sadeghi asked about her life in Dubai.

"I can't talk any more, excuse me," Tooba answered, as she sniffled and wiped at her face.

The officer asked if she wanted food or a washroom break.

"I want my children," Tooba answered, sobbing louder.

Mehdizadeh, watching in the monitor room, thought that there seemed to be no chemistry between the women; Sadeghi was getting nowhere. He knocked on the door of the interview room, arriving like a polite passerby, and was invited in by Sadeghi. Tooba had been in the small, windowless room for one hour and seventeen minutes. She had shown no sign that she was, as police hoped, the weak link among the three suspects. But Mehdizadeh would use different tactics. Tooba stood and smiled to greet him and, unlike a devout Muslim woman, shook his hand when he extended it. The inspector's tone was calm and polite as he took over from Sadeghi, who remained in the room but stopped asking questions.

"I have come here to speak with you because I know you are thinking a lot," he said. "I apologize for being with you in such a place. You know why you are here, for the murder of four people." Mehdizadeh sighed, as if to

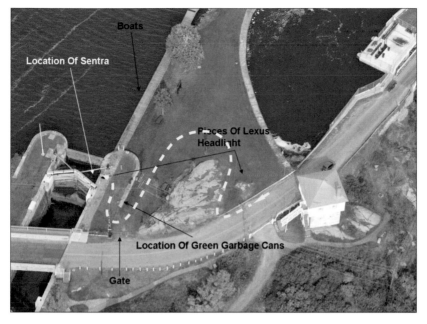

20. Aerial photo of Kingston Mills, looking north. The building at right is the blockhouse; the body of water at top left is Colonel By Lake, and the body of water at top right is the mill pond. The yellow line (added by author) denotes the path that police believe the Nissan Sentra took to the water. The Nissan approached from the east, hopped the low curb near a large rock outcropping, steered around it, drove up the grass embankment, made a hairpin turn and then drove along the ledge before tumbling off the stone lip into the water.

21. Aerial photo of Kingston Mills, looking west. At top middle is the visitor information centre, a building with public washrooms on the ground floor. Immediately left of the information centre is the turning basin. Police believe that the victims may have been drowned either in the turning basin or in the washrooms before they were placed inside the Nissan Sentra.

22. The scene at Kingston Mills, a few hours after the car was found underwater and before it was hoisted out of the canal. Arrow (added by author) shows the spot where the Nissan fell off the stone ledge into the water. The view is looking north from Kingston Mills Road, at the locked gate that would have permitted a car easy entry to the property, had it been open.

23. Two pieces of clear plastic, later determined to have come from Mohammad Shafia's Lexus SUV, were found about thirty metres east of the spot where the Nissan plunged into the canal. These pieces were crucial in establishing that the Lexus was at Kingston Mills on June 30.

24. Two silver letters, *S* and *E* (*next to evidence marker #3*), were found in the grass by Parks Canada workers. Investigators believe the letters proved the damage to the Nissan Sentra's rear happened on land, before it plunged into the canal near marker #2.

25. The Nissan Sentra, being hoisted out of the Rideau Canal after the bodies of the four victims had been removed. The grey wooden doors of the northernmost of the four locks at Kingston Mills are visible behind the car.

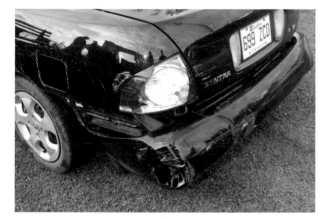

26. The Nissan Sentra, after it was hoisted out of the canal. Investigators later concluded that the damage to the driver's-side tail light was caused when Shafia's Lexus SUV rammed the Nissan from behind to push it into the canal.

27. Detective Steve Koopman documented the damage to the front driver's-side corner of the Shafia family's Lexus SUV, parked in the driveway at 8644 rue Bonnivet. Hamed had reported that the damage was caused when he collided with a guardrail in an empty parking lot in Montreal.

28. Tooba clutches to her face a photo album containing pictures of her dead daughters, as she cries during an interrogation on July 22, 2009, in Kingston. Constable Azi Sadeghi (*right*) began the interrogation, which was completed by another officer.

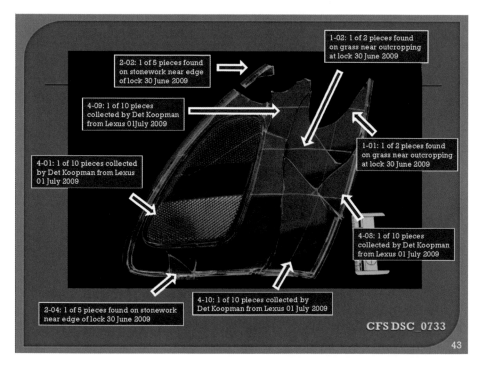

1-02: 1 of 2 pieces found on grass near outcropping at lock 30 June 2009

2-02: 1 of 5 pieces found on stonework near edge of lock 30 June 2009

4-09: 1 of 10 pieces collected by Det Koopman from Lexus 01July 2009

1-01: 1 of 2 pieces found on grass near outcropping at lock 30 June 2009

4-01: 1 of 10 pieces collected by Det Koopman from Lexus 01 July 2009

4-08: 1 of 10 pieces collected by Det Koopman from Lexus 01 July 2009

2-04: 1 of 5 pieces found on stonework near edge of lock 30 June 2009

4-10: 1 of 10 pieces collected by Det Koopman from Lexus 01 July 2009

CFS DSC_0733

43

29. An image assembled by the Centre of Forensic Sciences in Toronto, showing pieces of the Lexus headlight assembly that were recovered by police at Kingston Mills and in Montreal. The match of the pieces proved that the Shafia SUV was at the scene where the victims died.

30. Rona's diary, discovered by Kingston Police officers in the Shafia home in Montreal during a search on July 21, 2009. The diary documented abuse and humiliation at the hands of Shafia and Tooba.

31. The three Kingston Police officers who formed the command triangle and headed the investigation: (*from left*) Detective Constable Guy Forbes, Staff Sergeant Chris Scott and Detective Constable Geoff Dempster.

32. Shafia and the police officer who arrested him, Staff Sergeant Chris Scott, on October 20, 2010, during one of Shafia's many preliminary appearances at the Superior Court of Justice in Kingston.

33. Moosa Hadi speaks to reporters on the steps of the Superior Court of Justice in Kingston after testifying at the trial on November 16, 2011. Hadi was first hired as a defence translator but struck a secret deal with Shafia to investigate the case. He recorded a conversation in which Hamed gave a different account of what happened at Kingston Mills the morning his sisters and Rona died.

34. The luxurious six-thousand-square-foot home that Shafia was building in Brossard, an exclusive suburb southeast of the Island of Montreal, as it appeared, partly completed, in September 2011. Shafia sold the house and property in the summer of 2011, more than two years after he was arrested.

35. Latif Hyderi (*left*), Tooba's paternal uncle, and his son Reza, at Hyderi's home in Montreal in February 2012. Latif Hyderi testified at the trial that Shafia told him, in two separate phone calls from Dubai weeks before the four women died, that Zainab was a "whore" who had dishonoured him and that Shafia would have killed her if he had been in Canada. Shafia denied making these statements.

36. The mujahedeen identification card issued to Latif Hyderi when he joined the rebel movement fighting the Soviet occupation of Afghanistan, which began in 1978. Hyderi was a principled and proud man who loved his country, but he was horrified by Shafia's distorted thinking about family honour.

37. Jake Suarez, Sahar's classmate at Antoine-de-St-Exupéry high school. Jake says that Sahar liked him and gave him a chain as a gift.

38. The chain that Jake says he received from Sahar as a birthday gift in the fall of 2007, during their first year at Antoine-de-St-Exupéry.

39. In the days after Zainab, Sahar, Geeti and Rona were found dead, strangers placed flowers and cards at the edge of the canal at Kingston Mills.

40. The graves of Geeti, Sahar, Zainab and Rona, at a small Islamic cemetery in Laval, Quebec, just north of Montreal.

signal his comprehension of the enormity of the events. "I know that now you want and you think, 'Why I am here?'"

Tooba looked directly at the officer, bright eyed, as he answered the question for her.

"What do police have on me that they arrested me and brought me in Kingston? And, you are not alone. You are here, your husband, and your son Hamed. The police here in Canada don't arrest people for no reason and put shackle on them and take them here and there for nothing."

Mehdizadeh knew from the wiretaps that Tooba, Shafia and Hamed were eager to learn what evidence police possessed linking them to the deaths. He expected he could engage her with a promise of revelations. But it would be a barter. He noted that she had given stories to other police officers and journalists. "And I really apologize if I tell you that please sit here and repeat all this for me again," the officer implored.

At first, she balked. "It's better you tell me first what it is," Tooba said. "I myself, you know about everything I have said, what I have done."

Mehdizadeh pressed her. He had not heard the story first-hand, he complained. They had just met, and he had "lots of things" to tell her. He asked her again to tell him what happened when the family was returning home to Montreal from Niagara Falls. "Tell me the story and then after that I will tell you our story," the officer pledged. "The answer will be transparent, will be transparent that why we came and put the shackle to your hand, your husband and to your son's and brought you here, from all the people in Canada, why just you."

Tooba, anxious to know what police knew, agreed to speak first. She provided a four-minute narrative with more detail than she had volunteered previously.

"This was my story," Tooba said, when she completed the account. "This is the story and now you tell me your story, that what is yours."

Mehdizadeh ignored the request. He told her that he had some questions about her account. He asked if the family had stopped in Kingston on the way to Niagara Falls from Montreal.

They had stopped for a washroom break in Kingston, Tooba recalled.

"I don't know the place," she said. "I haven't read the sign and I don't know the place where it was." This statement was remarkable for what it lacked. Tooba did not say that "the place" where the family stopped for a washroom break on June 24, on the way to Niagara Falls, was Kingston Mills, the very spot where her daughters died six days later.

Tooba had been there again just four days earlier, on July 18, accompanied by Kingston Police officers. She had wept, looking down at the dark water where the bodies were found in the submerged car. Now, inexplicably, she did not tell Mehdizadeh about this coincidence. He let the omission slide and moved on.

"When you were in Niagara, your son Hamed were there all the time?" the inspector asked. "I mean, for the whole time when you were in the hotel he was there?"

This question was not innocuous. Police knew from cellphone records and from interviews with the other three children that Hamed and Shafia had left Niagara Falls in the Lexus early on June 27 and returned late that night. The cell records placed them in Kingston around 8:30 p.m. Investigators believed it was a final reconnaissance by the conspirators, who were checking to ensure that Kingston Mills was a suitable location to complete their plan. Tooba insisted that Hamed and Shafia were in Niagara Falls the entire time. Mehdizadeh accepted her answers without challenge. He was collecting her inconsistencies.

He went back over her account of arriving in Kingston in the dark, early on the morning of June 30. Tooba was driving the Nissan Sentra, with passengers Zainab, Sahar, Geeti and Rona. She pulled over on the roadside while the others went to find a motel in the Lexus. She couldn't say with certainty where she had pulled over.

"Are you sure that your daughters, all of you, came to the motel?" Mehdizadeh asked.

"Yes, I'm certain."

"I want you to tell me the truth," he responded, hinting to her for the first time that he did not believe her.

"I tell you the truth."

He told her, as part of his bond-building exercise, that "it is very important that we believe each other," and then he began a lesson. He asked her if
she knew how police would go about investigating a murder. He suggested
she try to think like a police officer. What would they do?

"You, you want to find proof then," Tooba, the eager student, responded.

"To find proof, okay," Mehdizadeh said, writing with pointless dramatic
flair the word "Proof" in marker on a sheet of paper. Tooba seemed to revel
in her accomplishment. She smiled at Mehdizadeh as he taped the sheet of
paper to the wall of the interview room, telling her, "We make you a police
now."

"Yes," Tooba said, returning the smile.

The officer began to enumerate the tasks of investigators. They conduct interviews, he said, writing "Interview" on the paper tacked to the
wall. Officers look for people who have pictures related to the events.
Mehdizadeh also provided a crude lesson in the mechanics of cellphone
towers. He explained that a phone uses different towers as the person
moves around. Police can track this. Officers collect physical evidence, he
said. The officer paused in his inventory to ask Tooba if, given these things,
she would change her story. She grinned and said no.

Mehdizadeh pulled two sheaves of paper from a large stack of material
he had carried into the interview room. He explained that Sahar had used
her cellphone a lot. Hamed used his too. Police could tell from the records
of their calls, he said, where they had been and at what times. The officer
told her that he had forgotten to add another item to the list of police
methods: police can listen to the people they investigate.

"That is called what? Wiretap," Mehdizadeh said, quickly writing the
word on the wall. He changed subjects again and returned to Tooba's
account of the roadside stop during the family's drive from Montreal to
Niagara Falls.

"Are you sure you don't remember where you had stopped for washroom and stuff?" the officer asked.

"No, believe me, I don't remember," Tooba insisted.

"Do you think it was close to where the car was drowned, the car, the road?" Mehdizadeh had drawn the link for her, giving her an opportunity to confirm what police knew.

"It was very dark," Tooba explained. "It was dark. I don't know. I didn't pay attention where it was."

Mehdizadeh knew it was not dark when the family's caravan stopped at Kingston Mills. Cellphone records showed they arrived just after 8:30 p.m. on June 24, three days after the summer solstice, the longest day of the year. The sun did not set in eastern Ontario until after nine on June 24. It had been a beautiful summer day. The sky was clear and it was still twenty-two Celsius when the family arrived at Kingston Mills.

"What time were you here?" Mehdizadeh asked. "I don't think it was dark."

Tooba held fast. It was dark, and Kingston Mills was not the place they stopped.

Mehdizadeh had circled long enough. It was time to confront his quarry. He asked again about her contention that Hamed and Shafia never left the family while they were in Niagara Falls.

"Yes, they were there with us," Tooba repeated.

"Okay, I say this is lie," Mehdizadeh said, as he clapped his hands together once. He was still standing at one end of the rectangular table, because Constable Azi Sadeghi, who had begun the interview, was still seated in the other chair.

Tooba did not shrink. Her arms were crossed on her chest, and she was looking directly at the officer as he called her a liar.

"I, I say they were with me," she shot back.

Mehdizadeh showed her the records that placed Hamed's cellphone in Kingston on June 27. He reminded her that her other children had told police about the disappearance of Hamed and Shafia on that day, but Tooba insisted that it "never happened like that."

Mehdizadeh's congeniality and facade of deference were dissolving. He had called her a liar and she had not recoiled. "I am telling you that you have done this," he said. He wanted to know why they were killed, so he asked her to talk about her children and the difficulties she had with them.

Tooba willingly offered a detailed account of Zainab's failed marriage to Ammar Wahid. She had warned her daughter not to marry him, because "this guy is not right for you." She said she struggled to stop Zainab from ruining her life. The dutiful mother could not divert all her energies to this one wayward child because she had many burdens.

"My husband used to go to Dubai," she complained. "All the house responsibilities were on my shoulder such as shopping, groceries, I mean, cooking for the kids and bring the kids home from school, wake up the next morning and take the kids back to school. All these. I also advised her but she didn't listen, so she did it herself. I didn't."

It is the responsibility of a mother to advise a child, if she will listen, Mehdizadeh commiserated.

"I did my duty," Tooba said.

"I can tell you I, I, I really have respect for you," Mehdizadeh continued, seizing the idea of motherhood. "Because when we talked with your kids—"

"Yes."

"—the kids have said that you are a very good mother."

"Thank you very much."

Mehdizadeh heaped praise on her. He said he knew that Tooba protected her children from beatings. "I know that your husband, Hamed, these men, had been hitting the kids to force them not do bad things," he said.

"Yes," Tooba agreed, though moments later she corrected herself, adding that "Hamed has never hit the kids." She described him as "a very good boy."

Mehdizadeh decided to test her truthfulness again. He asked about Rona's relationship to Shafia. Tooba lied. She said Rona was a cousin, the daughter of Shafia's uncle.

"Was I crazy to marry a guy who had a wife and I was a young girl?" she scoffed. "How would I marry him with his wife? I wouldn't be crazy, would I?" She offered no further details of Rona's background, simply the circular argument that *she* wouldn't marry a married man, so Rona couldn't possibly be Shafia's wife.

Four people were murdered, Mehdizadeh repeated. Following a classic interrogator's strategy, he presented the accused woman with an opportunity to preserve her humanity by acknowledging what was done and by explaining how it was done. She could find some redemption in the truth, the officer intimated. It was a monstrous act but surely she was not a monster.

"I am saying that I don't think that any mother would kill her own children," Mehdizadeh told her earnestly.

"Yes."

"Because this is the hardest thing for a mother. They are the children of your heart." There was redemption in motherhood, and piety. "You are Muslim, right?" Mehdizadeh asked.

"Yes."

"So you are a very good Muslim? So you didn't think that they had wanted to do this? You were looking after the kids."

Mehdizadeh noted that every good Muslim believes that God decrees the date of a person's death. Over the following ten minutes, the officer larded his accusations with affirmations that he did not believe Tooba was evil.

"When I speak with your families, I realize that you are good people."

But police were certain that someone played God that night.

"I have already told you that I have a lot of respect for you."

Science had revealed that the Nissan could not have fallen in on its own.

"You are a very good person."

Investigators had proved that the Nissan was pushed into the water.

"Either you have killed them—"

"No."

"—or you know what has happened to them and you have helped. These two things, I am certain about it. I am certain hundred percent. The first one, I hope not to be, because I think you are a good mother, a Muslim woman and a good mother." Sometimes by telling the truth, "your heart will be opened up a little," he said.

Tooba repeated her claim that she did not know of a plot. "I have told you," she began firmly. "I have already told you and I am telling you now,

I am saying again about this, Shafia hasn't told me anything that he would kill them or, 'I would leave them,' or something. He has never told me. If he had told me that he would kill the children, especially Zainab, I would go to the police with my children."

Mehdizadeh, now alone in the room with her because Sadeghi had departed, piled more evidence in front of Tooba. The officer explained that a witness had seen two cars at Kingston Mills early on the morning of June 30. He showed Tooba photos of the fractured bits of headlight lens found there that proved the Lexus was at the locks. Damage on the Nissan and on the stonework revealed how the smaller car had been pushed over the lip. The damage on the Lexus matched the Nissan.

Tooba interrupted him and zeroed in, detective-like, on a key question: "Excuse me now, the important . . . the important . . . now, the important thing is to specify the person, who was that person who hit it with the other car, pushed it into the water?"

Mehdizadeh reminded her that each of them had explained that Hamed had the Lexus.

"No," Tooba insisted.

"We know, Hamed himself has told us."

"Believe it," she said, her voice rising.

"Madam."

"Believe it, Hamed, Hamed, in fact, doesn't do this."

For another hour, Mehdizadeh bludgeoned her denial with evidence, motherhood and Muslim ideals.

Police had listened to Shafia, Tooba and Hamed talking in the minivan. They heard her say that all three of them were "there" that night.

"How much were you crying? I know you love your daughters."

Police had talked to Tooba's brother. He had told the detectives that Shafia had asked him to help kill Zainab.

"You can do whatever you want to do with me or to anybody else, you can lie, but you are a good Muslim."

Tooba pushed back. If he would not accept denial alone, she added faulty memory.

"Give me one night so I can relax my mind as nothing comes to my mind, believe me."

"Madam!" Mehdizadeh snapped.

"I don't remember anything. I have forgotten."

"Madam!" he scoffed.

"I have forgotten."

People don't forget such things, he insisted. Mehdizadeh said he had killed a suffering animal fifteen years ago and still remembered every detail of it. "Fifteen years," he said, tapping on a large photo he had put in front of Tooba, a ghastly image of the bodies of her daughters after they were lifted out of the canal. "One month ago, not even month ago, four people, three of your daughters, have you forgotten?"

"No," Tooba said softly, staring down at the table. "Never I forget." The shrill tone of indignation was gone from her voice. Mehdizadeh had moved close to her in his rolling chair. She seemed trapped between the corner of the small room and the table, with her side turned to him.

"I am not a stupid person," he said. "I know you haven't forgotten it." He thought she was vulnerable.

"I know this is shameful," he continued, as he reached toward her with his left arm and, committing an act forbidden by her culture and religion, clasping his hand around her right shoulder. "I know it. It's not a simple thing. Telling the truth is a very hard thing. But this is the right thing you have to do." He had lowered his voice.

Tooba did not retreat from Mehdizadeh's touch. She continued to stare blankly at the table. Sometimes people suffer shock and forget, she said.

Mehdizadeh held onto her and implored her to do "the right thing," to explain what happened to her "three beautiful daughters." The officer removed his hand after a minute but kept up his pleading, leaning on his knees close to her so that his face was little more than a foot from hers.

She would not look him in the eye, but she listened.

"Tell me the truth," he said. "I know, do your motherly job. Tell me the truth. Tell me how your daughters have become like this. How have their lives ended?" Mehdizadeh had dragged her to the brink, with his refusal to believe her lies and his explication of the evidence, so he waited to see which way she would turn. He sat silently for twenty seconds, staring at her, leaning in close enough that she could smell him.

She began slowly. "I told you, somewhere on the way, I said in one part that I changed the car with my husband, right?"

"Yes."

"I went to Hamed in the Lexus," she offered, providing a new variation on the narrative the family had repeated many times. Her disclosure was conditional: "But I request you one thing, that never tell my husband," she said.

"I will not tell your husband these things," Mehdizadeh said, making a pledge he knew he could not keep.

"Never tell my husband that I have said this."

She seemed to believe she had found not only redemption, but extrication from her maternal predicament. "I want my children not to be raised in different houses. I want to be with my kids and have them round me, under my wings." She crossed her arms and clasped her shoulders in a mock embrace.

In her revised story, she explained that she was driving the Nissan with the four passengers and parked it along a road in Kingston while Shafia and Hamed went to find a motel. All five of them were awake in the car, waiting. Shafia and Hamed returned without the other three children, and Shafia got behind the wheel of the Nissan. Tooba said she "ran" to the Lexus, driven by Hamed, and fell immediately asleep. Her long-held account that she drove the Nissan to the motel was erased.

"And then I don't know what happened after that, whether the kids came or Shafia brought them in to the hotel or not, I don't know this," she said. "From this point on, I don't remember anything."

Mehdizadeh pressed and she offered more.

The morning of June 30, in the dark, Shafia drove the Nissan into that grassy area beside the "big river," the one "that I had come a week ago and saw."

"I know it was dark, very dark," she continued. "I know that Shafia brought us there, before, Shafia brought us there."

"So he had brought you here before?" the officer asked, recognizing that she was changing another important component of her story.

"Yeah."

"When you were going to Niagara Falls?"

"Yes." She had suddenly given up the contention that she had never been to Kingston Mills before her visit with police on July 18. She had been there, on June 24, at the spot where the four died. She said she did not go onto the grass near the canal.

"We went with the children and with that lady, was with us too," she said, refusing to acknowledge Rona by name.

Tooba had been in the interview room by now for four hours and showed no signs of weariness, anxiety or anger. She sparred enthusiastically when her interrogator suggested that her convenient conclusion—she slept after she got into the Lexus and didn't remember anything—was a lie.

"No," she shot back.

"These are—"

"It's not lie," she said forcefully, speaking over Mehdizadeh.

"—lies."

"Believe me, they are not lies."

"Madam!"

"I tell you the truth."

Tooba volunteered that she had not heard anything if the victims were being murdered. "If I was awake and they were pressing and putting them into the water, I might have known it," she said. "As a human, I would have been shaken or would have heard a sound of splashing or something but that time, believe me, I don't know nothing about the detail of this story, how it happened."

This was an unnecessarily detailed denial of an accusation not made. Mehdizadeh had never suggested that Tooba saw or heard the victims being drowned—"pressing and putting them into the water," "splashing"—before the car was pushed into the canal.

"These girls, did these girls ever come into the motel?" the officer asked. "Did this car ever come to the motel? Tell me the truth."

"No, I told you, no."

He seemed surprised by her firm repudiation of another long-held claim. "This car has never come to the motel?"

"No."

The previous story, told to police by Shafia, by Hamed and by Tooba, that Zainab asked for the keys to the Nissan at the motel, was a grand lie, in the light of this new revelation. The explanation that the family had provided for the deaths, of a doomed joyride, was no longer plausible. Tooba's new account brought Zainab, Sahar, Geeti and Rona to Kingston Mills, where they were "sitting calmly" in the Nissan, in the dark, until Shafia and Hamed returned from depositing the other three children at the motel. The victims were not sleeping or unconscious, Tooba said. And then they were dead, drowned in the sunken car.

Mehdizadeh pointed out the obvious gap in her narrative: "How these four women have come into the water with the car without fighting with anybody, without defending themselves, just the car goes into the water and all four of them are drowned in the water and died?" he said. "Tell me the true story so I can understand how this is possible. I know you know what have happened."

Tooba was defiant, but she had backed herself into this corner. "No, believe me, I don't know," she said, "I know this much, that Shafia brought them here."

She amended the tale. She said that when Shafia and Hamed returned to the place where the Nissan was parked, she did not get directly into the Lexus. She and Hamed stood by the side of the road.

"I was talking with him that I heard a sound," she said.

"Hmm," Mehdizadeh murmured.

"Did you understand? But I ask you not to tell Shafia about this."

"No."

"Believe me, don't tell Shafia."

"No."

"Tell me," the officer encouraged.

"I heard a noise. Hamed and I heard it. We both ran and we saw that a car was in the water. This car has fallen into the water."

Mehdizadeh asked her to describe again more clearly where the Nissan was parked while she waited for Shafia and Hamed. How, he wondered, did the Nissan get to the edge of the canal, while Tooba and Hamed, by her new account, stood talking? Tooba said Shafia disappeared into the darkness and she did not see what he did. Mehdizadeh asked if Shafia pushed the Nissan into the water.

"I don't know this, whether he has done it by hand or by the other car," she responded, casting blame fully, for the first time, on her husband.

"By hand, it's not possible," the officer said.

"I, I, just, just saw that when the noise came from the water, since Hamed and I was a bit far away, Hamed was walking around and we were chatting, when the noise of the water came, I, when the noise of the water came, we ran. We ran and came. We came. At that moment, I became so stressed, as I didn't understand where the Lexus was or where this car was."

"What were the girls doing when the car went into the water?"

"Nothing I, believe me, I fell down."

"No?"

"I screamed and fell down."

"Okay."

"I screamed and fell down so I didn't understand that this car, where the Lexus went, what happened to this car. Just when I realized that this went into the water, I screamed and fell down. I screamed and fell down so—"

"No one," the officer interrupted.

"—I became unconscious."

"Nobody has screamed over there."

"I did."

Mehdizadeh reminded her that there was a witness. There was no scream. Tooba insisted that her remarkable new account, in which Shafia was solely responsible for whatever happened, had climaxed with her collapse. In Dari, she said *behoosh,* she became unconscious.

"I, I, at that moment that we ran, Hamed and I ran, we ran and we saw that the car was in the water. After that, I don't remember. Believe in God that I didn't understand anything. I grab my hair and fell down, fell down, then I didn't understand." Her unconsciousness lasted until they arrived at the motel. "When I got to the motel, I was still not thinking that the girls had been fallen into the water. I thought that their dad had already taken them. I was thinking like this. Do you understand?"

"No, it's impossible because you knew that the girls were in the car."

"They were in the car but I was thinking this . . ."

"You were thinking?"

" . . . why these girls didn't come down after me because they were always coming after me. Wherever I was going, they were following me. I was thinking like the car had fallen empty."

At the motel, she said she came to and saw that Shafia was driving the Lexus.

"Hamed held my arms and his father put me in the room," she said.

Mehdizadeh asked if she saw Shafia driving the Lexus when it was used to push the Nissan into the water.

"I didn't see it by my eyes," she replied. She had only heard the sound of the water.

"Then you saw this?" the officer asked.

"Then this, gone into the water. When I ran towards the water, I didn't know what happened to me."

"Did Hamed go? Did he go to save them?"

"Yes, Hamed and I ran screaming. Hamed ran too."

"Hamed went into the water to save them?" Mehdizadeh asked incredulously.

"Into the water, no. He couldn't go into the water."

"Why?"

"He couldn't go, that we ran and I fell down."

"Nobody called the police?"

"To the police? I don't know anything after that. I don't know anything."

Mehdizadeh praised her for telling "a bit" of the truth.

"I never say lie to you," Tooba insisted.

"You, you first thought that you could lie to me."

He began to tug at the loose threads of her story.

No one called the police when four family members disappeared into the canal, yet Hamed called promptly after a minor collision with a pole in Montreal.

The Nissan was stuck on the stonework at the water's edge, yet Tooba did not see Shafia drive the Lexus into the rear of the smaller car to push it in.

The four people were awake and calm in the Nissan just before their vehicle plunged into the water, but then made no effort to escape the sinking car.

Hamed drove immediately back to Montreal after watching his sisters and Rona drown.

"The only true thing that you have told me so far is that you and Hamed and Shafia had been there when the car went into the water," the officer concluded.

For the next forty-five minutes, Mehdizadeh peppered Tooba with one demand, an explanation for this absurdity: three healthy young women and Rona made no effort to escape the car. "What has happened that all these four people, not even one of them, has ever wanted to come out of this car, not even one?" he asked again and again. "You just tell me one reason. I am not saying give me ten reasons, just one reason. Don't tell me that they were asleep because it's not a reason."

"Uh, unconscious, they were unconscious?" Tooba offered tentatively, worn down by his persistence. She was alert to the motive for the officer's dogged pursuit of this answer. "If they were unconscious, all those medical examinations have been completed, why it hasn't shown anything in the test?"

For another hour and forty-five minutes after this, the inspector would beg her, beseech and plead with her to show respect to her dead daughters by being truthful. When he pointed out that, according to Tooba's new story, she watched her daughters drown and then went to the motel and slept, the mother scrambled to escape.

"I have become completely confused," she said, as she pressed her fingertips into her temples. "I have become completely confused, believe me."

She pushed her fingers through her thick, dark hair and held her hands behind her head for a moment as she spoke. "I don't know what I am saying."

Mehdizadeh reminded her what she had told him.

"I can't talk with you any more. I have become confused. I don't know what I am saying. Whatever comes out of my mouth, I am saying it, I don't know."

He pulled his chair close to her and banged on the small table with one hand as he demanded to know the truth. He chastised her. Her persistent lying was akin to spitting in his face, he said. She was showing no respect for her dead children. She was a mother "with a heart like a rock." He offered to get down on his knees and kiss her hands and feet, if only she would tell him what happened.

"God forbidden," she said, recoiling from the gesture.

Her eager attention to Mehdizadeh's inventory of the evidence was spent. She began to slump in her chair and her head flopped to the side. She had stopped looking at the policeman.

He assailed her one last time. "Have you killed them?"

"No."

"Hamed has killed them?"

"No."

"Shafia has killed them?"

"No, I don't know."

"Nobody?"

"I don't know what has happened. What has happened, I myself don't know somebody else has killed them."

"Are you afraid of Shafia?"

"No."

20

Interrogated

HAMED OBVIOUSLY CONSIDERED HIS INTERROGATION, conducted after Tooba's, an opportunity to quiz police about the evidence that incriminated him and his parents. Although he acknowledged his lawyer had cautioned him not to speak to any officers, he told Detective Steve Koopman that he was willing to speak to him.

Koopman continued to play the slightly dopey, polite flatfoot who was out of the loop. If the ploy failed, another officer was waiting in the wings to step in and play the heavy.

"I feel I'm in a different position than some of the other officers," Koopman lied to Hamed. "I'm just saddened that you and I have to sit here tonight in regards to the fact that you're under arrest for this."

He feigned surprise at the turn of events and asked Hamed to "help me understand" what happened on June 29 and the morning of June 30.

Hamed wanted to know why he was under arrest for murder. He had read the allegation on the warrant that the officers showed him before they searched the family's home. "I just wanted to know, like, ah, how could they be so certain about something?" he inquired politely.

Koopman lied twice, telling Hamed that he'd been on vacation and wasn't privy to the information considered when the warrant was drafted.

Hamed talked but said nothing of substance for the next hour and twenty minutes. He retold the story he had always presented, complete with preposterous explanations for his actions, including his solo trip to Montreal after the family checked into the motel in Kingston, and his early-morning collision with a pole in an empty parking lot. It was the same bland accounting for puzzling events.

Koopman challenged him, gently: "I guess in terms of where we are tonight and why you're sitting here, I just gotta ask, should I believe everything that you've told me tonight?"

Hamed insisted he had not lied. "Yeah, if it wasn't the truth, I wouldn't tell you but then if, uh, if you're saying uh, if you're asking me, like, uh, asking me, if you believe me or not, then, you know, it's up to you," Hamed replied.

Koopman asked Hamed if police had made a mistake, or perhaps there had been a misunderstanding. "You know, if, if, if you show me a mistake, then I'd be able to correct it, right?" he asked, slyly.

Koopman, still masquerading as the ignorant officer, offered to go and speak to his boss. He left the room and when he returned four minutes later he had a different tone. He let out a long sigh as he sat down.

"Just opened up my eyes a little bit there," he told Hamed. He said his sergeant had filled him in on the gist of the evidence. "From everything put together, okay, there's absolutely no doubt in my mind, from everything, in the totality of evidence, okay, that you and your mom and your dad, okay, are responsible for what happened with your sisters and Rona," Koopman said.

His masquerade over, Koopman demanded to know why Hamed's cellphone was in Kingston on June 27.

"I don't know," Hamed answered weakly. "I don't know what you're talking about."

Koopman suggested Hamed didn't want this to happen. He was a reluctant conspirator, but he was lying. Broken pieces of Lexus headlight were found in the grass at Kingston Mills, the detective explained.

"You're saying they belong to the Lexus?" Hamed asked. "That's what you're saying?"

Scientific analysis proved it, Koopman answered.

"And how, how, how is this, how are you involving me and my mom in this or my dad or me or any, any of us?" Hamed stammered.

The officer reminded Hamed that he had said he drove the Lexus that night. Koopman laid out the police theory that the Nissan with the four victims inside became stuck at the edge of the canal and was pushed into the water by the Lexus. Hamed then drove the Lexus back to Montreal, faked an accident and hid the SUV in the garage. As Mehdizadeh had done with Tooba, Koopman offered Hamed some hope for redemption.

"The thing for me is that I know it wasn't done cold-blooded," the officer said. He said he had seen the tears in Hamed's eyes.

Hamed was downcast, slumped in the chair, his arms crossed and tucked tightly against his body. His head hung forward.

Koopman spoke slowly and quietly. "Did you mean to get this involved with this?" he asked.

"No," Hamed answered, in a barely audible voice.

Hamed seemed on the cusp of some revelation, but when Koopman asked if it had always been the plan to use the Lexus, Hamed seemed uncertain.

"No, I really wanted to go with the Lexus to Montreal," he said.

Koopman changed direction. "How's your mom been handling it?" he asked.

"She's not doing well. My mom, she doesn't, uh, have anything to do with it."

Koopman did not ask what "it" was that she had nothing to do with, but his opportunity seemed lost. Hamed's answers became vague and imprecise. He asked the officer if he could see his mother. Koopman said no. The officer asked him to explain why the broken pieces of Lexus headlight were found at Kingston Mills.

"I don't know that," Hamed said. "How come, uh, there are not tire tracks or anything over there?"

"I'm not saying there aren't," Koopman shot back. "You keep searching for what we have on you and your parents—"

"No, no," Hamed interrupted.

Koopman prodded for a further seventeen minutes, but Hamed had retreated to safe ground. He insisted he had told the truth and did not know anything about a plot conceived by his father.

Koopman left the interview room, and four minutes later Sergeant Mike

Boyles, who had been watching from the monitor room, stepped in. He pulled the interviewer's chair close to Hamed, and he leaned in and made it clear that he would not be polite and gentle.

"We've got a lot of concerns about what you're telling us today," Boyles said. "You understand that?"

"Yeah."

Boyles announced that Hamed's phone was in Kingston on June 27. "That's a fact, Hamed."

Hamed complained that it wasn't true but Boyles continued.

"And I'm telling you, you killed your three sisters."

"Well . . ."

"You understand that?" Boyles barked, without waiting for a reply. His voice was loud and aggressive. "And the evidence tells me that. I'm not making it up. There's millions of people in this province, Hamed."

Hamed looked away but Boyles wouldn't allow it.

"Look at me," the officer demanded.

"Yeah."

"There's millions of people in this province. Everything's pointing to you, your father and your mother."

Boyles was preparing to startle the young man. Hamed did not know about his mother's admission to Mehdizadeh that the trio was at Kingston Mills early on the morning of June 30.

"I've spoken to your mother. Your mother has spoken to police for five hours, okay? Your mother has decided what's right and what's wrong and when to draw the line. She's made the right decision."

"The right decision?"

"You have not made the right decision."

"The right decision, her right decision, my right decision, it's the same thing which is—"

"It's not the same thing," Boyles interrupted. "'Cause she's made the right decision and you're doing the opposite. You're continuing to lie. You're not telling us the truth so you're making the wrong decision. You understand that?"

"No, I don't," Hamed responded.

"Is your mom a truthful lady?"

"Yeah."

"Is your mom lying?"

"No."

"Does she ever lie?"

"No."

"So if she told us certain things tonight, would she be lying to us or telling the truth?"

"Telling you the truth, I guess," Hamed said.

"Okay, so if your mom says all three of you were at the locks . . . on the night, if she told us you were all there, would that be a lie or the truth?"

Hamed hesitated, perplexed by Boyles's revelation-question.

"If your mom told us that?" the officer continued.

"I don't believe that my mom says this."

"I'm asking you, if your mom said that, would it be the truth?"

"I wouldn't believe that, uh, she said that. I wouldn't believe it."

"Well, I'm telling you she said that. I witnessed it with my own eyes."

"Well, if she was there, I don't know, but I wasn't," Hamed insisted.

"She said you were there."

"Uh, that's impossible. Either you're making it up or—"

"It's not impossible," Boyles said, cutting him off. "I'm not making it up."

"Well, I don't know who's making it up."

The revelation did not weaken Hamed's resolve, so Boyles reviewed the young man's account of events and accused him of lying repeatedly. Hamed rejected the assertions and made it clear that he understood police were trying to wear him down and that he was certain they would fail.

"I could, I could, I could say the same thing all night, man," he told Boyles. "I could say the same thing all night, you know, it makes no difference."

SHAFIA WAS LAST TO FACE INTERROGATION. Mehdizadeh knew that the patriarch, accustomed to dominating people and controlling conversations, would resist force. The interview was conducted the next morning, after Shafia had spent the night in a holding cell at the police station.

As the interrogation began, Shafia sat with his arms folded across his chest, his body turned sideways in the chair so that he was not facing Mehdizadeh directly. The officer showed deference in his demeanour and his approach. His chair was not pointed directly at Shafia, but toward the wall. He had not pulled his seat close to him.

Shafia said he understood, after speaking with his lawyer, that he was not required to talk to the police. But he agreed to listen, when Mehdizadeh said he had things to say. The officer said he knew that Shafia was wondering why he had been arrested.

"This is a violation of my right," Shafia said. Soon afterward, Shafia professed anguish. "My life has been ruined," he said.

"Yes, anyone's life has been ruined," Mehdizadeh agreed.

"Yes, with my children, my kids. I loved them with my heart, with my heart," he said, tapping at his chest. "In fact, I don't have any problem with my family."

"Yes."

"Neither I have now nor I had it before."

It was too soon for Mehdizadeh to challenge him, to remind him of his recorded slurs. The officer said he wanted the truth to come out. He wanted to know why "four good women" died.

"I also want this, the truth to come out," Shafia parroted. "I too want to know." He agreed with the officer that telling a lie was a sin.

Mehdizadeh said he wanted to pay respect to Shafia, a "good Muslim gentleman," and together they could discover the truth, but he did not tiptoe around the principal question, as he had with Tooba.

Nine minutes into the interrogation, he confronted Shafia: "Have you killed them yourself?"

"No."

"Have you helped in killing them?"

"No."

When Mehdizadeh asked why he should believe him, Shafia flipped the question back.

"Why or for what reason I should do this to my children?"

The officer explained that police had done a thorough investigation and collected proof, as the law required, that all three of them were guilty.

"I have come to this country for its laws," Shafia offered.

Mehdizadeh asked him to speculate as to why someone would want to kill Zainab, Sahar, Geeti and Rona. Shafia said *he* had no reason because "they were pure and sinless kids," a starkly different characterization from "treacherous liars" and "whores." He recalled that one of Zainab's boyfriends had called and had threatened to kill her.

Only minutes after Shafia called his children "pure and sinless," he acknowledged that some of them had sought to leave home by calling a child protection agency.

"The kids were lying too much," Shafia said.

"The kids were lying?" Mehdizadeh asked.

"They were lying."

"Your kids were always lying?"

"They told a lot of lies. I give you an example."

"Which one of your kids lies the most?"

"They don't say the truth, ah, these five of them, for example, Zafar, Sahar, Geeti, Zainab, Sahar because this, once, I always give my kids money for their expenses. I used to give them hundred dollars each month."

Shafia recounted that Geeti and Mina were caught shoplifting at Walmart two days after Zainab's failed wedding reception. He was perplexed because the girls had hundreds of dollars with them. When police came, Shafia claimed the girls told the officers that their father and mother beat them.

"Yes, then all of your children are liars?" Mehdizadeh asked.

"They are lying."

"What about your wife? Is your wife a liar?"

"Wife, no." She was a "very good woman." Hamed also earned his father's praise. The older son helped with his businesses in Dubai and Afghanistan and always "says the truth." Shafia seemed blind to the contradictions. While Hamed and Tooba were honest and kind, his children were "pure and sinless" kids who lied a lot, though lying was a sin for a good Muslim.

Mehdizadeh apologized in advance for the accusation, then told Shafia he was lying. The stories the family had told for the past three weeks were false. "All of them are lies," Mehdizadeh said. Shafia did not respond to the accusation. The officer said Shafia had planned the murders but "this was done with a little mistake." He promised to prove it.

Shafia said only, "Okay, please go ahead."

Mehdizadeh didn't conceal his strategy, to chip away at Shafia's confidence.

"This story, you should have made a better story," the officer chided.

"No . . ."

"Listen to me, listen to me."

"Yes."

"You should have made a better story."

As Mehdizadeh marched through his Criminology 101 lesson, just as he had with Tooba, he asked Shafia if he had any questions. The father seemed uninterested. He repeated that he had nothing to do with the deaths.

"They are my children. I loved them at the price of my life."

Shafia was willing to acknowledge some facts he had not disclosed before. The family had stopped in Kingston on the way to Niagara Falls, he said, though he did not know the date. Mehdizadeh pressed Shafia to acknowledge that he and Hamed had driven to Kingston from Niagara Falls on another day, while the rest of the family remained in Niagara Falls. Shafia agreed, unknowingly contradicting Hamed.

"Hamed was with me," Shafia said. He said a family member had called from Niagara Falls before he and Hamed reached Montreal, so the pair turned around and drove back to Niagara Falls.

"Okay, okay, this is right, what you are telling me," Mehdizadeh said. He pointed to a map created by police that charted the location of cellphones belonging to Shafia family members, based on their activity. Mehdizadeh pointed to the marker that showed Hamed's cellphone using a tower in Kingston on June 27. Hamed had insisted he was not in Kingston on June 27, scouting the location for the murders, as his interrogators suggested.

"But twenty-seven shows that Hamed came here," Mehdizadeh said, pointing to Kingston on the map. "And returned back, his cellphone, and returned quickly, had returned to Niagara Falls."

"Yes, because they had called, yes," Shafia agreed. Mehdizadeh pounced.

"Hamed has lied to us so far," the officer explained. "First, he had wanted to lie to us because Hamed said, 'No, it is impossible, I have never come here,' and now you are saying that you have come."

"Yes," Shafia said, still apparently unaware of the predicament.

"Hamed is a liar, very, and you tell me he is a good boy!"

"No, he is not lying," Shafia shot back.

"He is very, ah, sir!"

"He is not a liar."

"Mr. Shafia, he has lied to me. He has lied to everyone now."

"Maybe it has been unintentionally, I don't know," Shafia offered. He said he wasn't sure of the date he and Hamed drove to the Kingston area.

Mehdizadeh explained that cell records don't lie; they show with precision where and when a phone was operating. The officer had a thick stack of pages in front of him, records that showed Sahar was using her cellphone a lot, he explained.

Shafia leaned forward with his arm extended, palm toward Mehdizadeh.

"Four hundred dollars, three hundred dollars the bill was coming!" he said in a loud voice, emphatic about how much she had cost him.

"Yes, I know it."

"I said I couldn't pay it."

Mehdizadeh told Shafia that the records revealed that just before 11:00 p.m. on June 29, Sahar suddenly stopped answering calls or texts, though in fact the records showed clearly that Sahar completed her last call at 11:31 p.m.

"Yes, you mean that they went to the water at ten o'clock and some minutes?" Shafia asked. "This is what you are saying?"

No, the officer said, but it was suspicious.

Shafia was becoming more combative. He insisted Zainab wanted to drive. She had even asked to drive during the highway trip. He claimed he was not upset by the actions of his older daughters. "I mean when my daughters were doing boyfriend stuff or something, I had already talked with them and resolved it," he said.

He insisted Rona had not been his wife. She was his cousin.

Mehdizadeh said he was lying and showed him that day's front page of the *Kingston Whig-Standard* newspaper, which carried a wedding photo of Shafia and Rona next to a story about the arrest of the trio.

"No, I am not lying," Shafia said. "I, see, if this was my wife, she should have children."

Mehdizadeh told Shafia that some women cannot have babies.

The officer thrust photos in front of Shafia. They were images of the broken pieces of Lexus headlight assembly collected from Kingston Mills and the damage on the Nissan. Shafia waved his hand in the air dismissively and insisted that police had debris from the Lexus only because Shafia had given it to them, in Montreal. Mehdizadeh explained that the pieces proved the Lexus was at the canal that night.

"And these broken pieces—"

"It's impossible."

"—are from your car."

"It's impossible," Shafia repeated, speaking loudly over the officer's words.

"Go and tell this in the court."

"I am going to the court."

Mehdizadeh warned Shafia that every time he lied, he was sinning.

"Where is your honour?" the officer demanded.

"My honour is honour."

"You don't have honour."

"No, don't say this word," Shafia snapped.

Mehdizadeh said everything out of Shafia's mouth was a lie. "You were there that night," the officer announced.

"I wasn't."

"Your wife said you had been there."

"No."

"Your wife said you—"

"No."

"—Hamed and you were there."

"No, no, it's impossible."

"Your car was there that night."

"No."

"Your car was there that night."

"Our car was at the hotel."

Shafia's childlike insistence that the Lexus was not at Kingston Mills branded him a liar. Police had proof that the Lexus had been not only to Kingston Mills, but also to the lip of the canal. As Mehdizadeh reeled off the evidence and the accusations, Shafia simply shouted louder that they weren't true.

"We can prove it, your car—" Mehdizadeh said.

"Our car was at the hotel, at the hotel," Shafia insisted, interrupting the officer.

Shafia was not worn down. He seemed energized by the officer's attempts to impugn his story with facts. Mehdizadeh warned Shafia about going to court with "a heart like a rock" and nothing but bald-faced denials.

"I swear to the God who had created, has taken life, I don't lie," Shafia responded, wagging the first finger of his right hand at the ceiling and then accusingly at Mehdizadeh. "For thousand times still, my word is not a lie."

"Okay, then Hamed has done, then Hamed has done?" Mehdizadeh shot back.

"Hamed hasn't done it, neither Hamed—"

"Hamed . . ."

"—nor my wife has done."

" . . . all of you."

"No."

"All of you have said that Hamed had this car," Mehdizadeh reminded him, tapping his finger on a photo of the Lexus on the table.

"Hamed was taking the car—"

"Listen!"

"—but he hasn't done this work."

Mehdizadeh insisted that someone had used the Lexus to push the Nissan into the water.

Shafia interrupted him, shouting the officer's name. "Mr. Shahin! Mr. Shahin!" he said, as he snatched from the table a photo of his dead daughters after they were pulled from the water. "These children were not kids as someone could come—"

"I know it."

"—and kicks their ass so they go into the water," Shafia said, punching his right fist into his left palm. His voice was loud and shrill.

"I know," Mehdizadeh said.

"They were not kids. You tell me, you are sitting like this. I have suffered so much," Shafia said in a near yell, bouncing his hands near his chest. "I have lost my heart."

"You haven't suffered so much because I had been listening to you, how much—" Mehdizadeh began sarcastically.

"No!"

"—you were suffering."

Shafia had an explanation, for the first time, for the foul curses that police had heard. "No, suffering, that word, whatever word I am saying, it's to calm down the others because they were saying they wanted to kill themselves, 'What is the point of being alive without them.'" Shafia insisted that he had said those things "for the sake of the other children." As to the ones who died, he said, "I loved them with my heart. I wish God would have taken my life and spared their lives. I would have been ready."

The interview had run for nearly two hours and Shafia had resurrected the same emotionless assertion that he had offered in the first five minutes: he loved his children with all his heart.

Mehdizadeh knew that to question him further was pointless. He began to collect the paper and photos strewn across the table and inched his chair away from Shafia. He stood and loomed over Shafia, who remained seated in the corner of the room.

Mehdizadeh said the Nissan became the grave of four women and the person who did this was the "worst, dishonourable person in the world."

Shafia agreed.

"You are also a liar," Mehdizadeh said, still standing, wagging his finger at Shafia.

"No."

"You are also a liar. Your son is also a liar."

Shafia mumbled unresponsively.

"Both of you are dishonourable persons," the officer said.

"No, excuse me—"

"You don't have even a little honour," Mehdizadeh said, his voice rising.

"—don't say this word."

"No, I say it."

"No, no."

"I say it because I can prove it as well."

"No, no."

"Both of you—"

"This is an ill word that you are saying."

"The son is like the father."

"No."

"Both of you are dishonourable people."

"No."

"Your wife is—"

"This is not right."

"—your wife, her honour, the honour of your family—"

"Umm."

"—the honour of your family—"

"Umm."

"—is in the hands of your women."

"No, you are not saying the right word."

"The honour of your family is in the hands of your women."

"No, this is not a right word to say."

Mehdizadeh left the room and Shafia glanced up at the video camera, just as he had done when the interview began.

AFTER HIS TWO-HOUR INTERROGATION OF SHAFIA, Mehdizadeh met again with Tooba. One night in a police station holding cell had transformed her memory. She repudiated most of what she had told the officer in the final third of her interrogation the previous evening. Her account of the accused trio being together at Kingston Mills on the early morning of June 30, in the dark, was not true, Tooba insisted. Her admission that she had heard the sound of water and had seen the Nissan in the canal was a lie, she said. Her recollection that she arrived at the motel in the Lexus was faulty. She reverted to her original account, the one that corresponded with the accounts provided by her husband and son. She had driven the Nissan to the motel, where Zainab asked for the car keys and disappeared, along with Sahar, Geeti and Rona.

PART SIX

Trial by Motive

"These were all lies that I said."
—Tooba Mohammad Yahya

21

Saboteur

MOOSA HADI WAS SHOCKED when he heard that police had arrested three members of the Shafia family. He didn't know them but he shared their culture. Born in Afghanistan, Hadi came to Canada in 2004. He thought the allegation that three members of one family had murdered four others was unbelievable, and he didn't understand the suggestion that it was an honour killing. Hadi, who was completing a mining engineering degree at Queen's University in Kingston, visited Kingston Mills hoping to understand the deaths, but he left more puzzled. Would someone really choose *that* place to commit a murder disguised as an accident? he wondered, while weighing his belief in the integrity of the police. Surely, they wouldn't arrest people without reasonable grounds.

THE CALLER ON THE PHONE, a man who spoke halting English, wanted to know if Peter Kemp would defend Mohammad Shafia. He had a lawyer, the caller said, but he needed a new one.

This kind of call wasn't unusual for Kemp. Sometimes they came directly from Quinte Detention Centre, the regional jail just west of Kingston where nearly everyone arrested in the area was held for court appearances, whether they were accused of selling drugs or committing a heinous murder. Kemp had Quinte on speed dial. After more than three decades in local courtrooms, he had earned a reputation as one of the area's most successful criminal defence lawyers, a fierce, sometimes ruthless adversary who had won acquittals and lenient sentences for many clients in the two dozen murder trials he had handled. Kemp was adept at deconstructing the testimony of Crown witnesses on the stand and skilled at playing to juries. At Quinte, Kemp's name was often suggested when a prisoner sought advice from cellmates about hiring a defender.

Nabi Neda had not chosen Kemp because of his record of success or his reputation as a smooth-talking litigator. Not knowing any lawyers in Kingston, Neda had leafed through the Yellow Pages and found Kemp's advertisement. It trumpeted Kemp's thirty-five-plus years of experience and announced that he was available twenty-four hours a day. Neda was looking for a lawyer because he didn't think Waice Ferdoussi, the Montreal lawyer Shafia had hired, was the right man for this big case. Neda was shocked when the Kingston lawyer said his hourly fee was $500; he figured Kemp must be a good lawyer at that price. Kemp also recommended local lawyers for Tooba and Hamed, David Crowe and Clyde Smith. Each person needed a lawyer, he explained, even though they were charged jointly. Separate lawyers would be critically important if one of them decided to co-operate with police and provide evidence against the others.

TWO WEEKS AFTER THE ARRESTS, Hadi read a newspaper story that quoted Kemp, who had taken over Shafia's defence. Kemp told the newspaper that his client was not doing well behind bars. "He can't see his wife, he can't see his son, and he can't see his three kids who are in Montreal and he's isolated in the detention centre where I suspect very few, if any, people speak his language, so it's a difficult go," Kemp said. He had discovered that his client spoke and understood limited English and was barely literate in his first language, Dari. The lawyer added that the language barrier would be an obstacle: "It's going to be a serious barrier for the whole trial."

Hadi knew the frustration of life in Canada for a non-English speaker. When he immigrated, he spoke only Dari, but now he had a good command of English. He sent an email to Kemp offering his services. He wasn't a trained interpreter, but he was fluent in English and Dari. The Ontario government department that oversaw the court system had an inventory of Farsi interpreters available but only a handful who were fluent in Dari.

Hadi was articulate and seemed sincere. Kemp hired him as a translator and had him sign a confidentiality agreement. Hadi would be privy to the lawyer's intimate conversations with Shafia. Hadi also would provide services to Crowe, who represented Tooba, but he had no agreement with Smith, who could communicate with Hamed in English.

Hadi accompanied Kemp to a meeting with Shafia at Quinte Detention Centre for the first time on August 27. Shafia complained that he had been arrested based on false allegations by extended family members who held grudges against him. Hadi thought Shafia seemed sincere. During the car ride back to Kingston, Hadi asked Kemp if he could visit Shafia on his own, as a fellow Afghan and friend, because he felt sorry for the imprisoned father. The lawyer explained that Hadi's visits would be personal and would not be covered by confidentiality.

Four days after the August 27 meeting, Hadi returned alone to the detention centre and visited Shafia again. He did not repeat what Kemp had told him, that this personal meeting was not governed by any rules of confidentiality. Hadi told Shafia that he understood him and empathized with his predicament. He asked for permission to review the evidence that police had collected.

"I may be able to uncover the truth," offered the twenty-seven-year-old university student with no training in the law or forensic sciences.

Shafia agreed that Hadi should investigate and gave his consent for Kemp to release to Hadi the evidence that police had disclosed. Hadi was given a portable hard drive that included copies of the secret police wiretap recordings. Over ten weeks, Hadi reviewed the recordings and other evidence, and spent roughly fifty hours at the detention centre interviewing

Shafia, Tooba and Hamed, without the knowledge of the three defence law-yers. He quit his job as a clerk at a convenience store and dropped half his university courses so that he could spend more time on the investigation. Shafia paid Hadi $5,500. Shafia did not tell Kemp about his arrangement with Hadi.

In interviews with Hadi, Shafia and Tooba repeated what they had told police, that they didn't know what happened to the four family members. Hamed provided a troubling account of events that he had not disclosed to police. Hadi came to a very different conclusion about the deaths than police investigators and decided that, in the interest of justice and his civic duty, he had to bring his findings to the attention of authorities, regard-less of any agreement he had with the lawyers. Hadi did not tell Kemp, or the lawyers representing Tooba and Hamed, what he planned. It would be tantamount to tossing a grenade into the defence camp.

DETECTIVE GEOFF DEMPSTER WAS AT WORK on November 11 when he heard a page over the building's public address system. Barbara Webb, the civilian who first took the missing person report from the family on June 30, was asking for an investigator working on the Kingston Mills case to come to the front reception desk. Webb handed Dempster a large manila envelope that had been delivered to the police station. It contained a DVD and three copies of an eight-page letter written by Hadi.

He wrote that he had been deeply saddened by the tragedy at Kingston Mills and shocked by the arrests. Hadi explained that he had spent two hundred hours on an independent investigation of the case.

"I have never made any promise to Mr. Shafia to defend him and his family, but I have made every promise to uncover the truth and I have been paid directly by Mr. Shafia to do this job," Hadi wrote. He explained that he had recorded an interview with Hamed at Quinte, and the DVD in the envelope contained a copy of the digital audio file. The letter continued:

Eventually Hamed has given me a story that to the best of my knowledge matches with the existed evidences, including evidences on the scene, statements of the witnesses and audio recordings of conversations between the accused persons. I have not shared this story with the two other accused persons or any other individual. I also encouraged Hamed to speak with detectives and he agreed. Audio recordings of the conversations between the three accused persons confirm Hamed's claim that he was the only one who was aware of what happened to the four family members.

Police were floored when they listened to the three-hour recording made by Hadi at the detention centre. On it, Hamed revealed a terrible secret that he claimed he had kept for four months. Investigators immediately concluded it was a preposterous lie.

Hamed claimed that Zainab got into the Nissan in the parking lot of the Kingston motel soon after the family arrived there around 2:00 a.m. on June 30.

"My sister said that she wants to drive the car and just go for a spin and then come back soon," Hamed told Hadi. He tried to dissuade her and went to his parents' room, intending to tell them about Zainab's scheme, but they were asleep so he didn't wake them. Instead, he decided to drive the Lexus and follow the Nissan, to make sure the group was safe. Rona was in the car with Zainab because she wanted to buy a phone card. Sahar and Geeti were also in the Nissan.

Zainab drove north on Highway 15, Hamed told Hadi. She passed the interchange for Highway 401, turned left onto Station Road and then left onto Kingston Mills Road. At the Mills, Zainab stopped the Nissan suddenly and Hamed was unable to avoid a collision. The Lexus rear-ended the Nissan.

"I hit the back but not hard, just the glass was broken, the glass of Lexus car," Hamed said he discovered, after jumping out to inspect the damage. He began collecting broken pieces of the Lexus and chastised Zainab for driving to the dark, isolated spot. The Nissan's front wheels appeared to have jumped the curb onto the grass, and the car seemed to be stuck, Hamed said.

"There was a sound, 'shooo, shooo,' something like that," he said, mimicking the noise of spinning wheels. Hamed said his sister told him she wanted to follow him. She would turn the car around and he could lead in the Lexus. Hamed thought she would drive around the large rock outcropping and bring the car back onto the road. Near the rock, "or somewhere like this, I saw them for the last time."

The conversation between the two men, mostly in Dari, was matter-of-fact and seemingly devoid of emotion. Hamed did not cry or falter as he recounted the final few moments of life of his four family members.

"Okay, so you were busy with the Lexus car," Hadi suggested.

"Yes."

"To find out what part had damaged?"

"Yes."

"And to pick all the pieces that had fallen on the ground?"

"Yes," Hamed answered. "I had them in my hand when I heard the splash."

"The splash" was the sound of the Nissan plunging into the water. Hamed told Hadi that he ran to the stone lip of the canal and, although it was very dark, he could see what had happened.

"At that moment, I think one of the lights was showing," Hamed said. "There was a bit of light showing that I understood that it had fallen here." In his rush to investigate, Hamed still carried the broken pieces of the Lexus that he had been collecting by the road.

"I put all those pieces around here that I had had in my hand," Hamed said, explaining that he deposited the chunks of automobile debris at the lip where the Nissan had tumbled into the water, at the very spot where police had found pieces.

There seemed no sadness or anxiety in Hamed's voice as he told Hadi what steps he took to save his drowning sisters and Rona, after setting down the broken Lexus parts. Hadi encouraged him as he recounted his rescue effort.

"Then after that you went back?" Hadi said.

"To the Lexus to fetch something."

"Okay, to bring something."

"Yeah, yeah, before that, the boy says, 'I heard a horn sound,' right?" Hamed seemed to remind himself.

"Yeah," Hadi said, which prompted Hamed to explain that he had done exactly what was necessary to explain the sound reported by young witness Dylan.

"I sounded the horn a bit to see if there was anyone," Hamed said.

"To help you?" Hadi asked.

"Yes, yeah."

Hamed said he sounded the horn once, for five seconds, or perhaps twice, but no one came to help so he returned to the edge of the canal with a length of rope that had been in the Lexus. He dangled the rope in the water.

"Okay, you put the rope into the water?" Hadi asked.

"I put it in the water, nothing happened."

Hamed figured that his waterside rescue effort lasted seven or eight minutes. In that time, he shouted into the darkness: "Zainab, Sahar, Geeti, Rona." He wiggled the rope.

"I thought they are coming out, but they didn't," he recalled. If the brother, watching four family members drown in a submerged car, felt any fear or panic, he did not recall it for Hadi. His inventory of his actions was plain and pathetic: the horn, the rope and calling out. He did not call 9-1-1. He did not leap into the water. He did not run to the houseboat moored nearby to seek help. He was conscientious about one thing: He picked up the broken chunks of the Lexus that he had dropped at the ledge, though he later acknowledged he might have missed some of them in the dark.

"When they didn't come out, I came back to the car with those pieces. I came back here, then I stood there for a few minutes."

Hadi asked Hamed why he didn't call police when he realized the Nissan went into the water.

"First, I thought that if I call the police, they would blame me that she didn't have licence and, 'You brought her here,'" Hamed answered.

"Okay, so you thought that the police put the blame on you that, why?"

"For example, they will tell me, 'This person doesn't have a licence and came here,' so I was scared and changed my mind. I decided with myself not to say that I was with them."

Hamed then decided to drive on to Montreal, as he had planned, leaving his three sisters and Rona underwater.

"When I went to Montreal, first I didn't think about the accident," he told Hadi. "First, I went home. I had the key. I opened it and sat there thinking. I didn't think of doing what I was supposed to be doing. I didn't know what to say to my mom and dad."

In addition to being unable to determine how to tell his parents that he'd witnessed the deaths of four family members, he simply hadn't found the time. "Later on, I decided that I should tell them, but there wasn't any opportunity to inform them," Hamed said. He was scared too that Shafia would be upset that Hamed failed to stop his sister from taking the car and that he didn't tell his father of her plan.

"He might have become very upset," Hamed said. "He would have sworn. He would have lost his temper badly as, 'Why they have gone with the car without permission?'" For all these reasons, he called no one for help and he told no one what had happened.

Paradoxically, the young man who so feared police that he would not call them as his sisters and Rona drowned overcame his fear in Montreal, where he faked a collision and called police to report it. "I took the Lexus and hit to a post a bit," Hamed said, explaining that he conceived the ruse to explain the damage that the Lexus suffered when he rear-ended the Nissan at Kingston Mills. He placed a piece of the Lexus near the parking lot pole.

"I put one of the pieces," he said. After a Montreal police officer investigated the minor collision, Hamed put the piece back in the Lexus, where police would later find it, before he drove the SUV to the apartment on Bonnivet and parked it in the garage. He returned to Kingston in the family's other vehicle, the Pontiac minivan.

Beyond its overall implausibility, Hamed's new account had specific problems.

He said that when he rushed to the edge of the canal, "I think one of the lights was showing." The Nissan's headlight switch was in the off position when the car was recovered, and because the ignition was off also, the car's daytime running lights would not have been illuminated.

Hamed said that Zainab drove the Nissan to Kingston Mills, but after the collision with the Lexus, she switched with Sahar. No one was in the driver's seat when the police diver descended to the sunken Nissan. Sahar was in the back seat.

Hamed told Hadi that eventually, he decided he should tell his parents what really happened, but "there wasn't any opportunity." The family members were together, after the deaths, for three weeks, before they were arrested and separated. Hamed had one ideal opportunity to unburden his secret to his father: the two sat together in a police car for hours on the day they were arrested.

Hamed claimed that the Nissan ended up at Kingston Mills because Zainab was hunting for a place to turn around. To get there, she had driven past dozens of driveways and two large, illuminated carpool lots before turning off onto Station Road, an unlit, two-lane blacktop that cut through the dense woodland south of Kingston Mills Road. To suggest she had not passed a good turnaround was absurd.

Hamed's disclosures to Hadi were irrefutable evidence that Hamed was a liar. His secret was a modern *deus ex machina*, a brilliant reply to key evidence against the family. The tale explained the broken pieces of the Lexus at Kingston Mills. It accounted for the eyewitness evidence of eight-year-old Dylan, who saw two vehicles there in the dark on June 30. It made sense of Hamed's nonsensical collision with a pole in an empty parking lot in Montreal.

Hadi met with Dempster the day after the package was received at the police station and agreed to a videotaped interview. It was soon obvious that Hadi was a peculiar young man who believed himself a more sophisticated investigator than police or the lawyers. He was contemptuous of the defence lawyers, who he believed had failed their innocent clients. Hadi thought many of the translations of the intercepted wiretap conversations were badly flawed and misrepresented the nature of Shafia's anger when he cursed his dead daughters. He believed Inspector Mehdizadeh, who had interrogated Tooba, had acted unprofessionally and should be investigated.

Hadi also told Dempster about conversations he had had at the detention centre with Tooba.

"Even she suggested me, okay, 'If I could be instead of Hamed in prison, I'm the one who accept the responsibility, but I don't want my son to be in prison, you know, it's not okay, you know,'" Hadi said, recounting Tooba's words.

Hadi told Dempster that Tooba was very upset when he met her inside the detention centre. "She's crying so badly and just, 'Okay, I don't want anything to happen to my son,'" Hadi recounted. "You know what, yeah, just she said, like, 'Okay, what if the father take responsibility? Because I don't want, Hamed is like, he, he's such a, like baby, I can't see him inside the prison but the father, he's like older. He can, uh, even if he's prison, it's maybe less difficult for the father, so can you just, like, tell the father to take responsibility instead of the son?'"

Hadi told Dempster that he cautioned Tooba: "I told, ya know what, if, if somebody take the responsibility instead of the son, he has to answer the, lots of questions."

Hadi, who claimed that he had uncovered the truth that it was really just a terrible accident, mistakenly concealed by a frightened young man—a "baby," in his mother's words—had implicated Tooba in a conspiracy to shift the blame either to her or her husband, in a bid to save Hamed.

22

Voluntary

AMONG MANY SKIRMISHES over what evidence could be presented to jurors, the pretrial battle over Shahrzad Mojab was critical to lawyers on both sides. The diminutive, middle-aged professor was just a few inches taller than five feet, with mostly grey, wispy hair that fell to her collar, but she would be a formidable witness for the prosecution. The defence lawyers desperately wanted her kept out of the courtroom.

Mojab, a native of Iran, had been studying violence against women, primarily in the Middle East, for more than a decade. She had interviewed women in Iraqi Kurdistan who survived honour-based violence. She had authored more than five hundred publications, including refereed articles, chapters, conference papers and lectures, primarily focused on honour-based violence in the Middle East and in immigrant communities around the world. She had advised the United Nations on honour-based violence. She had held prestigious positions and was considered one of the top academic experts in Canada on honour killings.

Crown prosecutors hoped to call her as a witness because Mojab could provide the context for Shafia's wiretapped rants about his honour and the shameless behaviour of his daughters. Mojab was the "why?". By decoding the motive, she could lend credence to a theory that twelve ordinary Canadians might otherwise find preposterous: three members of a family, including the mother and father, conspired in cold blood to murder four others to restore the family's honour. The defence lawyers would fight to block her from testifying, arguing that her research wasn't up to rigorous social science standards that would position her as an expert, and that permitting her to give evidence would afford the Crown the unfair opportunity to frame these events as typical of other honour killings.

Two months before Shafia, Tooba and Hamed were arrested in 2009, Mojab appeared in an Ottawa courtroom as an expert witness for the prosecution in the trial of Hasibullah Sadiqi, a young man from Afghanistan who had pleaded not guilty to two counts of first-degree murder. Sadiqi had shot and killed his twenty-year-old sister and her fiancé as they sat in a car in a parking lot. There was no doubt that he was the shooter. The big question was, why? Other witnesses testified that Sadiqi believed his younger sister had shamed the family by failing to seek her father's permission to marry. Mojab testified during his trial that in some cultures the murder of a woman perceived to be misbehaving is seen as an act of purification that restores the family's tarnished honour. Sadiqi was convicted and sentenced to life in prison with no chance of parole for twenty-five years.

In October 2010, Mojab sat in the witness box in the main courtroom of the Superior Court of Justice building in Kingston. The spectator benches were empty. Shafia, Tooba and Hamed, shackled at the ankles, were confined in the prisoner's dock. Mojab spent six hours answering questions from the Crown and defence lawyers. She explained her research and her belief that honour-based violence is far more complex than the forms of domestic violence that are prevalent in western societies. Honour killings often involve conspiracies that include extended family members, the murders are sometimes endorsed or tacitly approved by the wider community and, in some cases, the victims are compliant, cowed into acknowledging that their acts have shamed the family and that their death is the only solution. In some cases, victims commit suicide to spare the family the difficulty of concealing a murder.

When Mojab was asked if honour-based violence is a problem in Canada about which Canadians needed to be educated, she added a call to action: "I can't stress the urgency of this matter enough. It is a very serious problem."

Supreme Court Judge Robert Maranger ruled that Mojab would be deemed an expert who could provide evidence at the trial. She would be permitted to testify about the concept of honour killings, but the Crown could not ask her if she thought the deaths of Zainab, Sahar, Geeti and Rona were honour killings.

Mojab was one of forty people who testified during thirty-three days of pretrial hearings and a preliminary inquiry. In many cases, the testimony was a trial run, so that the lawyers on both sides could see how witnesses would perform on the stand. Battles were also fought about what evidence was admissible, including Tooba's seven-hour interrogation on July 22.

Her lawyer, David Crowe, argued that her incriminating statements in front of the camera weren't voluntary because she was offered inducements, a legal no-no for interrogators. There was, he argued, the implied inducement that if she told police the truth, her three surviving children would somehow not be denied access to their mother; there was a general statement that if Tooba helped the police they would help her; and there was a promise sought by Tooba that police would not tell Shafia what she revealed to the investigators. Crowe also complained that she was tired, under duress and had tried to assert her right to remain silent in the face of the officer's badgering. For these reasons, prosecutors should be barred from using some or all of the statements she made during the interrogation, he argued.

Judge Stephen Hunter, who presided over the preliminary inquiry, said Tooba was "intelligent and perceptive" and demonstrated a "consistent search for what proof the police had," evidence of her free will in operation, the hallmark of voluntariness.

Armed with the rulings on Mojab, the Tooba interrogation, and the surprise acquisition of the Moosa Hadi interview of Hamed, the two prosecutors assigned to the case were confident and anxious to get on with the trial. The Crowns were uniquely qualified. Laurie Lacelle was fluent in French and English, a valuable skill in a case replete with francophone witnesses. She was meticulous, focused and unflappable. Gerard Laarhuis, a lanky lawyer who stood more than six foot five, was zealous and known for his fierce cross-examinations. Laarhuis also knew a thing or two about the struggles of a big immigrant family. He was the fourth of seven children of a Dutch immigrant who had survived a Nazi concentration camp during the Second World War before building a successful family farm in a tiny community in rugged central Alberta.

Even before the rulings, the prosecutors had a mountain of circumstantial evidence, the damning wiretap recordings, the statements of extended family members about a murder plot and undeniable evidence that all three accused lied to police. And the evidence had improved over time.

Some of the wiretap recordings, particularly those from the minivan, had frustrated investigators because they were muddied by background noise. Chris Scott knew that skilled audio analysts might be able to enhance the recordings—and he knew where the best experts were located. He had seen the prowess of the FBI's forensic scientists when he attended the bureau's training program. When he reached out for help, the bureau was happy to assist a graduate. An American official from the U.S. embassy in Ottawa rushed to Kingston in early August 2010 to collect the digital files and ferry them to the FBI lab at Quantico. A week later, the enhanced files were returned to Scott, who was astonished. A further 30 percent of the conversations were discernible.

23

The Routine

THE ALLEYWAY AT THE EAST END of the century-and-a-half-old stone building was speckled with the first fallen leaves, splashes of orange and yellow
along the path of the prisoners. October 2011 was warm and bright. Shafia
had traded worn brown sandals for polished black shoes. Tooba wore crisp
grey trousers. Hamed's hair was shorn military short. Shafia grinned and
waved when a journalist shouted, "Salam," from behind the two-metre-tall
wire fence that had been erected as a temporary barrier.

The trio marched single file from the white police van that had pulled
into the alley. Each had emerged from a separate stainless steel compartment. They walked to a stairwell and descended eleven steps, shackle chains
jangling on cement, to a locked steel door. This routine would be imposed
on them for forty days over the next three months.

Shafia was accustomed to giving orders, not following them. He had commanded his children to return home nightly before dark. He had decreed
that his daughters not consort with boys. But Shafia was ordered into the
windowless basement prison within the courthouse, his son and wife trailing
behind him. A square space, six by six metres, it had three cells and a bathroom-sized command post where an officer could monitor video feeds on a
computer screen and control the lights. Shafia was instructed to kneel on one
of two black vinyl chairs, his face toward the wall, while a guard unfastened
the shackles that bound his legs together. His handcuffs were removed and
he was placed inside the first cell, nearest the door. The special constable slid

the barred steel door shut and turned the locking mechanism with a large brass key. Hamed entered the second cell and Tooba took the third, each similar in size and configuration to Shafia's.

Each cinder-block cell, two and a half by three metres, had garish yellow walls lit by a steel box of fluorescent tubes. The cell had only two places to sit, either a narrow concrete bench or the stainless steel toilet, concealed behind a half wall. The prisoners were not given blankets or pillows, books, magazines or any other comforts. There was no radio, television or writing equipment. They could lie on the bench, or the concrete floor.

The process of unshackling was reversed when word came from the second-floor courtroom that the judge, lawyers and interpreters were ready. Shafia, Hamed and Tooba retraced their steps. They exited the courthouse through the same basement door. They marched up the concrete steps and through the fenced alleyway to another door at the east end of the building. They entered the second-floor courtroom, with fifteen-foot ceilings and wood-panelled walls through a door beside and to the rear of the judge's dais. They walked into the centre of the courtroom, to the prisoner's dock, a rectangular enclosure of wood and bulletproof glass. Spectators in the public benches watched Shafia shuffle to the farthest seat on the right. Hamed sat next to his father, to his left, and Tooba sat to the left of Hamed. The sequence of the procession was not random. The president of Babul Ltd., his son and wife no longer chose where they sat. They had been instructed to take these spots so that they would be behind their respective lawyers, who were seated at a long wooden table in front of the dock.

THE TRIAL SEEMED TO BE BARRELLING TOWARD AN EARLY END as soon as it began. In the first five days, thirteen Crown witnesses completed their testimony, a breakneck pace for a complex murder trial. Only a few faced serious questioning by the defence lawyers. Witness number fourteen would be different: he was vital to the Crown's case. Constable Chris Prent had produced a detailed, ninety-three-page collision reconstruction report. His conclusions deflated Shafia, Tooba and Hamed's explanation that the deaths were the result of a joyride that ended in tragedy.

The thirteen witnesses before Prent had laid the groundwork for his analysis. Jurors had heard from the first police officers to arrive at Kingston Mills on the morning of June 30. Police diver Glen Newell recounted the "perplexing" death tableau he found underwater. Clerk Robert Miller had recalled the early-morning appearance at his motel of Shafia and Hamed, who seemed confused about the number of people checking in. Two forensic analysts told jurors that bits of jagged plastic recovered at Kingston Mills and in Montreal had come from Mohammad Shafia's Lexus SUV.

Chris Prent's scientific analysis explained what the Lexus was doing at the water's edge that morning. Prent had measured every inch of the canal, the stonework, the machinery, the drop to the water from the edge. He calculated the weight of the Nissan that night—Zainab, Sahar, Geeti and Rona added 228 kilograms to the total—its centre of mass, its angle of deflection when over the lip. He studied, down to the millimetre, the dimensions of the Lexus and Nissan. He compared the contact areas on the two vehicles where damage appeared to match. He analyzed the pattern of scrapes on the Nissan's undercarriage. From all of this evidence, Prent concluded that what happened on the early morning of June 30 was not an accident.

The Lexus had pushed the Nissan into the water. The small car was driven to the precipice but had become stuck on the stone ledge of the canal when its frame fell onto the stonework after its front wheels cleared the lip. Prent concluded that the SUV was driven in behind the Nissan and used, snowplow-like, to propel the small car forward until it teetered and tumbled into the water. As the car was pushed over the ledge, the SUV's front left corner butted against the Nissan's left rear, causing the small car to rotate counter-clockwise. It tumbled 2.03 metres before hitting the water and sinking.

Prent's testimony was spread over two days. On the second day, after the Crown had carefully led the officer through his analysis and his findings, the defence had its turn. Patrick McCann, an Ottawa lawyer who had taken over Hamed's defence before the trial began, took the lead for the defence in questioning Prent, part of a coordinated strategy among the three defence lawyers. With most witnesses, each lawyer asked questions, but often each focused on a different portion of the testimony. McCann launched a spirited, hour-long attack on Prent's conclusions, aware that jurors would soon hear about his client's jailhouse conversation with Moosa Hadi. If jurors accepted Prent's findings, it was an easy inference that Hamed's tale must be a fabrication. Both scenarios could not be true.

McCann cherry-picked an exculpatory passage from Prent's report and carefully offered the witness the chance to affirm it. McCann referred to page 34 of the report, where Prent had outlined two scenarios: the car was inadvertently driven into the canal, or it was pushed in with the aid of another vehicle.

"And those are, in your opinion, two possible scenarios?" McCann asked, mindful of the golden rule for litigators—do not ask a question if you're uncertain of the answer you'll receive. He knew how this would play out.

"Yes, sir," Prent answered. "That's my opinion."

"Okay. And that was after thoroughly reviewing all of the material that you reviewed with us, yesterday?"

"Yes, sir."

"So, I take it, then, that you cannot rule out the possibility of that vehicle being inadvertently driven into the canal?"

"Well, I . . . There's always the possibility. The problem is, um, there's too many things that, um, point to the contrary. Um, and—"

"Alright, sir," McCann said, interrupting. "I appreciate that, in your opinion, the second scenario is the more likely, but your words, in your report, are pretty clear, that there's a possibility, it's a possibility that can't be totally discounted. Right?"

"Correct."

McCann seemed to have wrested an admission from the Crown's expert that an accident was possible. The lawyer had done it by paraphrasing Prent—"the second scenario is the *more likely*"—when no such language existed in Prent's report.

When Laarhuis had the chance to re-examine his witness after the defence lawyers, he asked Prent again about his final assessment based on the two possible scenarios explored in his report.

"So, but what's your conclusion?" the prosecutor asked.

"My conclusion," Prent replied, "is that the vehicle was pushed over the edge of the canal, by means of the Lexus."

FAZIL JAWID SWORE ON THE QUR'AN to tell the truth during his testimony. He was not the only extended family member who had agreed to testify for the Crown. Latif Hyderi had followed through on what he had told Shafia in 2009: "I would not be a partner in your crime with you. I will be the first one to call the police." But there was a price. Hyderi says he began receiving threatening phone calls at his Montreal home soon after he gave a video-taped statement to police in July.

"Don't create problems for yourself and others," a man on the phone said tersely, before hanging up. He did not give his name, but Hyderi thought he recognized the voice.

"They're innocent, don't go against them," Hyderi was warned in another call. He wasn't dissuaded. Hyderi believed he had to stand up for the four who died and tell the truth. He was convinced that Shafia was the master-mind who had forced Tooba and Hamed to help him commit the murders. Hyderi's son Reza claimed he had heard this from Tooba.

"Dear cousin, you have no idea what kind of person Shafia is," Reza recalled her saying, during the crisis over Zainab's pending marriage to Ammar Wahid. "He's going to come back from Dubai and make my son kill Zainab and put him in prison." Reza was not interviewed and did not testify at trial.

But Latif Hyderi had spoken directly to Shafia, by telephone, weeks before the four died. Hyderi had told police that Shafia told him he "would have killed Zainab" if he'd been in Canada.

Hyderi considered himself a principled man. He was a good Muslim who regularly attended mosque, and a proud warrior. During the Soviet occupation of Afghanistan, he had eagerly joined the mujahedeen, the resistance movement bent on driving the Red Army from the country. Hyderi was among tens of thousands of jihadists who were killed or captured by the Soviets. On the day that Hyderi travelled to Kingston to testify, he carried with him the Afghan government document that explained that he had been granted amnesty after serving four years of his eight-year Soviet-imposed jail term. He was prepared to look Shafia in the eye.

When Hyderi took his seat in the witness stand, an elevated platform enclosed by half-walls of chestnut-coloured wood, he met Shafia's stare. The accused father's place in the prisoner's dock put him less than five metres away, almost directly in front of Hyderi. The retired rebel with leathery, olive skin was not cowed. This was the right thing to do. His only anxiety was about repeating Shafia's disrespectful slurs in public.

Prosecutor Laurie Lacelle asked him to recount what he had heard in May 2009. Hyderi said that he got a call from Tooba who said she had a problem and wanted to see her uncle.

"And a few minutes later, maybe five, ten minutes later, I receive a call from Shafia, and for sure that was from Dubai, and he said, 'Latif, do you know that Zainab . . . ' and he said some very bad things about her, and swear at her, and he said, 'She wants to dishonour me,' and some bad words he said for her," Hyderi testified, without articulating the "bad words."

"Can I interrupt?" Lacelle interjected. "What were the bad words?"

"I am ashamed to repeat those words, but it was very insulting, very insulting. The words should not be said to a human being."

"We need to know what the words were, sir. Can you tell us what they were? We know you mean no disrespect."

"I'm sorry. I offer my apology to the souls of those martyrs when I'm just repeating these words on my tongue. He said, 'She is a whore. She is a dirty . . . She is a curse of the father, and a curse to me, if I'm the father. She is a dirty woman,' and that subject."

After Hyderi had spent an hour and a half on the stand portraying Shafia as an arrogant tyrant, Shafia lost his composure. He stared at Hyderi and mouthed curses.

"Don't move your lip," Hyderi snapped at Shafia. "Confess, confess!"

Defence lawyer Patrick McCann jumped to his feet. "Your Honour, this is getting out of hand," he said.

Supreme Court Judge Robert Maranger swiftly adjourned the trial for lunch and the brief confrontation ended.

AMMAR WAHID ARRIVED IN KINGSTON on Sunday, November 20, to meet with the Crown lawyers and prepare for his testimony the following day. The young man was nervous about confronting Shafia. He had ignored his mother's warning to stay out of the police investigation. She had told him she feared he'd end up dead. Ammar didn't believe he was a target, but his mother's fear infected him. He occasionally looked over his shoulder. *If he is capable of killing four family members, maybe he'd come after me too,* he imagined. But he felt compelled to go to court. He could have done more for Zainab when she was alive, he believed. He owed her this.

Standing beneath the towering stone portico of the courthouse Sunday evening, in the informal smoking area outside the front doors, he remembered Zainab's gushing emails about their love, their marriage and the obstacles they faced. Ammar realized he had not given the emails to police, even though he had mentioned them during his testimony at the preliminary inquiry. Police had never asked to see the messages, which were still in his Hotmail account. After the prelim, Ammar had completely forgotten about them, including Zainab's first warning: "be aware of my bro."

"I think it's some pretty good evidence, some pretty heavy stuff," Ammar told Lacelle. He explained that his laptop was at the hotel but he could forward the emails later. Police and prosecutors were floored by the content of the emails they received that evening. Ammar had not exaggerated. The emails weren't *good* evidence. They were remarkable, damning evidence. Lacelle would use them to lead her questioning of Ammar the next morning.

The Crown lawyers provided copies of the emails to the defence lawyers Monday morning, before court began. They explained that they had not disclosed the messages sooner because they only acquired them late the previous evening. The defence was not happy and objected as soon as Lacelle began questioning Ammar about Zainab's first cautionary email.

The jury was sent out of the room to permit a voir dire, one of many such mini-hearings during the trial. Disputes about the admissibility of evidence in criminal trials are argued out of view of the jurors. Defence lawyer Patrick McCann complained about the last-minute disclosure. He said the emails were vague and unfairly prejudicial because jurors might draw inappropriate inferences from them. The Crown argued that the emails were reliable and clear evidence of Zainab's conflict with Hamed, and the language in them was not inflammatory. The judge ruled that the emails could be presented as evidence.

Ammar's testimony was completed the following day. Inexplicably, he never mentioned the threats Zainab had told him Hamed made at their wedding celebration. He admitted that he had a criminal record, an unrelated conviction for uttering threats in 2007, but it did not seem to undermine his credibility. His insistence that Zainab was afraid of her father and of her brother Hamed, and his account of the details of her flight from home, were consistent and detailed. Ammar, thin with coal-black spiked hair, looked sullen on the witness stand. He often cleared his throat nervously and he spoke in a soft voice that prompted regular reminders from the lawyers to speak up. But he convincingly brought to the courtroom the intimacies of a young woman's desperation. In the parade of witnesses—the computer expert, the collision reconstructionist, the interrogator, the cellphone analyst—Ammar was the first who had loved Zainab. He seemed lost without her.

24

"We May Never Know"

TWENTY-FIVE WITNESSES INTO THE TRIAL, some jurors had shed their appearance of neutrality. They could be seen occasionally scowling at the defendants. But the prosecutors had not yet offered any evidence to show how the victims were killed. The question had to be looming in the minds of jurors. How were three healthy girls and a woman subdued without suffering any obvious injuries? Why didn't any of them try to escape the sinking car, if they were conscious when it went into the water?

Geoff Dempster, who was at the courthouse most days helping with witnesses and evidence, believed he knew the answer, but he had not been asked about his theory when he testified three weeks before Ammar. The detective, who had interviewed all of the accused, believed the victims were incapacitated with some substance that the doctors and scientists were unable to detect. "We may never know, not unless one of them . . ." Dempster said, leaving the thought unfinished as he gestured from the foyer toward the closed double doors of the courtroom. A woman who had been briefly double-bunked in a cell at Quinte with Tooba had told police in March 2011, seven months before the trial began, that Tooba confided to her that the victims were poisoned before the car was pushed into the canal.

"I believed her," Dempster said. "She wasn't asking for anything."

After Treena Maxwell told police what she claimed Tooba had told her, police obtained authorization to bug the cell. Tooba did not say anything about poison once the recordings began. Maxwell, whose past included convictions for fraud and other petty crimes of dishonesty, was not called as a witness at the trial. Without corroborating evidence, it would have been difficult for the Crown to present her account as credible.

"They would have looked stupid to call her," defence lawyer David Crowe sneered. Maxwell's account of Tooba's alleged jail-cell conversation was "all bullshit" as far as Crowe was concerned.

DR. CHRISTOPHER MILROY, a bulky man with thick lips, bright blue eyes and grey hair, immediately seemed brilliant and likable. He reeled off his qualifications, in a thick British accent, with genuine modesty—more than four thousand medical-legal autopsies performed, more than half a dozen certifications and degrees including the highest level of qualification as a forensic pathologist, even a law degree. He had been working full-time as a forensic pathologist for nineteen years by the time he was asked to examine the bodies of Zainab, Sahar, Geeti and Rona. Once the chief forensic pathologist of the Forensic Science Service of the United Kingdom, Milroy had been lured to Ontario in 2008, after he played a key role in a provincial commission of inquiry that examined dramatic failures in pediatric forensic pathology in the province.

If anyone could tease out the truth about how the four were killed, surely it was Milroy. But the plain-speaking doctor knew just one thing for sure: all the victims drowned. "I cannot say with any certainty whether they were conscious or unconscious when they drowned," Milroy testified. Even his diagnosis of drowning had a fraction of uncertainty. Drowning is a diagnosis based on circumstances, the exclusion of other causes and the observation of expected features in the body, he explained. How well a doctor can see those features depends on the freshness of the body.

Milroy's testimony followed a week of evidence from nine Montreal teachers, school administrators, shelter staff, social workers and youth protection investigators who had looked inside Zainab, Sahar and Geeti in a way that the doctor could not, even with his scalpel. The nine were saddened by what they had seen—lost girls, desperate for affection and freedom.

Milroy found the typical signs of drowning—expanded, overlapping lungs and frothy fluid in the airways. The bodies were fresh and were not undergoing any changes that would obscure the indicators. He concluded that there was no explanation for the deaths other than drowning.

But he could not say whether the victims were dead or alive when the car sank. He could not say where or when they drowned, though it had happened recently. Milroy cautioned that there was no conclusive test to identify the origin of water found in a drowning victim's lungs or stomach. Unlike fictional forensic investigation in which super-machines solve all medical mysteries, no magic device can detect all toxic substances, no matter how obscure, in the human body. Multiple tests are required for different varieties of substances, he explained. Routine tests had been made to look for roughly 150 substances, but because investigators postulated that the victims were incapacitated before the Nissan plunged into the water, Milroy had ordered additional tests that are not routinely completed.

Scientists looked for carbon monoxide, cyanide and ethylene glycol— the poison in antifreeze—in part because "antifreeze" was found in a text file hidden inside the computer seized by police. Sophisticated testing was done to detect sedatives such as diazepam, and morphine and other opiates.

"There's nothing that we could have tested for that wasn't really tested for," Milroy testified.

The results were negative. The only substance found was gamma hydroxybutyrate, GHB, a substance known as a date-rape or party drug. Milroy said the body manufactures it and the small amounts found were consistent with typical and natural post-mortem changes.

The pathologist had made one puzzling discovery beneath the scalps of the victims. Rona, Zainab and Geeti had bruises on the tops of their heads. Rona had the largest of these injuries, two adjacent bruises that covered an area six centimetres in diameter. It was a "fairly substantial" fresh injury, caused before her death, up to as long as thirty-six hours before she died.

Milroy said the "moderate impact" injury could have caused unconscious-ness, and resulted from a blow to her head or her head striking something solid. The doctor also found bruising in the large muscle of the neck, near her left ear and in the muscle over her voice box. He believed these were "agonal" injuries caused when a person violently thrashes about in the moments before death.

Zainab had two small bruises that appeared to have come from two "minor" bumps to the head. She also had bruising in her right chest, beneath the skin, that could have resulted from seizures during the dying process but might also be explained by "force against restraint."

Geeti had two small bruises on her head, the result of an impact greater than the injury Zainab suffered, and some bruising over the right collar-bone. The collarbone area injury was not in the muscle and was not agonal, Milroy said, but more likely caused by pinching of the skin.

Sahar did not have any fresh injuries, and Milroy could not explain the bruises he found on the heads of Zainab, Geeti and Rona. "It clearly requires explanation and what is somewhat unusual is that they have three areas of impact to the head and there is a relative absence of injury else-where on the body," he testified.

It was possible that Zainab, Geeti and Rona bruised their heads when they banged into the roof or window of the car as the vehicle crashed into the water, Milroy said, in response to a question from Kemp. When Crown prosecutor Laarhuis had a chance to re-examine the doctor, he asked about the likelihood that the bruises on the heads of the three victims occurred when the car toppled into the canal.

"I think it's difficult to put any specific probability," Milroy answered. "What the jury will have to consider is, in a scenario where you have four people entering the water, in that hypothesis alive and in the dark, why you only get bruises in one area with the potential to impact a number of dif-ferent areas."

BEFORE MONTREAL LAWYER SABINE VENTURELLI TESTIFIED, jurors were sent out of the room so lawyers could discuss "another one of those hearsay situations," as Laarhuis described it. Venturelli had been working on Rona's immigration file, helping her to obtain permanent resident status. Rona had arrived in Canada November 6, 2007, on a visitor visa that had been renewed twice.

Venturelli had testified in February 2010 at a preliminary hearing that she had received a call, in either April or May 2009, from Zarmina Fazel, Tooba's aunt, who lived in Montreal. Fazel, a confidante of Shafia's, was also a native of Afghanistan. She spoke English fluently and accompanied Shafia and Rona whenever they visited Venturelli's law office. Venturelli testified at the hearing that Rona's application for permanent resident status was going smoothly and was at a stage where a final interview would soon be scheduled. The lawyer expected that Rona's application would be approved.

In the phone call, Fazel told Venturelli that Rona was "causing problems to the family and that Mr. Shafia was asking me to close the file of Mrs. Rona and to have her sent back to Afghanistan . . . and he was offering me an honorarium of $10,000." Venturelli thought it was a moment of anger over a family dispute and not a serious attempt to bribe her. After the bizarre call, Venturelli never heard again from Rona, or Fazel.

Prosecutor Gerard Laarhuis argued that jurors needed to know what Venturelli had heard on the phone, even though it was admittedly hearsay—evidence recounted by a person based on information from others rather than personal experience, in this case the words of Shafia as reported to Venturelli by Fazel.

Kemp argued that if the prosecution wanted evidence of the call placed before jurors, they could call Fazel to testify. Laarhuis acknowledged that was "another matter," but didn't explain further. At the preliminary hearing, Fazel said that, at Shafia's request, she spoke to Venturelli about cancelling Rona's residency application, but said there was no discussion of any specific amount of money, just that Shafia would pay whatever the lawyer's costs were. Laarhuis agreed to "proceed in a very cautious manner." Questioning Venturelli in front of the jury, he did not ask about the phone call.

SHAHRZAD MOJAB WAS THE FIFTIETH AND FINAL CROWN WITNESS. The expert on honour killings would not testify about Zainab, Sahar, Geeti and Rona. She would testify about imaginary girls and women who were guilty of affronts to family honour. She would explain the motivation of families who killed for honour. It was a charade of hypotheticals that could not have seemed hypothetical to anyone in the courtroom. In a long-running battle over Mojab's testimony, the defence had failed to block her appearance at the trial but won this concession. She could explain what an honour killing was, but she could not offer an opinion about whether *this* was an honour killing.

Mojab testified that in patriarchal and patrilineal societies across the Middle East and South Asia, gender inequality is embedded. Women are the property of men. They must be obedient and passive to ensure the dominance of the patrilineage, and their subservience is a public acknowledgment of the patriarch's control. Family honour is tied to the patriarch's ability to control women's bodies, their sexuality and their freedom. Women must guard their virginity and chastity through modesty and through adherence to strict rules of dress and behaviour. If they stray from the rules, signalling that the patriarch has lost control, the family will be dishonoured in the eyes of the wider community. The death of the offending woman cleanses the shame. These codes are not the product of religion, she said, but ancient and tribal in origin.

A long list of perceived offences might tarnish family honour: revealing family secrets publicly, refusing an arranged marriage, dressing immodestly, being the victim of sexual assault, seeking a divorce, even from an abusive husband, committing adultery, consorting with males not approved by the patriarch, engaging in sexual relations outside of marriage. Even suspicion can be a trigger.

"It could be only even a rumour could cause the killing of a young woman," Mojab testified.

No one listening to the professor's inventory of insults to honour could not correlate it with the conduct of Zainab, Sahar, Geeti and Rona. They had done almost *all* of it. In those chaotic last few months of life, according to the professor's checklist, the girls had offended family honour dozens of times: running away, revealing abuse to authorities, painting their nails and baring their legs. Even Geeti had shamed her father by refusing to remain under his control and by making her wishes to be placed with a foster family known publicly. Insolent Rona had encouraged the shameful westernization of the girls she cherished. She too bared her arms, shunned her headscarf, painted her face and asked for a divorce.

Mojab testified that honour killings, unlike domestic violence, are often not the act of a lone perpetrator. Families, particularly male members, can hold meetings to discuss or even plan killing an offending female. Sometimes mothers are involved, she said, in allowing the conditions to exist for such crimes, by taking part in the planning or participating in the killing. Mothers have an unusual role in strict patriarchal families, in which they must negotiate with the males who hold power, usually the father and oldest son, Mojab testified.

"There is a tendency of protecting the female members from the patriarchal structure," she said. By acquiescing to the wishes of the men, in a bid to shelter her children from harm, a mother perpetuates the patriarchal dominance, she noted.

Peter Kemp cast aside the pretense that all this was not about Shafia, Tooba and Hamed.

"If you have an honour killing that is disguised as an accident, can the patriarch still restore control, and therefore his honour?" the lawyer asked.

"Um, yes. Yes, because it is the larger community that, um, still perceives the restoration of the reputation of the family, by eliminating the cause of this reputation."

"Okay, but if the larger community perceives that what happened was an accident, as opposed to an honour killing, then, if there was any shame to be purified, it wouldn't happen, right?" Kemp suggested.

"Um, you know, these are hypothetical questions, and it would be very difficult for me to make a proper judgment on one way or the other. The only thing is that, even in a patriarchal community, larger community relations, even if it is perceived as an accident, everybody, in their hidden conscience, they know that this was an act of honour killing."

25

Cruelty of the Children

PETER KEMP BELIEVED, EVEN BEFORE THE TRIAL BEGAN, that his client would have to do what many accused murderers do not: he would have to testify. The burden of proof was with the Crown, so Shafia did not have to prove his innocence, but he did need to explain the angry rants about his dead children that had been captured on the police wiretaps. The Crown's case turned on the recordings, for which the only reasonable explanation seemed to be that an angry, honour-obsessed father had trumpeted his murderous accomplishment and sought to secure the silence of his accomplices with exhortations about the necessity of what they had done.

The risk in testifying was cross-examination. The Crown would be free to prod Shafia with leading and accusatory questions. The prosecutor could parse his sentences and demand explanations for every discrepancy in every statement he had given to police, and there *were* inconsistencies to be exposed and amplified. There was always the danger that, badgered for better answers than those he gave police, Shafia might offer another version of the truth, a flash of spontaneity that would paint him as a liar.

Removed from the glass-walled prisoner's dock, the diminutive man with a balding head, deeply lined face and rounded shoulders looked small and soft. He calmly sketched his biography: dropped out of school after Grade 6, worked full-time by age eighteen, was given money by a grandfather to open an electronics shop, fled civil war in 1992, eventually settled in Dubai.

"The case was that those people who came to Afghanistan, they were against the women, and the women didn't have the right to go out," Shafia explained, his interpreted words beamed throughout the courtroom to wireless headsets. "The girls' schools were closed, because we were living in Kabul city. My family was a liberal family, and all the time we were under pressure and threats from them, so we left the country, Afghanistan."

When Kemp asked about the transfer of Shafia's business from Afghanistan to Pakistan and then Dubai, numbers were the only detail offered.

"When I transferred my stocks from Afghanistan, I lost $200,000," Shafia boasted. "I just transfer my goods, to the value of $1.5 million to Pakistan."

When Kemp asked about his success selling Panasonic products in Dubai, Shafia recalled a company party: "There was two hundred people, and, between those two hundred people, they gave me something, and my company name was written there, and also they gave me $50,000, a gift."

Kemp asked about a house that Shafia owned in Afghanistan.

"I sold that house, in the year of 2008, for $900,000," he explained.

He insisted that everything he did, he did for his children, even the family's upheaval in 2001 when they moved to Australia in search of better opportunities. Shafia said they returned to Dubai in 2002 because the children were unhappy. He was not challenged by the Crown and no witnesses were called to refute his claim.

When Kemp asked about Zainab's failed marriage, the businessman became a grieving father. Shafia's face flushed red and he began to cry as he explained how Zainab had apologized for impetuously marrying Ammar Wahid.

"Zainab came, and she told me, 'Daddy, please forgive me.' I told her, 'There is nothing, don't worry.' I gave her hundred dollar, and I kiss her face," he said, wiping away tears. Thirty minutes after his tearful recollection, he revealed bitterness about how his children had treated him.

"My children did a lot of cruelty toward me," Shafia said, recalling his discovery of photos of Sahar hugging her boyfriend, Ricardo Sanchez. He swore and cursed her, he said. But it was not motive to kill her. He insisted that he did not see the snapshots until several weeks *after* her death.

"Cruelty" was not a mistake or a mangled thought. Shafia made no attempt to reconsider his words. *He* was the victim. Kemp asked what he had seen in the photos that so upset him.

"One of the picture, what I saw, here, she had a short skirt, and the guy had hug her. And she and all my children and her mom, she just hide this from me. I'm not sure if the mom knew about that, knew about that. I'm not sure if my other children knew about this or not, but they hid that from me. I was upset. I might have . . . I swore, because I say that I didn't expect this thing from my children. I was not happy about that."

The cruelty inflicted on Shafia—his daughters wore short skirts and cavorted with boys—left him angry and vocal. He showed the photos to Tooba and cursed some more, he recalled. "I swear at my children. I told them they did this treachery to me. They lied to me. They did everything hidden from us."

He insisted that he didn't force his children to wear head coverings and to dress modestly. "I never interfered in the clothing that my children wear," he said. "It was up to them, whatever they wanted to wear. I didn't have any interference in that, just wear or not, veil doesn't take her out of Islam."

This was the pattern established for his testimony, a jumble of paradoxes that could not be reconciled. They were good children who did bad things. He didn't care how they dressed but was enraged when they wore short skirts. He loved them but hated their conduct. He cherished them yet despised their treachery. Shafia's creased face and his body language betrayed no guile or subversion.

Shafia acknowledged his bad conduct. He had lied about Rona's status as his wife, but only to ensure he could get her into Canada. He had slapped Geeti, Zafar and Mina, but only once, because they came home late. But there was nothing sinister about the slurs heard on the wiretaps, he explained.

When he said of his dead children, "May the Devil shit on their graves," it meant "so, the Devil will go and check with them, in graves. If they have done a good thing, it will be good. If they have done bad, then it would be up to God what to do."

When he said, "I say to myself, 'You did well. Would they come back to life one hundred times, for you to do the same again,'" he meant that if they came back to life, one hundred times over, he would give them good advice and caution them not to do bad things.

Shafia did not deny that he had called Sahar a "whore" or dismiss it as an irrational, emotional outburst. "When I . . . when I saw that, the pictures, when I saw the pictures with them, of course, Sahar's pictures, of course, before Sahar was deceased, I had so much trust in Sahar, and I don't even raise my voice on it," Shafia stammered. "I loved Sahar very much. But when I saw that, I wasn't, I couldn't even believe that would be Sahar's pictures. Sahar was a very good girl. When I saw the picture, I thought, you know, she betrayed me. She lied to me. She lied to me. She was not a liar. She was sitting right next to me. If she was telling me, 'Father, I love this boy,' I would have . . . 'I want to marry this person,' I would have asked the boy, I would have talked to that boy, and if that boy would have been a good person, of course, I wouldn't have any problems. If he was a bad person? Like Zainab, I would have given her the same advice. When I saw the pictures, and I'm telling you the truth, I was upset when I saw them. And I did not expect this from my children, never."

Shafia insisted he was an honest man, save for one lie. He had not told the truth about Rona. "Any other thing which I said, to this date, I never lie. I never want to lie in my life, and that's what I don't like."

Shafia was indignant when Crown prosecutor Laurie Lacelle suggested to him that he had continued to lie about Rona, even after her death, because he considered her no more than a servant.

"I beg you, dear respected lady, no one would help a maid, a servant to that limit which I helped financially, in our home, and she was a member of my family," he responded. "In all my life, I spent more money for her than Tooba. When she went to France, I just gave her $7,000, in order for . . . to cover her expenses. You don't deal with a servant like that."

Clothed. Fed. Paid. These were the hallmarks of Shafia's benevolence. He never passed up an opportunity to itemize his largesse.

Lacelle reminded him that when he visited Kingston Mills on July 18, he was captured on a wiretap cursing his "filthy and rotten" children.

"Yes, I saw the locks," Shafia said. "I went home and before that, I saw the pictures. I told them, because, respected lady, when they went, they just killed themselves. They didn't kill themselves alone; they killed us, too. Me, three of my children, they are in people's house. They are living outside our house. And three of us, we are in prison. It's not four people who's just lost, or killed. It's just ten people. They're all killed."

Lacelle pointed to the kindness that was reserved for Hamed. She reminded Shafia of a conversation in the police vehicle the day they were arrested: "And do you recall saying to Hamed, 'I commend you to God'?"

"Yes, I said that, 'I will just hand you to God.'"

"And you never once spoke that way about your dead daughters, did you? You never commended them to God. You said, 'May the Devil shit on their graves.'"

"Yes. If I said that, to commend, that, 'We are innocent, so God will help us.' That's what I said, and there's no other reason."

Shafia denied that he had told Latif Hyderi that he wanted to kill Zainab: "I never said this thing to Latif, at all."

He had been on the witness stand for nearly five hours before Lacelle asked any questions about the critical events between June 23 and June 30. Shafia admitted he was a lawbreaker. The family had driven to Niagara Falls in 2008, all ten people in the Lexus. Shafia was behind the wheel when they were caught in a police radar trap near Kingston. He was clocked at more than 150 kilometres per hour, 50 kilometres over the speed limit, and there weren't enough seat belts for all of the occupants. The vehicle was seized. The family booked motel rooms in Kingston while Shafia and Hamed took a train back to Montreal to retrieve their minivan so that they could continue the trip. Shafia recalled that it cost him $650 in fees to recover the Lexus at a later date, in addition to hefty fines.

They didn't make the same mistake when they headed for Niagara Falls on June 23, 2009. The family was split between the Lexus and the Nissan Sentra. The vacation destination was originally Vancouver, he testified, and that was why the family drove to Grand-Remous, a wilderness community more than 250 kilometres northwest of Montreal. A direct route to Niagara Falls, Ontario, did not pass anywhere near Grand-Remous.

Lacelle suggested that the stop there had something to do with Hamed's visit to the isolated locale four days earlier.

"I don't know that area, that where we were, but we wanted to go some places in order, regarding our business, or to see a place," Shafia answered. "But I didn't know the name of that place, exactly. I'm not, I'm not familiar to many places in Canada."

Shafia said he had never been there before, he didn't know Hamed's cellphone had been tracked to the place four days earlier and he didn't know that the area had been searched on Hamed's laptop.

The family had a picnic by a river and stayed in a motel there, Shafia said.

"And you deny that you called Fazil, and told him that you would take Zainab on a picnic, and throw her in the water?" Lacelle abruptly asked.

"I don't have any relationship with Fazil, in such a way, and even I didn't like to hear his voice. I never called him. He called me, in Dubai. And when he told me, 'I'm Fazil,' I just hang up on him," Shafia answered.

The next day, the family drove into Ontario and stopped at Kingston Mills early in the evening. "We didn't know anything, any place by name of Kingston Mills locks, but, because we needed washroom, we went there," Shafia explained.

Lacelle quizzed him about where they parked at the site, how well he knew the spot, whether he saw the water. She reminded him that many photos of the site, including aerials, had been displayed on the big televisions in the courtroom during the trial.

"But you say that you were there two times, the year before, as well?" Lacelle asked, in reference to testimony Shafia gave earlier.

"Yes, 2008."

She was circling, not yet prepared to challenge him about his admission.

"So, you would be very familiar with the site?"

"We went to washroom there. We are not familiar in this area, to say that we always came here, no. When my children were there, I came with them."

The prosecutor asked about the family's stop at the motel on June 30, the highway interchange they chose to take, the signs they had seen. She was preparing to pounce.

Shafia explained that they had stopped at Kingston Mills the first time, in 2008, accidentally. On June 24, 2009, they chose it. It was a good spot for a family of ten, he said, because they didn't have to worry about gas station or restaurant rules requiring washroom users to buy something. On June 29, 2009, it was Hamed's choice, Shafia said, to take the Highway 15 exit from Highway 401. It was the nearest interchange to Kingston Mills.

Lacelle looked directly at the accused father. "Sir, if you had been at that place two times in 2008, why didn't you tell the police that in any of your interviews?" she demanded.

"I was not familiar with this place. I didn't know that by name. Even if police would have told me that, 'Did you come to Kingston Mills locks?' I would have said, 'No,' because I didn't know the name of that place."

"Well, you say, sir, when you're captured on the wiretap, on July 18th, that what you're worried about is the fact that you've been there, three times, before. So, you knew, on July 18th, you'd been there?"

"Yes, when police brought us there, and showed that area, and say, 'That's the spot that your children were drowned, there,' that was the time when we realized that we came to this washroom."

"And you didn't tell the police that, on that day, did you?"

"Police didn't ask any question from me. And that was a question that came to me, that, yes, we came here before, and we used that washroom."

Shafia offered no further rationalizations for how this strange coincidence came to be. It was his stark assertion: He had been to this very spot three times before police officers escorted him there on July 18, 2009, to show him where four family members died. It was one of the few places in Kingston he had visited. Though he pledged to investigators, when he met them June 30, that he would do whatever he could to help solve the mystery of the deaths, he did not tell them, at any time in the weeks before his arrest, that his family had visited Kingston Mills three times before the Nissan was found there.

He did not tell investigators this, even on the day they took him to the spot, because *police didn't ask*.

Lacelle was not done.

"And then, five days later, you're interviewed by Inspector Mehdizadeh, and you don't mention it to him, either?"

"I'm telling you, again, that when police told me that, 'Your children were drowned here,' he didn't say, he didn't use the word 'Kingston Mills lock,' plus, I didn't know that stuff by the name of Kingston Mills lock."

"Well, he showed you photos?"

"Yes, showed me the picture of house, and showed me, 'This is the place.' He didn't ask me, or didn't tell me that, 'If you're familiar with this place.'"

"I'm going to suggest to you, sir, if any of that had been true, and you really wanted police to investigate, and know the truth, you would have mentioned it," Lacelle said.

"Whatever I knew, whatever I remember, I told the police all of that," Shafia insisted.

Lacelle asked a final question on the matter, though the answer was unimportant. The question was the conclusion that any witness to the exchange had surely drawn.

"You didn't tell the police that you'd been there before, because you knew it would be suspicious?" she asked.

Shafia denied it.

The prosecutor next headed for another weak spot in Shafia's narrative.

"One of the things that you knew was suspicious, sir, was the fact that Hamed's cell phone was recorded in Kingston, on June 27th. Correct?" Lacelle inquired.

Shafia said that on the 27th, while the rest of his family was in Niagara Falls, he was alone in the Lexus, driving on Highway 401 near Kingston, when a cellphone in the vehicle rang. He didn't know that Hamed's phone was in the Lexus. It was Sahar calling, telling him that the rest of the family wanted to go home to Montreal. Shafia said he turned around and drove back to Niagara Falls. He had been headed to Montreal to deal with business issues.

Lacelle pointed out that this was not what he had told Mehdizadeh during the interrogation on July 23. He told the inspector that he left Niagara Falls on June 27 with Hamed.

"I didn't say, never, that on twenty-seven Hamed was with me," Shafia protested.

Lacelle read from the transcript of the interrogation, "You say, 'Hamed, um, what, we came here, if here, to go to Montreal.' The inspector asks, 'Who came there?' You say, 'Hamed was with me.' The inspector says, 'You and Hamed?' And you reply, 'Hamed.' The inspector says, 'The children were not there?' You say, 'The children were not there, because we were going to Montreal, and one car was there.' The inspector says, 'One car was in Niagara with the children?' You say, 'Yes.' He says, 'With your wife?' You say, 'Yes. One was with us.'"

Lacelle asked again for the seemingly inescapable answer: "You and Hamed were in the Lexus on the 27th?"

Shafia clung to his new truth. He was alone in the Lexus on that day.

Lacelle pointed out that he didn't tell the inspector that he was alone, with Hamed's cellphone in the SUV.

"He didn't ask me," Shafia replied. "I said I was alone."

It was, he claimed, another fact investigators lacked because they didn't ask the correct question.

Lacelle continued to review the interrogation, in which Shafia referred repeatedly to travelling toward Montreal with Hamed on June 27. Lacelle noted that the other children had told police that Shafia and Hamed left Niagara Falls *together* on June 27 and were gone for a lengthy period. Investigators believed it was a final reconnaissance at Kingston Mills.

"Did you and Hamed go to Montreal, on business, at any point in time between the 24th and the 29th?" Lacelle asked again, drawing an unexpected answer that would extricate Shafia from this predicament.

"We might have gone, yes," he said, suddenly suggesting that there had been *another* trip from Niagara Falls to Montreal during the five-day period.

"And that's something that you never told us, either yesterday, or in your previous interviews?" Lacelle asked.

Shafia clutched at a familiar lifeline to explain his oversight: "I haven't been asked."

Some jurors smirked and spectators snickered. But Shafia's sudden recollection of another trip from Niagara Falls to Montreal explained his insistence that he was alone on June 27. Hamed was with him on that *other* trip.

The prosecutor drilled deeper into Shafia's uncertain account of events on June 29 and June 30. She noted that on June 30, hours after the events, when they should have been fresh in Shafia's mind, he gave Detective Constable Geoff Dempster three different accounts of how Tooba got to the motel in the Nissan with Zainab, Sahar, Geeti and Rona.

"I'm going to suggest to you, sir, you gave three different scenarios to Detective Dempster because you couldn't keep your story straight, because it wasn't true," Lacelle said.

"The story was that which I said, and that's the truth, and that's what I said," Shafia replied.

If he couldn't keep the story straight, because it was untrue, it was because Tooba did not bring the four family members back to the motel in the Nissan, Lacelle continued. They were killed and dumped into the canal.

Shafia said the Qur'an would not permit him to do this. They slept at the motel, and Zainab took the keys and the car.

"How is it a possible someone will do that to his or her own children, my respected lady?" Shafia asked.

"Well, you might do it if you thought they were whores," Lacelle shot back.

"No. Not. I will, again, respected lady, tell you it's only Zainab, which she did that, and Sahar, which I didn't know at that time. And two others, they were innocent, and one was just a child. And nothing, nothing can cause this, that a person with such a common stuff, do such a terrible and heinous thing. It's impossible."

Shafia acknowledged that he was concerned when he awoke early that Tuesday morning in the motel to discover that the Nissan, three daughters and Rona were gone.

"And I expect, if this was true, you would have become increasingly concerned, as time went on?" Lacelle asked.

"Yes, my worry was increasing. At first, I called Sahar. When she didn't answer, then my worry was increased, and I called Hamed."

"The phone records indicate that you called Sahar at 7:01 a.m. That's the call?"

"Yes."

"And you went to the police station at about 12:30 p.m.?"

"Hamed came, and then we came. Hamed came, I think it was 11:20, or 11:15. I can't tell exactly. It was after eleven. We drop the children at Tim Horton, and then we went to the police station."

"Sir, you say you were worried about your missing family members, but, between seven o'clock in the morning, and 12:30 p.m., you made exactly *one* phone call to Sahar's phone," Lacelle observed.

"I think I called once or twice."

"Well, we've had the phone records presented, sir, and I'm going to suggest it was one phone call. Would you agree?"

"That should be correct. Yes."

"You didn't keep calling, to see if she would answer?"

Shafia said he called Hamed, who told him that he had tried calling also, to no avail. He did not ask motel staff if they had seen the four because he didn't understand English. "I was not able to ask, to go and talk to them. If I had an interpreter, I would have done that. I might have done that, because I was not able to speak the language."

But he had two interpreters with him, Lacelle noted. Zafar and Mina, who were asleep at the motel, spoke perfect English.

"And you didn't wake up your English-speaking kids, so they could make the inquiries on your behalf?"

"No. Not."

Shafia had bought a phone card from the motel clerk in order to make the 7:01 call to Sahar's cell, but he did not ask the clerk if he had seen Zainab, Sahar, Geeti and Rona.

"And you didn't ask these things because you knew he hadn't seen them?" Lacelle suggested.

Shafia sat silently.

"You knew they were dead?" Lacelle continued.

"No. Not."

Shafia acknowledged that he believed the deaths of Zainab and Sahar were fated, the result of their treachery. "Yes. Indeed, they do, themselves," he said. "We didn't do anything wrong."

"Because you believed their actions brought about their rightful death?" Lacelle asked.

"Yes."

The prosecutor had, by now, been assailing Shafia for four hours. She returned to the wiretap recordings, reminding him that he had called his daughters "honourless" and "shameless girls," and he had told Tooba and Hamed, "This is my word to you. Be I dead or alive, nothing in the world is above than your honour."

"And for you, there's no value of life without that kind of honour?" Lacelle asked.

Shafia may have sensed that his confrontation with this "dear lady" was coming to an end, and he needed to camouflage the contradictions she had exposed. His answer was a dismissive diatribe.

"For each human being, honour and reputation for that person is important. And when I saw these pictures, after their deaths, in this part, I was angry. My honour is important for me. But the honour and reputation of a human being, to kill someone, you can't regain your reputation and honour. Respected lady, you should know that. In our culture and our religion, if someone kill his wife or daughter, there is no honourless person more than that person who did that act or commit that act. If someone do such a treacherous, such a betrayal, he can't, even that person doesn't kill that girl alone, because with do that, he will never regain his honour, but he will lose it, and it will be worse. When my girls died, people thinks and imagine different ways in different ways, but for me, for me, anyone who, in our culture and religion, anyone who killed his children, or daughter, that person really becomes shameless. That thing doesn't restore honour. Can you tell me in which religion you kill someone, and then that person gain honour? I don't call that honour."

Lacelle reminded him that in another wiretap, he told Tooba and Hamed, "There is nothing more valuable than our honour, and I'm telling you now, and I was telling you, before, that whoever plays with my honour, the words are the same: There's no value of life without honour."

"And that's how you felt, wasn't it?" Lacelle asked.

Shafia said everything he had done in life was for his children, including his flight from Afghanistan to take his family to safety, away from the oppressive Taliban regime.

"Yes, I'm Muslim. I don't deny that. But I'm not a killer, and I don't kill."

26

Whispers

TEN CROWN WITNESSES WHO HAD SEEN AND HEARD EVIDENCE that Sahar was sad, suicidal and desperate to escape an emotionally and physically abusive home had it all wrong, the handsome young man insisted. They didn't know the real story. Life at 8644 rue Bonnivet for Sahar was "joyful" in 2009, just before her death, because she was part of a big, happy family, the eighteen-year-old said. He should know. It was his home too.

Zafar Shafia, one of the four siblings who did not die on June 30, was the second defence witness. The teenager was stylish, with thick black hair. He wore a grey shirt that hugged his slender torso, black pants and grey sneakers. He smiled and high-fived a cousin as he strode into the courtroom on his first day of testimony. He smiled at his parents and brother, staring at him from the prisoner's dock. He would be the only Shafia sibling to testify.

He seemed to have an explanation for the most damning pieces of evidence and testimony that jurors had heard over the twenty-five days the Crown took to present its case. At the end of Zafar's two and a half days on the witness stand, spectators were shaking their heads and whispering, in the corridor outside the courtroom, about his testimony.

The teachers, administrators and social workers to whom Sahar had confided that she was scared and wanted to kill herself had been thoroughly deceived by a seventeen-year-old con artist, Zafar suggested.

"It was a story made to tell teachers," he said. They were lies invented "so we could get sympathy" from teachers and "get away with the stuff we used to do."

Oh, and it was fun too. He and Geeti were complicit in the charades, he added. Sahar would tip them off that a deception was in the works. "She would kind of give us a heads-up that, 'This is what I said.' And we would back her up on her stories." If teachers called youth protection workers or the police, the siblings would simply take back what they had said.

"You thought it was fun that teachers would worry, would call the DPJ, the DPJ would come to your house, and police would come to your house?" prosecutor Gerard Laarhuis sneered, referring to the Direction de la protection de la jeunesse, the Quebec youth protection authority. "You thought that was *fun*?"

"Um, no. I found, um, the part which is fun is that we got away with most of the stuff we did. That's what's fun." Zafar had begun to chew at the right corner of his bottom lip.

He could not explain Rona's diary entry describing a suicide attempt by Sahar at home. He claimed, instead, that *he* was the only child who was ever truly suicidal. After Zainab ran away from home in April 2009, he grew despondent and began to scour the Internet for advice about ending his life. He produced a new piece of information that he had not given police at any time in the previous two and a half years. The revelation explained the most incriminating discovery made by forensic examiners when they burrowed deep into the hidden memory of the family computer.

"We understand that there was, on June 20th, a search done for 'Where to commit murder.' Do you have any knowledge of that, or can you help us, at all, with where that might have come from?" Patrick McCann, Hamed's lawyer, asked Zafar.

"Um, well, I can say that, at the time, when I was suicidal, I was trying to find ways, and, um, I would make searches on the Internet about stuff like that," Zafar answered.

"Okay. But why 'where to commit murder,' as opposed to 'where to commit suicide'?"

"I think, um, I think I wasn't familiar with the, um, with the term 'suicide,' 'suicidal.'"

"Yeah?"

"So I, kind of, thought, murder meant the same thing."

"Like, kill yourself, or kill someone else, was the same?"

"Um, like, kill myself, yeah. That's . . . alright."

"Okay. You say you don't remember making that search, but it's possible you did make that search?" McCann asked.

"Um, yes, that's true. I made quite a few searches like that."

Police had not found evidence of "quite a few" searches like that one, although forensic examiners had recovered tens of thousands of bits of information from the computer. The June 20 search was found in a hidden area of memory along with evidence of other online searches for boat rentals, water, mountains, rivers, iron boxes and the notable query "Can a prisoner have control over his real estate." Zafar told Crown lawyer Laarhuis, during cross-examination, that he was not responsible for any of these searches.

Police had found one additional sinister electronic record.

"On the 16th of June, there was a Google search for 'facts and documentaries on murders.' That wasn't you?" Laarhuis asked.

"Um, I'm not sure about that."

"You're 'not sure' on that? You thought you'd need to, on the 16th of June, you would need to see a documentary on murders?"

"As I said, I'm not sure about that."

"Well, what do you mean, you're 'not sure'? Did you type, make a search?"

"Um, it was a long time ago, and, I'm sorry, I can't say I have or I haven't."

"Do you think you'd remember, if you did?"

"Um, well, as I said, I made a few searches back then, and I don't remember exactly what words I typed in."

Zafar agreed when Laarhuis suggested that his dark mood lifted in the weeks before everyone went on vacation together in late June. He was upbeat, happy to be going on the trip with his family. Zafar did not appear to see where the prosecutor was leading him.

Laarhuis asked a lengthy sequence of questions about Sahar's phony suicide stories, as Zafar had described them, and then switched subjects. He asked Zafar about his education in Dubai. Zafar acknowledged that he had attended an English school until he was thirteen.

"Okay. And you never heard words like 'killing yourself,' or 'suicide'?" Laarhuis asked.

"Um, I probably did, yeah."

"Okay. So, when you told us . . . that you didn't know those words, what you meant to say was that you did?"

"No. It's just that I probably heard, um, I know pretty well what 'kill,' I really, I knew what that meant, and I knew that word, but 'suicide,' um, I wasn't really aware of what it exactly meant," Zafar answered in his typically halting syntax.

"Okay. So, when you used the word 'murder,' you think, you may have, at some time, at some day, did you type in 'How to murder yourself'?"

"Um, no. Actually, I didn't really pay attention on what I typed. I just typed in, 'cause whatever you type in Google, they'll give you results. So, I typed that in Google, and, hoping that they'll give me a result."

"No, no, no. The exact words that were typed in, were, 'Where to commit a murder.' Those precise words were typed in. This wasn't just some random group of words."

"M'hmm."

"I'm asking you: Did you type in, 'How to murder yourself,' or 'where to commit a murder'?"

"Um, yeah, something. I would be making searches like that, at the time," Zafar repeated.

"You would?"

"Yeah."

"And this was on, what day, again?" Laarhuis asked.

"Um, well, after, it was written the 17th. Right?" Zafar responded, seemingly searching for the correct answer.

"No, it wasn't. You're wrong. It was during your happy period, the 20th."

"The 20th? Okay," Zafar said, surprised, perhaps aware of the problematic chronology he had constructed. His "17th" was April 17, but the date of the murder search was June 20, at a time when he had acknowledged his melancholy had lifted.

"Do you want to change your testimony about that, now?" Laarhuis offered.

"Um, no, not at all."

The contradiction was left hanging. Laarhuis had exposed the discord in Zafar's timeline and nothing he could say would rescue it.

There were more problems related to April 17, the chaotic day in the Shafia household when police came to investigate the complaint, made by Zafar, Geeti, Sahar and Mina, that they feared their father. Zafar had testified that he was "absolutely truthful" when he spoke to police who were investigating the deaths of his sisters and Rona and he was honest with the police who came to his home on April 17.

"Okay. So, when you told them that you were afraid, that you thought your dad was dangerous, that was the truth?" Laarhuis asked.

"Um, that was something, um, to make the police take us seriously. I wouldn't say, I wouldn't necessarily say that's true," Zafar replied, suddenly qualifying his truth.

"Well, you needed the police to take you seriously, because it was a serious situation?"

"Um, I wouldn't say that. I would say that all we wanted was the police to take us seriously, because they thought we were fooling them around, and they weren't going to take any action against us, against what we were saying."

"But you were trying to be truthful to the police officers, though?"

"Um, no. All I was trying to do, all I was trying to do was to, um, get the police to take us out of the house."

"So, you were manipulating the police, too?"

"Um, at the time, yes."

"So, you manipulated the police by telling them lies. You manipulated teachers by telling them lies?"

"Um, yeah."

"You manipulated workers from the DPJ?"

"Um, no, I don't think the DPJ. Because, whenever they came, we took back our words."

"So, where do you draw the line on manipulating people, and telling lies?"

"Um, I'd say, when it goes too far, I guess."

Zafar didn't explain what constituted "too far," but his past statements that he now professed were lies, concocted for various reasons, filled a large ledger.

It was a lie when he told police in April 2009 that his father had threatened, "I'll tear you apart."

It was a lie when he told police that his father had assaulted him three times that year.

It was a lie when he told police his father punched him in the face and Hamed pulled his hair.

It was a lie when he told a school vice-principal that things had improved at home, because he didn't want to admit he had lied to police about imaginary abuse at home.

Zafar readily admitted he had been a liar, but certainly not now, not while he was on the witness stand. He did not *say* that some Crown witnesses who had testified before him were liars too, but he contradicted them in ways that suggested someone was lying, or someone was terribly mistaken.

Ricardo Sanchez, Sahar's boyfriend, had testified that Zafar caught the couple in a restaurant together. Zafar said the encounter did not happen. He insisted he had never met Ricardo.

Erma Medina, Ricardo's aunt, had testified that Sahar told her she wanted to run away to Honduras with Ricardo to escape her controlling and abusive father. Zafar said Sahar was "very happy" at home and had no desire to leave.

Ammar Wahid had testified that Zainab was confined to the house and yanked out of school because the pair were caught at her home. Zafar said Zainab chose to suddenly quit school at that time for a break before switching schools.

Motel clerk Robert Miller had testified that after the family checked in around 2:00 a.m. on June 30, the large SUV left the motel and did not return in the thirty minutes he remained awake. Zafar said his father and Hamed left the motel and returned "in a few minutes."

Diba Masoomi and Fahima Vorgetts had testified that Rona had complained she was isolated and belittled by Tooba and sometimes abused by Shafia. Zafar said Rona was happy at home and was treated as an equal to Tooba.

Youth protection worker Jeanne Rowe had testified that when she interviewed Sahar on May 9, 2009, the girl was wearing a hijab. Zafar testified that his father never forced clothing on the girls and none of his sisters ever wore a hijab.

Zafar testified that his parents were loving and liberal, though his father had high expectations for his children. He wanted all of them to get good educations and he expected them to work hard, but he was never violent, save for a few mild slaps delivered on April 17.

Laarhuis wanted explanations for Zafar's cryptic comments during another turbulent period in the family's life, July 21 and 22, 2009, when the children were removed from their home in anticipation of the arrests. Early on the morning of July 22, Zafar called Hamed from an emergency foster home. In the conversation, secretly recorded by police, Zafar told his big brother that "you are one hundred percent caught," which prompted a cautionary rebuke from Hamed, "Don't say these stuff on the phone" because it could be "easily recorded." Zafar had whispered, in response: "Okay, you mean, okay, it's not safe to talk?"

"And your brother is telling you, 'Don't say anything on the phone, because it could be recorded?'" Laarhuis observed.

"Um, yes, that's right."

"Okay. So, is he afraid that you're going to talk about something that might help the police find out what happened to your sisters?"

"Um, no. It's just that I, I didn't believe the police, when they said it. So, that's why, if I believed anything they said, I wouldn't have did all the stuff I did, here."

"Sorry? You didn't believe, what about the police?" the prosecutor asked, baffled.

"When the police told me that they were one hundred percent sure what they did—that my parents and Hamed were involved in this."

"Okay. But Hamed's response to that is, 'Don't talk about that on the phone'?"

"M'hmm."

"I mean, what the police said to you, that's not private or secret?"

"Yes."

"But what is it that you weren't supposed to talk about on the phone?"

"Um, I guess, what, I don't know. I'm not sure," Zafar stammered.

"Well, it's clear that you and Hamed were both concerned that you had information that you didn't want the police to know?"

"Um, I don't think so, no."

"Neither you nor Hamed wanted the police to find out what had happened to your sisters?"

"I don't think that's right."

When accusatory questions invited direct denials, Zafar hesitated.

He *didn't think* that he and Hamed had information that they wanted to keep from police. He *didn't think* that he and Hamed did not want police to find out what happened to their sisters. He maintained that "one hundred percent caught" was just his repetition of what he had heard from the detective who had interviewed him late the previous evening, that investigators were certain his family members were the perpetrators.

Zafar knew otherwise. He testified that he was certain the deaths were an accident, the result of Zainab taking the car for a joyride. It wasn't surprising given what he knew. While the family was in Niagara Falls, Zainab often stole the car keys from her parents' room and secretly drove the Nissan around the parking lot. Zafar said that he was with her several times.

But Zafar could not prove it was an accident. He had fragmentary memory about key events the day his family members died. He was tired and half asleep in the Lexus when the family's two-car caravan pulled into Kingston sometime after 1:00 a.m. June 30. They stopped in a parking lot and the two cars pulled alongside each other. The drivers talked to each other through open windows. Though Laarhuis pressed Zafar for details about the locale, the boy insisted he could not say if it was a parking lot at Kingston Mills. On this detail, his memory was foggy.

Were there any buildings there? *Don't remember.*

Was the parking lot gravel or paved? *Don't remember.*

Was it far from the highway? *Don't remember.*

The location was a critical detail in the prosecution theory: Tooba remained at Kingston Mills in the Nissan with the victims while Shafia and Hamed, who were in the Lexus, dropped the three other children at the motel. The men returned to Kingston Mills to kill the four family members.

Zafar acknowledged that he and his sisters Mina and Fereshta were dropped at the motel. A few minutes later, he recalled, Zainab came into his motel room and asked to borrow his cellphone. He shooed her away. He awoke late that morning to the news that the four family members were missing.

Laarhuis observed that Zafar had a peculiar memory. As time passed, he remembered distant events more clearly so that he could inject vital new details, though only those that supported the innocence of his accused family members.

"So, all of those things, you have a better memory on, now, right?" Laarhuis asked.

"Um, yes."

"Okay."

"I had these memories, before, too, sir. It's just that I was not asked about it."

"Okay. But other stuff that's unhelpful to your mum and your dad and your brother, your memory hasn't improved at all?"

"If you ask me about it, I'll be happy to tell you."

It was a challenge the prosecutor could not pass up. "Well, where did the car stop, while your mother waited with the four of them in it?" Laarhuis asked immediately.

"Um, I don't remember that, sir."

"So, no better memory, there, right?"

27

"These Were All Lies"

TOOBA ARRIVED IN COURT with her thick chestnut hair knotted tightly behind her head. She smiled serenely with pursed, thin lips, swore on the Qur'an, kissed the Muslim holy book, and pledged to tell the truth. She explained that she was a liar. Even when she had not lied to police, her honesty had been qualified.

"As much as my brain worked, I wanted to say the truth, and tried to say the truth," she said. But *wanting* to say the truth wasn't the same as *saying* the truth and so instead, for half of her long police interrogation, she had concocted stories that incriminated her and her son and her husband. On the stand, she confessed deceit: "These were all lies that I said."

The lies washed away the incrimination, leaving behind confusion.

She would spend thirty hours on the witness stand, over five and half days, categorizing her acts and recollections by their relative validity. True. False. Uncertain. Forgotten.

Tooba's testimony was a shrill staccato. She was a harried narrator with too much script for the time allotted. The court interpreters could not keep pace, and often she was reminded to slow down. On her first day, dressed in a flowered blouse, she spoke clearly and confidently, looking directly at her lawyer as she responded to his questions.

She was one of seventeen siblings raised by a pharmacist father and stay-at-home mother in Kabul. It was a happy, middle-class life. Tooba's mother had been divorced and her father's first wife had died of breast cancer, she explained. She had four siblings, all brothers, who shared the same mother. She was selected as a suitable mate for Shafia when she was seventeen. She claimed that Rona and two other women came to her family's home to meet her, though there was no mention of this meeting in Rona's diary.

Tooba said she had great empathy for Rona's plight. When she was pregnant with Shafia's third child, the two women were home together, watching a movie called *Mother* that chronicled the anguish of a barren wife of a wealthy man.

"And that was a time when it affected Rona a lot, and she was crying," Tooba said, beginning to sob. "And she said that, 'This story is exactly like mine. I don't know why happened this to me, why God made it like this.' At that time, I was eight months pregnant, and when I looked at Rona, I was just crying. I was not able to stop my crying. And I stood up and hugged her, and I told her, I put my hand on my tummy, and I told Rona that, 'Rona, in two months, you will be a mom.' And she was crying, and she was laughing." When Sahar was born, Tooba handed the child to Rona to raise as her own.

Tooba's teary account did not match Rona's recollection, contained in her diary. Rona wrote simply that Tooba gave Sahar to her when the child was forty days old. "She is yours and you will have charge of her," Rona recalled Tooba saying.

Tooba's lie-filled police interrogation was momentarily overshadowed by this emotional recollection, but Gerard Laarhuis was a nimble interrogator too, and he was prepared to spend hours revisiting what Tooba had told Shahin Mehdizadeh on July 22.

She had prefaced her admissions with the plea that the inspector never, ever tell Shafia what she would reveal, that the trio were at Kingston Mills together early on June 30. The Lexus and the Nissan stopped in a parking lot on the south side of the property. She got out of the car and was walking with Hamed, in the dark, when Shafia drove the Nissan away from the parking area toward the water. Hearing a splash, Tooba ran toward the sound, cried out, clutched her head and collapsed in distress. The Nissan had crashed into the water. Tooba was helped into the Lexus and next awoke at the motel. This version of the truth had expired a few hours later, the morning after the interrogation. She had not been at Kingston Mills and did not hear a splash. She had driven Zainab, Sahar, Geeti and Rona to the motel in the Nissan. Zainab took the keys to the Nissan and after that, Tooba knew nothing.

On Tooba's second day of questioning by Laarhuis, he extended to her another opportunity to embrace the account of events in which she arrived at the motel in the Lexus.

"I was in my car with four people. I came, the thing which I said first to the police and what I said that yesterday in the court, that was the truth. The first police was truth, yesterday was truth but what I said to Shahin . . . I lied to him."

Discovering Tooba's truth would be a primary school exercise in pattern recognition. Her pattern was: truth, lie, truth, truth, if it was accepted that what she said in the courtroom was the truth.

Laarhuis responded in a drawl. "Soooo, when you said you fell asleep in the Lexus and that you didn't drive any more, what you meant to say was, you didn't fall asleep and you drove the Nissan?"

"I meant that I drove and I came to the motel."

Tooba said she had recanted because she had realized that this one big lie—that they were all together at Kingston Mills that morning—might cause more trouble for Hamed. She had invented the story to save her son from torture. Constable Azi Sadeghi, the Farsi-speaking officer, had told her that Hamed would have to "cool his heels" behind bars and that he would have to sit in jail and "drink ice water."

"Because, one of the torture in Afghanistan was, the accused, when they're being tortured, there's very cold water, and they would freeze in it, and become unconscious under the freezing water," she said. "And I didn't want to mislead that officer, but I just want to lie, in order to get my son out of that torture, and get him out of that situation."

She "wanted to lie" for another selfish reason, to escape the badgering of police who were calling her a liar and murderer: "It wasn't, sir, just Hamed, but all that pressure which I was under that, for the past twenty-three days, it made me to lie, in order to get away from the police."

While Tooba repudiated her admission that she was at the canal when the Nissan plunged into the water, she preserved a vital part of the original account that everyone had given police. The Lexus–Nissan convoy stopped somewhere—she could not say where—when they first arrived in Kingston on June 30. When they pulled off the highway, Shafia was driving the Nissan. After they stopped, Tooba took the driver's seat in the small car and Shafia returned to the Lexus. Tooba was tired, so she told Shafia and Hamed to go in the Lexus to find a motel and return to fetch her and her four passengers, who would wait in the parked Nissan.

This was a critical moment in the execution of the murder plot, the prosecution believed. Tooba's primary role in the killings was to babysit the victims, to keep them calm and unaware, while Shafia and Hamed dropped the three other children at the motel. Either the victims were already incapacitated by sedating substances or they were groggy and asleep, the Crown contended. This "mystery parking spot" where Tooba waited with the four was Kingston Mills, Laarhuis suggested. But Tooba, like Zafar, insisted she could not say where they had stopped. It was near the motel, she thought, close enough to see lights. It was not a parking lot. It was alongside the road.

Tooba could recall what she had said to Rona while they watched a movie together in Kabul twenty years earlier. She remembered the precise date when she acquired her driver's licence in Dubai, June 2004. But she could not remember where they had parked on the morning when nearly half her family died.

"Yes, because I didn't pay attention for that, there was no need for me to pay attention for that that where did we change the cars. I got out and he got in so what was the need for me in order to record that in my memory that where we were and I didn't know that such a thing will happen, such an event and then wrongfully I will be charged and I will be made in order to sit here and give testimony."

It was not the only gap in her memory. Tooba had difficulty recognizing Kingston Mills, though she claimed she had been there three times before police took her to the spot in July.

"Yesterday, you testified that you first recognized the locks on the 18th of July, when police invited you there. Do you remember that?" Laarhuis asked.

"After that accident, yes."

"And, at that time, you wanted to be helpful to police?"

"What do you mean by 'helpful'?"

"You wanted the police to find out what happened to four members of your family?"

"Yes."

"So, when you recognized this place, you recognized this very strange coincidence—that the place that your four family members died was the very place that your family had been, so many times before. You must have wanted to let the police know that—this strange coincidence that they died at a place where you had been only a few days prior, but also a couple of other occasions, as well. So, did you tell that to the police, then?"

"At that time, no one ask us, in order for us to tell that to the police."

Groans wafted from the public gallery.

"Right. But, you're there," the lawyer persisted. "You're at the place where now you know your daughters died. It's the first time you're there. And it must have struck you, immediately, 'Oh, my God. This is the place where we were, just a few days before, and where we had been, a couple of times, last year. I should tell the police that my family has died at a place that I recognize'?"

"At that time, it didn't cross our mind, sir, to tell this, right away, to the police. To that spot, which a family members dies there, and you see that place? At that time, it didn't cross our mind to say that to the police, and police didn't ask that question from us."

Just as Shafia had done, she blamed police: if only they had asked the right question.

There was a simpler explanation, Laarhuis pointed out. They concealed it because they knew it would be suspicious. No one in the family told police about the previous visits to Kingston Mills.

"So did you believe that the entire family had made the same mistake and had forgotten the very same three events?" Laarhuis asked.

"Yes, we didn't know that place, they asked us this question that, 'Were you there?' and we said, 'No.'"

"So you believed that all of you, Shafia, Hamed, yourself, Mina, Zafar, you had all made the same mistake and had all forgotten about the three other times that you'd been there?"

"No, we didn't forget sir, but we didn't know the place. We didn't know its name. After that incident, that place was famous which you told us."

But why, the prosecutor wondered, did Tooba not tell the inspector, during her interrogation on July 22, four days after she'd been to Kingston Mills, that she knew the place? "You were there and you lied to him, you said 'Never,'" Laarhuis snapped at her.

"But he was telling me that, 'That night you are involved in this crime with your husband and son,' he was telling me that, I was telling him, 'No, never.'"

Laarhuis threw Tooba's words back at her: "'I am certain you have been there,' and you answered, 'No, never,' you said that because you did not want him to know that you had been there."

"But sir, he told me that, 'No, you were there.' I thought that he's telling me that night which your husband and your son did that, you were there. I told him, 'No, never,' but he was not made that clear when I was there, which I would have been able to tell him clearly when I was there."

"You certainly weren't telling him what he wanted to hear, were you?"

"What I knew, I was talking about that, but what I told to Mr. Shahin it was not what was the truth. I was under a lot of pressure when I told him whatever I told him that was all lies."

"Right, but you said that you were under pressure and you were just saying what they wanted you to say to get Hamed out of the torture, right?"

"It was not just Hamed's case, sir. He put me there for six hours and I was not able to sleep in the room because of my other children. It was not just Hamed's issue. Three other daughters I lost that before, I lost Rona, I lost all my life. It wasn't just Hamed's problem. It was the problem of my seven children and Rona and all my life."

Her wiretapped anxiety about a camera and her denials to Mehdizadeh about having been previously to Kingston Mills did not make sense unless she had something to hide, Laarhuis said.

"You could have said to him at that point, 'Ah, I know why you're talking about the camera, I was here on the 24th. That's when I was here.' You were concerned about it and you never told him. You never told him you were there on the 24th or the 29th. Correct?"

"Sir, as I said to you before, he put me in a circle and that night, it was, 'You with your husband and your son,'" she said, her voice rising, as she drew a large circle in the air with her arm. The gesture seemed to captivate the jurors, who were staring at her. "First, I should have cleared that circle and then to say something else. I was repeating that to him that, 'Sir, I was not there,' and he was telling me, 'No, you are lying and you were there and you were helping them,' but I forgot about the other one, but he was telling me that, 'No you were there,' but I was telling him, 'No, I was not there, I was not there,' but I didn't know the time of that."

She denied it, but Laarhuis declared that the family had not visited Kingston Mills in 2008. It was a fabrication to explain why, on the wiretaps, they talked about having been at the canal three times. There were, the prosecutor announced, three visits: June 24, when they stopped en route to Niagara Falls; June 27, when Shafia and Hamed scouted the site to ensure it was a suitable location for a murder disguised as an accident; and June 30, when the plot was carried out.

Her husband's angry rants about his daughters, captured on the wire-taps, were also innocent, Tooba insisted. "Shafia had one custom: He used to talk a lot. And he used to talk a lot about things. He was persistent on something. He used to take some mistake which the children did, he used to go on, and continuously he was just swearing at them, and continuously talk about that, for weeks. That was what he did."

For this reason, she hid from her husband minor infractions of the children. She hid photos too, *those* photos, to dull his anger. The snapshots that inspired Shafia to damn his daughters as "shameless" and "whores" were found in the house sometime between July 5 and July 7, as the family was cleaning in preparation for the arrival of overseas visitors coming to pay respects, Tooba said. In the askew, arm's-length self-portraits, Zainab and Sahar were dressed only in underwear, or in bikinis, or they were seen in the embrace of boys. Shafia seethed.

"The picture which make him the most upset, made him upset lots, one of the picture was Sahar, God bless her spirit, it was she was with Ricardo, with a short skirt. And the one which make him very upset, that was a short, upper parts. And so that was the picture with the bra. And that was the picture which made very upset."

Tooba said she removed from the album the photos that Shafia found most offensive, dozens of them, and concealed them in the outer pocket of a suitcase. Some of these were photos whose origin appeared to be Sahar's cellphone camera, but no one could explain how they turned up as prints in Hamed's suitcase. Tooba hoped Shafia's anger would fade if the photos were out of sight. Her account of the discovery of the photos corroborated Shafia's claim that his rants were not evidence of a motive to kill his daughters because he had not seen the photos until *after* their deaths.

But there was evidence that the album had been discovered sooner than Tooba claimed. Laarhuis reminded her that the grieving parents had appeared in television news stories that were taped at their home a few days after the Nissan was found underwater.

"Now, would it surprise you to know, though, that, in those media interviews, you're actually looking at the very album that's an exhibit, here, in this courtroom, today?" Laarhuis asked.

"Sir, if I show my home to you, I have tens of albums, which they're all the same," Tooba shot back.

"Well, we see the album. It's got 'Princess' right on the cover; it's pink. Are you telling me you have ten such albums in your house?"

"Yes. If I would have been free, right now, I would have brought the same albums, many of them. There is not just one album of that in the world."

"Where were they, when the police searched your house?"

"What was where?"

"All these ten other photo albums that you have."

"Picture albums, indeed, they were in the closets, in the cabinets, in different places, in spots where a person puts his albums there."

Eventually, she conceded that there were only one or two pink "Princess" albums, including the one police had found on a table in the living room when they searched the apartment on July 21.

A clip was played from a television news story from July 3, 2009. Shafia appeared on camera, standing in the living room crying as he leafed through a pink "Princess" photo album.

In response to her own lawyer, Tooba had acknowledged that the album seized by police was the one from which she extracted the "shameless" photos. But, she said, summarily dismissing the Crown's suggestions, the one seen in the television clip was not the same album.

Another unusual discovery was made during the cleanup at home after the deaths, Tooba acknowledged. Shafia handed her three or four condoms that were found in the room where Sahar, Geeti and Rona most often slept. Tooba believed that they belonged to Zainab.

TOOBA INSISTED SHE WAS AN HONEST AND PIOUS WOMAN, despite her lies to the inspector. She prayed five times a day and she tried to instill in her children an understanding of the pillars of Islam. Her faith dictated that nothing may be forced on any child. She had told her brood that if she forced them to follow her commands, she would sin. But there were rules in the household.

"This was a thing which me and Shafia, and also Rona, we decided that, when the children were not graduated from school, and they didn't show their diploma to us, they're not allowed to have girlfriend or boyfriend, or to get married."

The rule applied to both the girls and the boys, including her adult son and daughter. There was a curfew too, nine in summer and four thirty or five in winter for all of the children, so they would be home early to do schoolwork. "So, they needed that curfew."

She explained to her daughters the religious importance of wearing a hijab, but she did not insist they wear it. "But you have to teach them. That's our job."

The girls never wore headscarves in Canada or in Dubai, she recalled, contradicting others. Ammar Wahid said Zainab wore a headscarf while she attended St. Pius X in Montreal. Sahar's schoolmates at St-Ex, who did not testify, saw her wearing a headscarf at school and crying because it had been forced on her. In Dubai, the older girls at Al Sadiq had been required to wear a headscarf as part of their school uniform.

Not only did Sahar reject the modest head covering, but she had a troublesome petulant streak, her mother explained. "Because, Sahar, she had one habit. Like, whenever, if she was missing a movie, not to watch, she would say, 'I will kill myself,' or even if she saw a clothing or something, if she was not able to get that, she used to say, 'If I can't buy this, I will kill myself.' And this was something which I was used to listening, that she used to say that."

It was a tactic the girl adopted beginning in Grade 6, Tooba said, so the wary mother began ignoring her child's threats. In the spring of 2009, when Geeti warned Tooba that Sahar was threatening suicide, Tooba dismissed it as meaningless. Sahar ate some preservative from shoe packaging but did not get sick, Tooba said. Despite having dismissed the threats, Tooba was adamant that she hadn't been callous about them. In response to the allegation in Rona's diary that she had said, "Let her kill herself," Tooba responded, "I never say anything like this."

Tooba acknowledged that she and Rona argued over Sahar's half-hearted suicide attempt, but she considered Rona her equal and co-wife. Rona was not abused, alienated or humiliated, as Rona's diary claimed, Tooba said.

She scoffed at the entry that offered evidence of Tooba's contempt for Rona: "You are not his wife. You are my servant."

"No, I never said anything like this to her."

Tooba insisted that Rona was like a mother to all seven children, but her observations diminished Rona's role as a wife. "At the time when I married with Shafia, I didn't see Shafia to sleep with Rona, or to have any husband-and-wife relationship with her," she said. She never saw Rona with a wedding ring.

TOOBA'S ANSWERS CONTRACTED as her week on the witness stand wore on. On her fifth consecutive day of testimony, her body seemed to stiffen and the sly grin that occasionally crossed her lips vanished. Her dislike for Gerard Laarhuis had ripened into contempt.

"Tomorrow will be one week that I'm under your pressure here and you're asking me one question for hundred times and you're repeating that and I'm telling you the same thing, that I don't know and I was under the same pressure when I was in front of Shahin which I told him, I don't know and I am in the same situation right now."

Tooba's lament for her predicament did not soften her questioner. Laarhuis confronted her with the prosecution's chronology of the crime.

Tooba sat with the four, in the Nissan, at the unlit and isolated canal property, waiting for Shafia and Hamed to return. The victims may have been sleeping. The front seats of the Nissan were reclined steeply when it was found. Zainab's cardigan was on backwards, as if she had been using it as a blanket. When the men returned, Tooba returned to the Lexus and Shafia and Hamed began drowning the four, one by one, perhaps in the shallow turning basin near the washrooms. Tooba knew this, Laarhuis insisted. She had telegraphed her knowledge during her interrogation by Mehdizadeh, when she said, "If I was awake and they were pressing and putting them into the water, I might have . . . heard a sound of splashing or something."

"These were not random words and they were not careless words," the prosecutor said, speaking slowly and softly. "Splashing" is what people do when they are in the water, he said.

Tooba said she simply repeated Mehdizadeh's allegations, in a bid to escape his insults and persistent questioning.

Laarhuis scoffed, "This wasn't an answer suggested by Shahin at all." The inspector had never said "splashing." He had told Tooba only about the recollection of the young boy, who saw two vehicles and heard a "splash."

"I'm putting to you that the 'they' that were pressing and putting them into the water were Shafia and Hamed and you saw it," Laarhuis persisted. "You said that because that's what you remember from that night, that somebody was pressing and putting them into the water."

"I never see those things and the gentleman was telling me all those things so all those things which I heard from him, so then I was making up something. I was telling him something in order for him to leave me alone, and get out of that insult and then I just wanted that he should leave me alone."

"I'm putting to you that if it wasn't Zainab who drove them to their deaths, only the three of you had the opportunity to have done anything because only the three of you were with them."

"We will never do anything like this. Don't say anything like this."

"I'm putting to you that one of you drove the Nissan to that place with the bodies inside and drove it to the edge of the canal wall and that the plan was that someone would drive it up to the canal wall. You needed a place where the car would drop straight down and be under the water. It couldn't be a place where the car would get caught driving into a lake or something like that. It had to fall and go right under the water and that, in part, is why you left the Pontiac Montana at home and bought a new car just one day before this trip. You wanted a car that was lower and cheaper. Do you agree with that?"

"No, not, never."

"And you took this lower and cheaper Nissan, you or Hamed or Shafia, with the bodies inside, and somebody drove it to the other side and somebody positioned it on that plateau at the edge of lock number one where the Nissan went in and somebody left the car running," he continued, as if narrating a horror story. "This was part of the plan—rolled down the window, put the gearshift in neutral, aimed the wheels of the car so that it would go between the two crabs that were at that location with the bodies inside, the seats reclined, the headlights off, the dome light off, the wipers off, got out of the car, closed the door, reached through the open window, put the car from neutral into gear number one, thinking that, on its own power, the Nissan would go into the water. What none of you expected, what was not part of the plan, was that the Nissan would get hung up. Do you agree with that?"

"Never, no."

"And that when the Nissan got hung up, there was an emergency because now you had bodies inside of a car hung up on the edge of a canal and you and Hamed or you and Shafia were in the Lexus and the emergency required driving the Lexus, positioning it behind the Nissan. There wasn't enough room so you had to do it at an angle which is what caused the Nissan to rotate as it was being pushed in, that we heard from the accident reconstructionist, or the collision reconstructionist, and that's what caused the damage to the headlight of the Lexus, the tail light of the Nissan. That's what rubbed the *S* and the *E* off of the back of the Nissan, two pieces that Hamed, for whatever reason, didn't pick up. Do you agree with that?"

"No sir, we are not murderers. We were a very sincere and collected family. This crime, we would never do such a crime. Don't ever tell me such a thing. I'm a mother. If you were a mother, if you were a mother, then you could have known what's in the heart of a mother for a child," she said, her mouth trembling, tears coming. "It's just a mom know that. No one else can feel that. Don't ever tell me that I killed my children. No. Never."

Her breathing was shallow and frantic, as if she were drowning in the words.

In addition to Tooba, Shafia and their son Zafar, the defence called five witnesses, including four who had no knowledge of the critical events in Canada between April and June 30, 2009, but who testified to the good character of Tooba and Shafia. A half-brother and a half-sister of Shafia, who had lived with him in Afghanistan, each told the court that they believed he was a liberal-minded man and a loving father who was incapable of murder.

Farida Nayebkheil, who travelled to Canada from Denmark to testify, mistakenly identified a photo of Sahar in a short skirt as Zainab when a Crown lawyer showed it to her. She didn't know that her half-brother called his daughter a "whore" after he saw the photo and was surprised by Shafia's reaction. She didn't know he held those beliefs, she testified.

Nabi Misdaq, an Afghan scholar and former head of BBC Radio's Pashto service, was the defence team's final witness. Misdaq, who was born in Afghanistan, was fluent in Dari, Pashto and English. He was permitted to testify as an expert on Afghan culture and language, but in a ruling, Supreme Court Judge Robert Maranger restricted the scope of his testimony and ordered the defence lawyers not to ask Misdaq about honour killings. Misdaq would not be permitted to reinterpret the translations of the wiretaps, Maranger instructed, noting that lawyers on both sides had already agreed to their accuracy.

Misdaq proposed an alternative explanation for Shafia's foul curses that had been recorded. He testified that language like "whore," "prostitute," and "cut them into a thousand pieces" is common among Afghan men, particularly within families, and that the words were "not to be taken literally."

The expression "may the Devil shit on their graves" may be closest to the western expression "to hell with them," Misdaq said.

Shafia's venomous expletives might indicate rage and anger at the predicament the family faced, which he believed was unfair, Misdaq testified. He said some concepts expressed in Dari are difficult to translate into English.

In answer to questions from Crown lawyer Gerard Laarhuis, Misdaq acknowledged he had never before been certified as an expert witness at a criminal trial, he had not done any studies of the use of profanity by Afghan men, and he had not read any literature on the subject. Misdaq was on the witness stand for one hour. When he stepped down, the defence lawyers indicated that they had no more witnesses to call, confirming that Hamed would not testify.

The defence laywers had one final opportunity, their closing addresses, to sway the jury. The three lawyers, collectively, spent six hours addressing the jurors.

Peter Kemp, Shafia's lawyer, moved the lectern to an arm's length from the elevated platform where the jurors sat and looked directly at them.

There was ample evidence of Shafia's concern for his family, rendering it unbelievable that he would want to kill them, Kemp told the seven women and five men.

"You would have to accept that the father of seven children, who had spent the last twenty years providing for them all around the world, who was in the process of building a large new home for them, for no apparent reason, became so black, so dark, so evil, that he would cold-bloodedly plan the execution of three of them and carry out that plan," Kemp said.

The lawyer argued that there wasn't time for the three family members to have killed four people and then for Hamed to drive to Montreal and receive a call on his cellphone at 6:48 a.m., given the prosecution theory that the victims may have been drowned elsewhere before they were placed in the Nissan.

David Crowe, who represented Tooba, pointed to the evidence of several prosecution witnesses who said they were told by some of the Shafia children that Tooba was "an angel," a loving and kind mother. There was no evidence, he said, that she ever abused any of the children, and even when she told an interrogator that the trio was at Kingston Mills on the morning of June 30, she did not say she was involved in the deaths in any way.

Hamed's lawyer, Patrick McCann, argued that the prosecution's case had a "huge hole." "There is no evidence, absolutely no evidence as to how the four women were incapacitated before being placed in the Nissan," the lawyer said.

He suggested jurors should discount the evidence of the teachers and school officials who testified that Sahar feared her father and oldest brother. Those witnesses may have been exaggerating or their memories may have been "sort of amplified" with the passage of time, McCann argued.

He said a key cellphone record introduced by prosecutors that had placed the family near the canal early on the morning of June 30 was not incriminating.

The record showed that at 1:36 a.m. on June 30, Sahar's cellphone received a text message that went unanswered. The phone was communicating through a tower one kilometre from Kingston Mills, but the records showed the phone could have been located in a tower sector closer to the Kingston Motel East than the canal, McCann noted.

"This, ladies and gentlemen, is perhaps one of the most important pieces of evidence in the trial that almost disproves the Crown theory," McCann told the jurors.

The lawyer suggested that the Crown theory that the victims were incapacitated, placed in the Nissan and pushed into the canal did not make sense.

"The only explanation that makes any sense at all is the one Hamed gave to Moosa Hadi," McCann said, which made the deaths a terrible accident, and not murder.

28

Honourless

THE TWELVE JURORS spent just fifteen hours deliberating secretly together before returning with their verdicts. Their speedy decision foretold the outcome.

"Please indicate your verdict on each accused as I call their names," the registrar of the court instructed. "Mohammad Shafia."

"The verdict is guilty, first-degree murder, all counts," the foreman responded, the verdict sheet vibrating in his trembling hands.

"Tooba Mohammad Shafia," the registrar continued.

"Guilty, first-degree murder, all counts."

Hamed slumped forward onto the wooden half-wall at the front of the prisoner's dock, his head collapsing onto his arms. His father patted his shoulder, then his head.

The registrar continued the roll call: "Hamed Mohammad Shafia."

"Guilty, first-degree murder, all counts," the foreman replied, for the third time.

Tooba began to weep, but Shafia's body and face had stiffened. His lips were pursed.

As required, the judge asked the convicted killers if they had anything to say before he passed sentence.

"We are not criminal, we are not murderer, we didn't commit the murder and this is unjust," Shafia said, in Dari, in a clear voice.

"Tooba Yahya, do you have anything to say before I pass sentence?" Supreme Court Judge Maranger asked.

"Yes, Your Honourable Justice, this is not just, I'm not a murderer, and I'm a mother, a mother!" she said, in Dari.

"Hamed Mohammad Shafia, do you have anything to say before I pass sentence?"

"Sir, I did not drown my sisters anywhere," Hamed replied in English, speaking for the first time at the trial. Until that moment, he had exercised his right to say nothing in his defence. Because he did not testify, he was never challenged on the remarkable story recorded by Moosa Hadi.

As is customary for judges, Maranger did not respond to their protestations.

"You have each been convicted of the planned and deliberate murder of four members of your family," he began, reading from a page of prepared remarks. "It is a verdict that is clearly supported by the evidence presented at this trial."

Maranger looked up from his page and stared at Shafia, Tooba and Hamed. In the headset that had delivered him the Dari translation of all the proceedings, Shafia heard his words used against him.

"It is difficult to conceive of a more heinous, more despicable, more honourless crime than the deliberate murder of, in the case of Mohammad Shafia, three of his daughters and his wife, in the case of Tooba Yahya, three of her daughters and a stepmother to all her children, in the case of Hamed Shafia, three of his sisters and a mother.

"The apparent reason behind these cold-blooded, shameful murders was that the four completely innocent victims offended your twisted notion of honour, a notion of honour that is founded upon the domination and control of women, a sick notion of honour that has absolutely no place in any civilized society."

The judge imposed life sentences with no chance of parole for twenty-five years, which were automatic for the crime of first-degree murder. If parole were ever granted, the trio would be flagged for removal from the country by immigration authorities.

His condemnation complete, Maranger slapped the page onto the desk and looked toward the jurors. "Members of the jury, thank you very much for your service, for your coura—" he said, stopping before completing the word. He seemed to have reconsidered the wisdom of praising them for an act of "courage" in convicting the trio.

"That's the end, thank you," the judge said.

29

Love

I WAS KINDA SCARED that somin' bad was gonna happen to her.

The feeling had gnawed at Jake since the catastrophic outcome of his peck on Sahar's cheek in the corridor of St-Ex in the fall of 2007. He had not forgotten the sight of the sad girl standing in the hall, tears trickling down her cheeks, as she explained that her dad got really mad and slapped her.

It was just one harmless little kiss.

She had never said that she was afraid of her father, but he believed that she was. If he'd slap her over a kiss on the cheek, what would be his reaction if he caught her doing something really bad? Jake had mostly stayed away from Sahar after that.

Word of the verdict spread quickly online among the handful of former St-Exers who had known Sahar and had stayed in touch. Many of them had left Montreal by the time the trial concluded on January 29, 2012. Jake was back in New York, living with his sick mom, when he heard that Sahar's father, mother and brother had been sent to prison. He wasn't surprised, but he was saddened and it stirred memories of the sweet girl who had pursued him.

wht do other girls hav that i dont?

pls go out with me

im in luv w you

He kept saying no to her, but never firmly enough to push her away. He enjoyed Sahar's attention, but he had a girlfriend and he was worried about that *thing* with her dad.

Still, he had felt a tinge of jealousy when that *crazy* text message from Sahar arrived in May 2009. Jake was at his job, at the building where he did janitorial work. He could not respond to messages. He wondered if it was a lie. Maybe she just wanted to get his attention, or make him jealous? Maybe it was a final, desperate ploy to get him to date her.

She was pregnant and she was having her boyfriend's baby, she had written.

Jake saw her at school, from a distance, once more, but they did not talk after the text message. He never found out whether her shocking claim was true. It was only weeks later that he heard Sahar, Zainab, Geeti and Rona were dead.

He was glad that he had something to remind himself of her. He still had the silver chain that she had given him in their first year together at school, and the memory of one magical afternoon they'd spent together at Old Port. It hadn't *really* been a date, but there had been no denying the feelings it had sparked.

She had invited him to go the waterfront with her and her big sister in April 2009. For the first time, he did not rebuff her, but he brought along his twelve-year-old sister, Jennifer. Sahar stepped out of the car when it stopped near the Metro station to pick up Jake and his sister. Jake tried not to stare, but he was agape at how *gorgeous* she looked. She was wearing a torso-hugging blue corset that exposed her arms and shoulders, tight blue jeans and high-heeled sandals. Eyeliner and mascara accentuated her big brown eyes. Her lips shimmered. He had never seen her like this. He had never looked at her like this.

Inside the car, Jake met Zainab and her boyfriend, Ammar, and his friend Wasi, who was driving. They stopped first at McDonald's and then drove downtown to Old Port. Sahar, Jake and Jennifer split off from the others and walked by the water. They told jokes and traded stories about St-Ex and their schoolmates. They stopped at a vendor and Sahar bought ice cream for the trio. Jennifer squealed with delight.

It was a sunny spring day and Jake thought Sahar seemed happy; she was smiling most of the time. They did not hold hands or kiss, but she was, at least, close to the boy she coveted. She trusted him with her secrets. Her father was a rich businessman who was building a big, fancy house for the family, she said. He was always away, travelling on business, never home with her and her sisters and brothers. She figured he didn't really care about them.

"He doesn't give us any love, just money," she told Jake. "That's all he cares about. He gives me money, not love, and that's what I want. I just want love."

Postscript

DURING AN AUTOPSY, pathologist Dr. Christopher Milroy found that Sahar was menstruating and was not pregnant. He detected no signs that she had been pregnant. But the doctor said that if she had been in the early stages of a pregnancy that ended in a miscarriage or an abortion, there might not have been any remaining evidence of it.

Three of Sahar's close friends at St-Ex, Herna Paul, Ray Fernandez and Lucy Lastragui, said that Sahar did not tell them that she was pregnant. Jake Suarez is the only person to say publicly that he heard the account first-hand, from Sahar. Jake never told anyone about the text because he didn't know if it was true. Jake was never interviewed by investigators.

Whether Sahar had ever actually been pregnant is perhaps beside the point. In families that adhere strictly to the cultural code that women must remain chaste and obedient to preserve the family's honour, sexual relations outside of marriage—or even the suggestion of them—are considered one of the most serious affronts to honour.

WITHIN DAYS OF THE CONCLUSION OF THE TRIAL, Shafia, Tooba and Hamed each filed notices of their intention to appeal their convictions to the Court of Appeal for Ontario. The appeals are not likely to be heard before 2013.

All three, who were placed in federal penitentiaries, declined to be interviewed for this book.

The Rona Amir Foundation has been established in Montreal. It will provide counselling and support for women and girls at risk of honour-based violence.

Zainab, Sahar, Geeti and Rona's names have been added to a stone cairn that stands at the entrance to the Kingston Police station and honours victims of domestic violence.

Acknowledgments

I AM DEEPLY GRATEFUL TO MANY PEOPLE who entrusted to me their memories, in the hope that this book could give new life to Zainab, Sahar, Geeti and Rona. A long list of people extended kindness, advice and invaluable assistance, particularly Jodi Mullen, and to them I am indebted.

Thank you also to those who shared my passion for this story. Daphne Hart, at the Helen Heller Agency, was my champion and cheerleader who found the perfect home for this project at HarperCollins. At HC, Jim Gifford was encouraging and enthusiastic. Kate Cassaday was the skilled editor every writer hopes for, someone as emotionally invested in and dedicated to the story as the author. She made me so much better. Peter Edwards pointed me in the right direction.

Thanks to copy editor Sarah Wight, legal counsel Alison Woodbury, Postmedia News and the Montreal *Gazette*.

Honour crimes are inextricably linked to a host of other oppressive concepts rooted in the subjugation and domination of women, including forced marriage and mutilation. Though these practices are not well documented, an insightful few have examined them. Their work informed my writing and I owe them gratitude and thanks for their courage. Jordanian journalist Rana Husseini's *Murder in the Name of Honor* (Oneworld), Turkish writer Ayse Onal's *Honour Killing* (Saqi Books), Jasvinder Sanghera's *Shame* (Hodder) and Ayaan Hirsi Ali's books, particularly *Infidel* (Simon & Schuster) are valuable resources for anyone seeking to understand the roots and scope of these scourges.

Photo Credits

1. Photo provided to author by Diba Masoomi; photographer unknown
2. Trial exhibit; photographer unknown; photo cropped by the publisher
3. Trial exhibit; photographer unknown
4. Trial exhibit; photographer unknown
5. Unaltered photo provided to author by Zubaida Siddique; photographer unknown
6. From the author's collection
7. Rob Tripp
8. Trial exhibit; taken from the Shafia home computer; photographer believed to be Zainab or Sahar
9. Trial exhibit; taken from the Antoine-de-Saint-Exupéry high school yearbook; photographer unknown
10. Trial exhibit; taken from a cellphone used by Zainab and recovered from the Nissan Sentra; photographer believed to be Zainab
11. Trial exhibit; taken from a cellphone used by Sahar and recovered from the Nissan Sentra; photographer unknown. Image cropped; originally captioned "25. Ricardo and Sahar – BTB on cell phone on 14 May 09 (also in black suitcase)"
12. Trial exhibit; taken from a cellphone used by Sahar and recovered from the Nissan Sentra; photographer unknown
13. Trial exhibit; photographer unknown
14. Trial exhibit; taken from a cellphone used by Zainab and recovered from the Nissan Sentra; photographer believed to be Zainab
15. Trial exhibit; taken from a cellphone used by Sahar and recovered from the Nissan Sentra; photographer is Sahar
16. Trial exhibit; taken from a cellphone used by Sahar and recovered from the Nissan Sentra; photographer is Sahar

17. Trial exhibit; taken from a cellphone used by Zainab and recovered from the Nissan Sentra; photographer is Zainab

18. Trial exhibit; taken from a cellphone used by Sahar and recovered from the Nissan Sentra; photographer unknown

19. Trial exhibit; taken from a cellphone used by Sahar and recovered from the Nissan Sentra; photographer is Sahar

20. Trial exhibit; Kingston Police; photographer is Constable Aaron Anderson. Image cropped; originally captioned "Aerial photo of Crime Scene Photo and labels by Ident Officer ANDERSON October 17th, 2009." Yellow line added by publisher

21. Trial exhibit; Kingston Police; photographer is Constable Aaron Anderson. Image cropped; originally captioned "Kingston Mills Road – Upper (north) Lock August 22nd, 2009"

22. Trial exhibit; Kingston Police; photographer is Constable Julia Moore. Yellow arrow added by publisher

23. Trial exhibit; Kingston Police; photographer is Constable Julia Moore

24. Trial exhibit; Kingston Police; photographer is Constable Julia Moore

25. Trial exhibit; Kingston Police; photographer is Constable Julia Moore

26. Trial exhibit; Kingston Police; photographer is Constable Julia Moore

27. Trial exhibit; Kingston Police; photographer is Constable Steve Koopman

28. Trial exhibit; Kingston Police; screen grab from a videotape of the interrogation of Tooba on July 22, 2009

29. Trial exhibit; Centre of Forensic Sciences, Toronto, Ontario

30. Trial exhibit; Kingston Police; photographer is Constable Rob Etherington. Image cropped; originally captioned "Pages of Rona's diary (Exhibit #810) Photo by Ident ETHERINGTON July 24th, 2009"

31. Rob Tripp

32. Rob Tripp

33. Rob Tripp

34. Rob Tripp

35. Rob Tripp

36. Rob Tripp

37. Jake Suarez

38. Jake Suarez

39. Dennis Arpin

40. Rob Tripp